MON

RESTORING AMERICA
AS THE LAND OF LIBERTY

By Stephen McDowell

Monumental: Restoring America as the Land of Liberty
By Stephen McDowell

All images are copyright free and obtained from:

Wikimedia Commons: http://commons.wikimedia.org/wiki/Main_Page

Nineteenth century resource books in the author's possession

The American Revolution, A Picture Sourcebook, 411 Copyright-Free Illustrations, Dover Publications

A few images are courtesy of WallBuilders, including *Forest and Flame in the Bible*, and *This Is the Enemy* poster.

Cover art and layout by Alex Dale

Printed in the United States of America

CONTENTS

SECTION ONE

The Founders'
Blueprint for Liberty

CHAPTER 1

The Forefathers Monument: A Matrix of Liberty

America has undergone a radical shift in recent times, from an exceptional nation – the most free, prosperous, and virtuous in history – to a nation in decline. The old nursery rhyme "Humpty Dumpty" provides an insightful picture of the condition of America today.

> Humpty Dumpty sat on a wall,
> Humpty Dumpty had a great fall.
>   All the king's horses,
>   And all the king's men,
> Couldn't put Humpty together again.

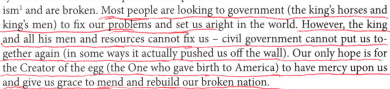

While the original rhyme was in part a riddle, where Humpty was an egg, the American people today can relate to Humpty Dumpty. We have fallen from a place of exceptionalism[1] and are broken. Most people are looking to government (the king's horses and king's men) to fix our problems and set us aright in the world. However, the king and all his men and resources cannot fix us – civil government cannot put us together again (in some ways it actually pushed us off the wall). Our only hope is for the Creator of the egg (the One who gave birth to America) to have mercy upon us and give us grace to mend and rebuild our broken nation.

Numerous signs point to the decay in the American culture. The most disturbing is the breakdown of the family. In 1960, 72% of adults were married. Today it is about 50%. In 1960, 65% of those filing taxes were married, and 35% were unmarried; today, 39% are married, and 61% unmarried. In 1980, 18% of children were born outside of marriage; today over 40% are born outside of marriage (and

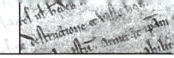

for the African-American community over 70%). Today, only 32% of people think premarital sex is wrong; 69% thought so in 1969.

In the 2012 elections, for the first time, voters in three states (Maryland, Maine, Washington) approved homosexual marriage. Before this, voters had rejected such initiatives every time (in 32 states). Nationwide polls show that 60% of the populace believes marriage is between one man and one woman. While that a majority believe this is good, it should be an overwhelming majority considering: 1) this has been the view of mankind since recorded history, 2) numerous studies show the detrimental effects on children of being raised in homosexual families, 3) the Bible is clear on the definition of family.

No more than 3.7% of the population is homosexual. Why then has this small minority been able to force their views upon so many Americans today? Why is the family breaking down so rapidly in recent decades? One primary reason is that the secularists have been very effective at taking control of state schools. They have successfully convinced the American citizenry that no absolute values exist (relativism) and that only government can solve our problems (statism).

Christians have been greatly impacted as well: 75% of youth raised in Christian homes who attend secondary public schools lose their faith, compared to 25% of those who go to Christian schools. Between 71% and 88% of Christians going to secular colleges deny the faith by the time they graduate. About 50% of those who attend Christian colleges deny their faith. Considering that 85% of Christian children attend government schools, it is no wonder we have decaying families. And remember, as the family goes so goes the nation.[2]

The family is God's chief instrument of dominion. It is God's primary tool for extending His kingdom — His government — in the earth. Children are arrows or weapons God gives the family to prepare and shoot into the culture to change the future (Psalm 127:4). If the family is faulty, the fulfillment of the mission wanes and the nation will decline.

The Christian family, with the arrows (children) it shoots, is becoming less an instrument of God's kingdom and more an instrument of man's kingdom. We have given the enemy our greatest weapon, our children. He has armed them and used them both against us and the cause of God. In the process the enemy has undermined biblical liberty and the foundations of the nation. This explains why so many people have embraced socialist government ideas, and why the culture is decaying.

The Declaration of Independence, the covenant upon which America is founded, declares we have God-given unalienable rights, which include the rights to life, liberty, and property. As we as a nation have abandoned the self-evident truths of our Creator, we have experienced not only the breakdown of the family and the secularization of education, but also the loss of life, liberty, and property. Consider a few recent actions of government and society:

 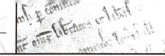
- Since abortion was legalized in America via the Supreme Court in 1973 more than 56 million 580 thousand unborn children have been killed.[3] Our national government not only considers abortion legal, but has recently used tax dollars to support abortions both in America and in other nations.

- Nearly half (46%) of all 15-19 year-olds in the United States have had sex at least once. One in three teen girls is estimated to get pregnant at least once before the age of 20. Of the 750,000 pregnancies among teens in 2006, around 200,000 ended in abortion.[4] The Center for Disease Control estimates that 19 million new sexually transmitted disease infections occur each year—almost half of them among young people 15 to 24 years of age. Among teenage girls, 1 in 4 (3 million) have a STD.[5]

- Over 10 million crimes are committed every year in America with a total annual cost of $675 billion. Every 3 seconds a crime occurs against someone's property; a violent crime occurs every 35 seconds. More than 1 in 150 Americans are in jail or prison (2.3 million behind bars), an all-time high that is costing federal, state, and local governments about $62 billion a year. The U.S. spends over $30,000 per year per inmate.[6]

- Government represents a great threat to liberty and economic growth with ever-increasing regulations and debt. With decades of deficit spending, by 2013 the U.S. federal government amassed over $16 trillion national debt (about $50,000 per person), saddling future generations with a massive debt burden. While 70% of Americans favor "smaller government with fewer services and lower taxes," current leaders borrow and spend with reckless abandon (with the 2010 budget deficit around $1.5 trillion); only 21% of voters nationwide say the U.S. government has consent of the governed.

- Through the new health care law (Obamacare), big government will be forcing every citizen to buy health insurance, and attempting to force business owners to violate their consciences and provide abortion services and medications to their employees.

- The IRS, the government institution that collects taxes and has the ability to confiscate property without due process, is assigned to implement and oversee Obamacare. It has shown its bias by targeting groups based on their political and religious views. The IRS has shown its ineptitude with wasteful spending on training programs and elaborate retreats.

- Big government intrudes into personal and business affairs, requiring citizens and businesses to file mountains of paper work to comply with government

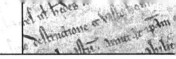

regulations and taxes. The state restricts how individuals use their private property, declaring areas to be wetlands or to contain supposed endangered creatures. Bureaucrats confiscate private property for development by private business, justifying such action as helping boost local tax revenue (as occurred in New London, Connecticut in 2000 and upheld by the Supreme Court in 2005[7]).

- Hostility to the Christian faith continues to increase in schools and colleges. Use of Bibles and prayer are restricted. Students are told not to mention Jesus or the Christian faith in graduation speeches. College students are denied degrees for adhering to ideas that are biblical and contrary to those that are "politically correct."[8]

We read similar examples of citizens' loss of life, liberty, and property on a daily basis. The problems are obvious. Can we do anything to solve them? Can we rebuild our nation making it once again the land of the free? Can we do anything to transform our nation? Did the Founders of America give us wisdom for building a free nation?

Yes, we can do something to rebuild, and yes, our Founders did give us wisdom and a blueprint of how to build. This blueprint or matrix is seen in the National Monument to the Forefathers.

National Monument to the
Forefathers

The Forefathers Monument

The National Monument to the Forefathers, located in Plymouth, Massachusetts, commemorates the Pilgrims, their planting the colony of Plymouth, and their contribution to the American nation at large. This 81-foot-tall granite structure also provides a matrix for how to build a free society based on the biblical ideas and worldview of these early settlers.

From the original concept in 1820 to the laying of the cornerstone in 1859 and its dedication in 1889, it was nearly three-quarters of a century in the making and contains in simple imagery the great wisdom of the founding era. The components of this significant, yet unknown, monument teach us how we can preserve America as a shining city upon a hill, an example of liberty to the world.

The builders of the nineteenth-century monument left us a template for constructing free nations based on the thinking of our forefathers. Their ideas worked, as they gave birth to the most free, prosperous, virtuous, giving, and just nation the world has ever seen. If we apply those same principles today, and build according to the successful pattern, we can expect the same results.

The monument is composed of numerous statues; the most prominent is *Faith*, standing with one hand pointed to the heavens and the other holding a Bible. At the base of the pedestal where Faith stands are four seated statues representing *Morality*, *Law*, *Education*, and *Liberty*. Flanking these allegorical figures are smaller engravings representing more components of the matrix of liberty.

Beneath the seated figures carved reliefs depict scenes from Pilgrim history.

Four inscriptions are engraved on panels on the four sides of the main pedestal. One explains how the "National Monument to the Forefathers" was "Erected by a grateful people in remembrance of their labors, sacrifices and sufferings for the cause of civil and religious liberty." Two other panels contain the names of the first settlers who came over on the Mayflower in 1620. The remaining panel contains a quote from Governor William Bradford's Of *Plym-*

First settlers, Mayflower 1620

outh Plantation and depicts well why these people have been called the "parents of our republic."

> Thus out of small beginnings greater things have been produced by His hand that made all things of nothing and gives being to all things that are; and as one small candle may light a thousand, so the light here kindled hath shone unto many, yea in some sort to our whole nation; let the glorious name of Jehovah have all praise.

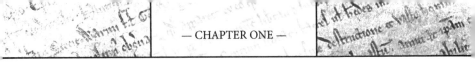

Review Questions

- Do you believe America has been in decline in recent times? Why do you think this?

- In addition to the things listed in this chapter that indicate our nation has abandoned our founding principles, can you give other evidence for this?

- What are the general components presented in the Forefathers' Monument that comprise the blueprint of liberty?

CHAPTER 2

Faith

Just as the statue of *Faith* is the central figure in the Forefathers Monument, the foundational building block of all societies is the faith of the people. All nations are religious; that is, all nations are built upon a set of ideas and principles that are ultimately rooted in the faith of the people. Every nation appeals to some authority to determine what they consider to be correct or lawful behavior. Each nation has some power they look to that they consider to be sovereign, whether consciously or unconsciously.

Some secularists proclaim they do not believe in a god and neither should a society appeal to any god, because religion has no place in public life. They say church and state must be separated. But secularists (and the various forms of secularism, like atheism, humanism, statism, progressivism, etc.) hold to an ultimate authority. To them, man is the ultimate authority in the earth; and in civil society this is usually man via the state.[9]

The faith of a people is the life-blood of their society. It should carry nutrients and oxygen to feed the national body. Yet, history has shown that most nations do not produce life, liberty, virtue, and prosperity, but death, bondage, corruption, and lack. Why? Simply because their faith has not been in the true and living God, but in gods of human invention. Most often men have fallen into the temptation of Adam and Eve in the Garden of Eden. In seeking to become gods themselves, they have sought to determine good and evil for themselves (Genesis 3:5). When man becomes his own god – his own source of truth and morality, his own standard of lawful behavior – then the nations he builds are not blessed but cursed. Blessing is the fruit of obedience to God (Deuteronomy 5:29). Nations that rebel go backwards, what He says will occur when we disobey (Jeremiah 7:23-24).

The Christian View of God[10]

The most important thing about a person is his view of God. The most important thing about a society is its view of God. This is true because we become like whom, or what, we worship. People always move toward their image of God. Since Christianity is the revealed truth of the Creator, cultures embracing Christianity have moved toward the true image and nature of God and the true state of reality within His universe. God has revealed Himself in His Creation (the law of nature) and more specifically in the Holy Scriptures — the revealed Word of God (the law of nature's God). Knowing and embracing the nature, character, and attributes of God affect individual lives as well as every aspect of society and culture.

Our view of God is the most important thing about us because we become like whom or what we worship.

Christians derive their view of God from the Bible, which presents an image of the living Almighty God — One who is omnipotent, omniscient, and omnipresent; a God who is just, but also forgiving, merciful, and loving. The true nature of God could never be created by the mind of man.

Man has made up all kinds of images of God. He looks many different ways to different people: He is like man, but bigger and stronger; He is harsh and stern, and sends judgment; He is found in rocks and trees and other parts of His creation; He is loving, gentle, not condemning, and allows all kinds of behavior (especially the evil things men want to do); and to some, God wants the government to be man's savior and provide all his needs.

Humanism and man-made religions proclaim "I made God in my mind." Christians need to be careful of creating their own image of God. We must have an objective source to identify God. The Bible is that source.

To correctly understand Christianity and the nature of God, one must understand the person of Jesus. Jesus is Lord and Christ, and sovereign over all Creation. He is fully God, yet fully man; although, unlike all others, He was and is a perfect man (and as man He mercifully veiled His Godhood least we be overwhelmed). He is seated at the right hand of God, "far above all rule and authority and power and dominion . . . in this age [and] the one to come" (Ephesians 1:20-23). All things are under His feet, in subjection to Him. He is the head over all things.

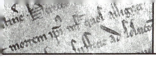
A FEW UNIQUE ASPECTS OF THE TRUE GOD INCLUDE:

The Triune Nature of God

The Trinity is a fundamental doctrine of Christianity. Three persons comprise the Godhead — the Father is God, the Son is God, and the Holy Spirit is God. The triune nature of God has many implications for mankind and for all creation. One, it reveals a unity with diversity in creation. All creation is unified because we have a common Creator; the creation reflects the Creator. Yet, that unity includes great diversity. For example, all humans are alike in many ways. We are all created in the image of God. We all have similar physical, mental, and spiritual features that set us apart from all other aspects of creation — there is unity among men. Yet, no two humans are alike. Each has unique external physical characteristics (like fingerprints and voiceprints) and internal characteristics (like talents, skills, attitudes, and callings). We display diversity because we reflect our Creator, and He is a picture of diversity. The Lord our God is one (unity), yet He manifests Himself in three persons (diversity).

Christian societies recognize the unity with diversity of its citizens. Thus such societies encourage all to develop their talents and skills so as to pursue the fulfillment of their unique calling. This has implications in many areas. For example, in the economy such an understanding promotes prosperity through division and specialization of labor.[11]

The nature of the Godhead also provides an example of love and service. The Son serves the Father, the Spirit carries out the wishes of the Son and Father, the Father lifts up the Son. Each member of the Godhead demonstrates love which serves as an example of how man should act toward his fellow man. Religions with a rigid monotheism (like Islam) do not present such ideas. Not surprisingly, these nations historically display less love and service compared to more biblical societies.

Justification by Faith, not by Our Works

In contrast to Christianity, all religions are works oriented. Thus, people say certain prayers or mantras to help themselves or others. Some lash their backs to show they are willing to suffer to follow their god. Some carve idols from stones and logs and worship them with ceremonies. Some attempt to gain right standing with their god by killing the infidels. Often the civil laws reflect that society's concept of justification. The resultant laws restrict freedom of worship, speech, assembly, and other liberties recognized and protected in a Christian society as God-given. Christian societies do not see the law as the tool for justification and salvation. Law cannot save man. Only Christ's redeeming work can save man, and this free gift of

 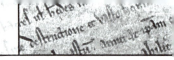

God is received by faith, not by works. Man's view of justification affects the laws of a society.

The Priesthood of the Believer

We can and must know God ourselves. This idea motivated Martin Luther to put the Bible in the common language of the people, and to write hymns in the common language — that all might know Him personally. This idea affects civil life in many ways. It leads to the promotion of education for all people, because everyone has the right and responsibility to know God and His Word for themselves. It also promotes democratic principles in a nation where each person has a voice in public affairs.

These examples represent just a few of the concepts that separate Christianity from other religions. The Christian idea of God has made an immense impact on many areas necessary to build free nations. The four statues surrounding and below *Faith* on the Forefathers Monument depict the role of the Bible in shaping such free nations.

Christianity Is the Foundation of Free Nations

The Founders of America, from the early Pilgrims and Puritans, who colonized many of the states, through those men who gave us our American Christian Constitutional Republic, understood that the foundation of free nations rests in true religion. True religion does not result where man is considered god. Neither do any of the man-made religions result in truth. The statue of *Faith* shows the two sources of true religion. She points to the heavens, to the Creator of all things, and she holds a Bible with the pages peeled open, indicating that true faith emanates from the living Word of God.

Central to the Christian faith is the message that God through Christ redeems man and gives him a living faith through a supernatural internal transformation of the heart. God via His Spirit gives man a new nature and writes His law upon man's heart. This internal transformation is the necessary first step to building godly nations. Since only the God of the Bible can bring about this supernatural transformation, only the God of the Bible can change a nation for good.

Biblical transformation moves from the internal to the external, yet God not only transforms the heart, He also gives principles and precepts in His Word for how we should live. He tells us how to effectively conduct the affairs of life. *Faith* has a star upon her head, indicating she receives wisdom from above. The four seated statues below *Faith* represent *Morality, Law, Education*, and *Liberty*; more specifically they represent Biblical Morality, Biblical Law, Biblical Education, and Biblical Liberty. The Founders understood the necessity of building the nation upon the Christian faith and worldview.

The people who settled the original thirteen colonies came to propagate the Gospel, to advance the Kingdom of God, as is clearly evidenced in the early constitutions, compacts, and charters. The Pilgrims' Mayflower Compact said they came "for the Glory of God, and Advancement of the Christian Faith."[12] The New England Confederation of 1643 says, "whereas we all came into these parts of America with one and the same end and aim, namely, to advance the kingdom of our Lord Jesus Christ and to enjoy the liberties of the Gospel in purity and peace." The colonies of Massachusetts, Plymouth, Connecticut, and New Haven joined together agreeing to this Confederation "both for preserving and propogating the truth and liberties of the Gospel and for their own mutual safety and welfare."[13] The Christian faith was central in the foundation of all the original colonies.[14]

The civil documents of the colonies also acknowledge God as the source of truth and law. For example, the Massachusetts Body of Liberties, which was the precursor of our Bill of Rights, states that no man's life or property can be taken except by some express law that has been sufficiently published, "or in case of the defect of a law in any parteculer case by the word of God."[15] What became known as the Blue Laws of Connecticut acknowledged "that the supreme power of making laws, and of repealing them, belong to

George Washington

God only, and that by him, this power is given to Jesus Christ, as Mediator, Math. 28:19. Joh. 5:22. And that the Laws for holiness, and Righteousness, are already made, and given us in the scriptures."[16] For these early Founders, the Bible was the standard for lawful behavior.

The men who gave us the Declaration of Independence and the Constitution understood and often spoke of the religious foundation of free nations. George Washington wrote in 1797: "Religion and Morality are the essential pillars of Civil society."[17] In his Farewell Address in 1796, Washington wrote: "Of all the dispositions and habits which lead to political prosperity, religion and morality are indispensable supports."[18]

James Madison wrote in 1825: "[T]he belief in a God All Powerful wise and good, is . . . essential to the moral order of the World and to the happiness of man."[19] Benjamin Franklin said:

I have lived, Sir, a long time, and the longer I live, the more convincing proofs I see of this truth—that God Governs in the affairs of men. And if

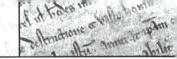

a sparrow cannot fall to the ground without His notice, is it probable that an empire can rise without His aid? We have been assured, Sir, in the sacred writings, that "except the Lord build the House they labour in vain that build it." I firmly believe this; and I also believe that without His concurring aid we shall succeed in this political building no better, than the Builders of Babel.[20]

Benjamin Franklin

Thomas Jefferson said:

Among the most inestimable of our blessings is that . . . of liberty to worship our Creator in the way we think most agreeable in His will; a liberty deemed in other countries incompatible with good government and yet proved by our experience to be its best support.[21]

The Constitution of New Hampshire of June 2, 1784 stated:

morality and piety, rightly grounded on evangelical principles, will give the best and greatest security to government, and will lay in the hearts of men the strongest obligations to due subjection; . . . the knowledge of these, is most likely to be propagated through a society by the institution of the public worship of the DEITY, and of public instruction in morality and religion.[22]

Last Will and Testaments

The Christian faith of the Founders is evidenced in their public and private writings and actions. Many of them clearly reveal this in their wills, which used to be called "Last Will and Testament" for a reason. Dozens of the men who signed the Declaration and Constitution clearly testified of their firm belief in Christ. A few examples follow:

In his Last Will and Testament Robert Treat Paine clearly reveals his faith in Jesus Christ.

John Dickinson (1732-1808), signer from Pennsylvania and author of first draft of the Articles of Confederation (1776), retired to write commentaries on the Gospel of Matthew. In his Last Will and Testament he wrote: "Rendering thanks to my Creator . . . to Him I resign myself, humbly confiding in His goodness and in His mercy through Jesus Christ for the events of eternity."[23]

Robert Treat Paine, signer of Declaration, plainly expressed his faith in his will:

"I am constrained to ex-press my adoration of the Supreme Being, the Author of my existence, in full belief of His providential goodness and His for-giving mercy revealed to the world through Jesus Christ, through Whom I hope for never-ending happiness in a future state."[24]

Richard Stockton – As he was dying from hardships of captivity during the war, he put his affairs in order, writing in his last will and testament:

Richard Stockton

"As my children will have frequent occasion of perusing this instrument, and may probably be particularly impressed with the last words of their father, I think it proper here not only to subscribe to the entire belief of the great and leading doctrines of the Christian religion, such as the being of God; the universal defection and depravity of human nature; the Divinity of the person and the completeness of the redemption purchased by the blessed Savior; the necessity of the operations of the Divine Spirit; of Divine faith accompanied with an habitual virtuous life; and the universality of the Divine Providence; but also, in the bowels of a father's af-

Samuel Adams

fection, to exhort and charge [my children] that the fear of God is the beginning of wisdom, that the way of life held up in the Christian system is calculated for the most complete happiness that can be enjoyed in this mortal state, [and] that all occasions of vice and immorality is injurious either immediately or consequentially—even in this life."[25]

Samuel Adams, signer of the Declaration and "Father of the Revolution," wrote in his will: "In the name of God. Amen…. Principally & first of all, I commend my Soul to that Almighty Be-

ing who gave it, and my body I commit to the dust, relying upon the merits of Jesus Christ for a pardon of all my sins."[26]

Myriad other statements from our Founders and from the early civil documents reveal their firm conviction of this principle. In later chapters we will examine many more of these.

Even the few other-than-orthodox Christian Founders saw the necessity of Christianity. Some today claim that America's Founders were all atheists, secularists, or at best deists, and hence any claim to America as a Christian nation is cast aside with disdain. These people readily proclaim America was in no way Christian, offering Franklin and Jefferson as examples of non-Christian Founders to prove their point. When pressed to name others, they struggle. That is because there were hardly any other Founders who did not embrace the Christian faith. In fact, all but two or three of the signers of the Declaration and two or three of the men who gave us the Constitution were orthodox Christians. The two most prominent unorthodox thinkers, Franklin and Jefferson, were not atheists or secularists. In fact, they were not even deists. Deists are those who believe in a supreme being, yet one who is removed from his creation. They are more accurately described as biblical theists. They essentially believed in a God as presented in the Bible, and held primarily to a biblical view of life. Jefferson even considered himself a Christian.

Thomas Jefferson

Jefferson was a member of the Christian church his entire life. In fact, he started a church in 1777 that met in the courthouse of his home town, Charlottesville, Virginia. He called it the Calvinistical Reformed Church. In the first few decades of the nineteenth century before any church buildings were erected in Charlottesville, the four major Christian denominations worshipped together in the Albemarle County Courthouse. He called this public building the "common temple," and he regularly attended these meetings, which he considered to be a great example of unity among the Christian denominational community. While President, Jefferson regularly attended church meetings held in the United States Capitol building. His view of separation of church and state was not to keep God out of public life, but to keep the government from restricting freedom of worship, wherever that restriction might occur, including in public buildings.[27]

In his early years none of his writings express anything but orthodox Christian views; however, in his later years of life, Jefferson expressed some doubts of the deity of Christ, finding the idea that the omnipotent Creator became a man very difficult to comprehend. Thus, while this professing Christian may not have been an orthodox believer, he, nonetheless, basically had a biblical view of life, and he understood that the Christian faith is the foundation of free societies. He wrote in 1809:

> The practice of morality being necessary for the well-being of society, He [God] has taken care to impress its precepts so indelibly on our hearts that they shall not be effaced by the subtleties of our brain. We all agree in the obligation of the moral precepts of Jesus and nowhere will they be found delivered in greater purity than in his discourses.[28]

Jefferson knew that God through Christ pushed the precepts of God's law into the heart of men. No other religion or belief system does this.

While not a professing Christian, Benjamin Franklin was greatly affected by the Christian culture of early America, which was seen in many ways. He often attended church, was friends with many Christian ministers (including the great revivalist George Whitefield), and even called the Constitutional Convention to prayer, where he declared that "God governs in the affairs of men" and spoke of God as actively involved in every detail of His creation.

Toward the end of his life, Benjamin Franklin wrote a reply to Thomas Paine seeking to dissuade him from publishing a work which spoke against Christian fundamentals. He told Paine that no good would come from his publishing his ideas, writing that "He that spits against the wind, spits in his own face." Franklin pointed out to Paine that "perhaps you are indebted to … your religious education, for the habits of virtue upon which you now justly value yourself…. Among us it is not necessary, as among the Hottentots, that a youth, to be raised into the company of men, should prove his manhood by beating his mother." Only evil would result if Paine's ideas succeeded, for, as Franklin wrote, "If men are so wicked with religion, what would they be if without it."[29] Many today in America are "beating their mother" when they seek to remove

James Otis

Christianity from our public life. Christianity is what has produced the liberty and prosperity that has allowed people to pursue such unwise action.

America's Founders understood the concept of sovereignty, of some ultimate authority to which a people look. They believed that the supreme civil power was not rooted in a president, or king, or parliament, or elected legislature, but in God. Revolutionary leader James Otis wrote:

> To say the Parliament is absolute and arbitrary is a contradiction. The Parliament cannot make 2 and 2, 5: Omnipotency cannot do it. The supreme power in a state … belongs alone to God. Parliaments are in all cases to declare what is for the good of the whole; but it is not the declaration of Parliament that makes it so: There must be in every instance a higher authority, viz. God.

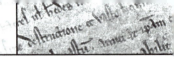

Should an Act of Parliament be against any of His natural laws, which are immutably true, their declaration would be contrary to eternal truth, equity, and justice, and consequently void.[30]

Our Founders believed that it was not just faith in any god or religion that formed the foundation of free societies, but it was specifically the Christian religion and faith in the only true God and His Word, the Bible. In a letter to James Madison from 16 October 1829, Noah Webster, the "Father of American Scholarship and Education" and author of the famous "Blue Backed Speller," wrote:

Noah Webster

The christian religion, in its purity, is the basis or rather the source of all genuine freedom in government. . . . I am persuaded that no civil government of a republican form can exist & be durable, in which the principles of that religion have not a controlling influence.[31]

In the Preface to his *United States History* book, Webster wrote:

Benjamin Rush

The brief exposition of the constitution of the United States, will unfold to young persons the principles of republican government; and it is the sincere desire of the writer that our citizens should early understand that the genuine source of correct republican principles is the Bible, particularly the New Testament or the Christian religion.[32]

Benjamin Rush, a signer of the Declaration of Independence and the Father of Medicine in America, wrote in 1806: "Christianity is the only true and perfect religion, and that in proportion as mankind adopt its principles and obeys its precepts, they will be wise and happy."[33]

The "Father of American Geography," Jedidiah Morse wrote, "To the kindly influence of Christianity we owe that degree of civil freedom, and political and social happiness which mankind now enjoys."[34]

The U.S. House of Representatives declared in 1854, "the great vital and conservative element in our system is the belief of our people in the pure doctrines and divine truths of the gospel of Jesus Christ."[35]

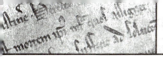
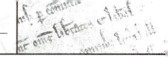

Public Proclamations

The importance of faith to our Founders can be seen by their public proclamations. The first Americans were predominantly Christians who embraced the doctrine of Divine Providence, seeing God in history as "directly supervising the affairs of men, sending evil upon the city … for their sins,… or blessing his people when they turn from their evil ways."[36] Looking to the Scriptures for the source of their law, both personal and civil, they firmly believed God's blessings would come upon those who obey His commands, and curses would come upon the disobedient (see Deuteronomy 28 and Leviticus 26). Consequently, during times of calamity or crisis both church and civil authorities would proclaim days of fasting and prayer; and when God responded with deliverance and blessing, they would pro-

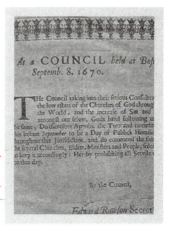

Possibly the first printed broadside for a Day of Prayer, September 8, 1670. Before this the numerous proclamations were written by hand.

claim days of thanksgiving and prayer. Such days of appeal to God were not rare, but a regular part of life in early America.

From 1620 to 1815 government (mostly colonial, and later state and national) proclaimed at least 1400 public days of fasting or thanksgiving. Such proclamations continued regularly throughout the nineteenth century, and in a smaller way up until today. During observances of fast and thanksgiving days, people would gather at their local meeting houses and churches to hear a sermon. State legislatures would also regularly invite ministers to preach on these days. Many of these sermons were printed and distributed for study.[37]

One example of a day of prayer occurred in October 1746 when France sent a fleet to attack Boston. Governor Shirley proclaimed a Fast Day and people everywhere thronged to the churches to pray for deliverance. God miraculously answered their prayers by sending a storm and pestilence to wipe out the French fleet. Everyone gave thanks to God.[38]

This not only occurred before independence, but also throughout the Revolution. During the Revolutionary War the Continental Congress issued at least seven different prayer and fast day proclamations and six different thanksgiving proclamations. These were issued after events such as the surrender of British General Burgoyne at Saratoga, the discovery of the treason of Benedict Arnold, and the surrender of Cornwallis at Yorktown. In response to the American victory at Saratoga in October 1777, the Continental Congress proclaimed a Day of Thanksgiving and

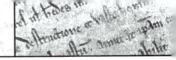

> TUESDAY, the 24th of MAY, 14 GEO. III. 1774.
>
> THIS House being deeply impressed with Apprehension of the great Dangers to be derived to *British* America, from the hostile Invasion of the City of *Boston*, in our Sister Colony of *Massachusetts Bay*, whose Commerce and Harbour are on the 1st Day of *June* next to be stopped by an armed Force, deem it highly necessary that the said first Day of *June* be set apart by the Members of this House as a Day of Fasting, Humiliation and Prayer, devoutly to implore the divine Interposition for averting the heavy Calamity, which threatens Destruction to our civil Rights, and the Evils of civil War; to give us one Heart and one Mind firmly to oppose, by all just and proper Means, every Injury to *American* Rights, and that the Minds of his Majesty and his Parliament may be inspired from above with Wisdom, Moderation, and Justice, to remove from the loyal People of *America* all Cause of Danger from a continued Pursuit of Measures pregnant with their Ruin.
>
> *Ordered*, therefore, that the Members of this House do attend in their Places at the Hour of ten in the Forenoon, on the said 1st Day of *June* next, in Order to proceed with the Speaker and the Mace to the Church in this City for the Purposes aforesaid; and that the Reverend Mr. *Price* be appointed to read Prayers, and the Reverend Mr. *Gwatkin* to preach a Sermon suitable to the Occasion.
>
> *Ordered*, that this Order be forthwith printed and published.
>
> By the HOUSE of BURGESSES.
> GEORGE WYTHE, C. H. B.

Thomas Jefferson, while a member of the Virginia legislature, penned this resolve for a day of fasting and prayer observed on June 1, 1774.

Praise to God. They stated:

Forasmuch as it is the indispensable duty of all men to adore the superintending providence of Almighty God, … and it having pleased Him in His abundant mercy … to crown our arms with most signal success … it is therefore recommended … to set apart Thursday, the 18th day of December, for solemn thanksgiving and praise.[39]

They recommended for everyone to confess their sins and humbly ask God, "through the merits of Jesus Christ, mercifully to forgive and blot them out of remembrance," and thus He then would be able to pour out His blessings upon every aspect of the nation.[40]

The individual states proclaimed numerous such days as well. The Virginia House of Burgesses set apart June 1, 1774, as a day of fasting and prayer in response to England closing the port of Boston. On the day British troops fired upon the minutemen at Lexington (April 19, 1775) the colony of Connecticut was observing a "Day of publick Fasting and Prayer" as proclaimed a month before by Governor Trumbull. Massachusetts set aside August 1, 1776, as a "day of solemn humiliation, fasting, and prayer" where they called upon the people "to humble themselves under the righteous hand of God; penitently to acknowledge their many heinous and aggravated sins" and asking Him to "pour out of his Spirit upon this people … and that he would spread the peaceful Kingdom of the Divine Redeemer over the face of the whole habitable world." New York set aside August 27, 1776, "as a day of Fasting, Humiliation, and Prayer to Almighty God, for the imploring of His Divine assistance in the organization and establishment of a form of Government for the security and perpetuation of the Civil and Religious Rights and Liberties of Mankind."[41]

The modern separationists often look to Thomas Jefferson to justify their beliefs, saying he gave us separation of church and state. But Jefferson was no strict separationist, as shown by many of his public actions. He penned the resolve for Virginia's day of fasting and prayer on June 1, 1774. While Governor in 1779, he issued a proclamation "appointing Thursday the 9th day of December next, a day of publick and solemn thanksgiving and prayer to Almighty God, earnestly recommending to all the good people of this commonwealth, to set apart the said day for those purposes."[42]

If in session, Congress and the state assemblies would even go to church together as a body to observe these days. In 1787 a committee of representatives of all the states, gratefully looking back over all the preceding years, set apart October 19, 1787, "as a day of public prayer and thanksgiving" to their "all-bountiful Creator" who had conducted them "through the perils and dangers of the war" and established them as a free nation, and gave "them a name and a place among the princes and nations of the earth."[43]

The first President, George Washington, issued days of thanksgiving and days of prayer as recommended by Congress. Most Presidents up until today have followed this example, with about 200 such proclamations being issued by national government leaders.[44]

These are only a few words and examples that reveal the Christian faith of our Founders and their belief that faith in God and conformity to His principles are the foundation of freedom. Some of those principles they considered essential in building a free nation are depicted by the statues on the Forefathers Monument and are presented in the chapters that follow.

In recent years, American culture has become increasingly hostile toward the Christian faith, causing some people to despair of ever being able to accomplish the godly task set before us – to transform America from its current fallen state. But with God there is always hope; a nation can be transformed for He is a living, sovereign, omnipotent God. That we are aware of the great need and are willing to take action is an indication that God is at work. He is not finished with the United States.

 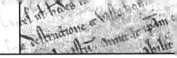
Review Questions

- Why is faith so important in an individual's life?

- Why is faith so important in the life of a nation?

- Choose one unique aspect of the Christian faith and explain how this affects public life in a society.

- Christianity was of central importance to the founders of America. Give a number of points of evidence for this statement.

- Why do you think Jefferson and Franklin, while not orthodox believers, clearly believed Christianity was essential for the well-being of the nation?

- Some people today say that while our founders may have believed in God, they were not Christians but deists. What evidence can you give to refute this idea?

CHAPTER 3

Morality

The first of the four seated statues below *Faith* on the Forefathers monument is *Morality*. The Founders of America saw man from a Christian perspective. They understood that man is a moral, yet fallen, being. This is in great contrast to what our society teaches today.

The Christian Idea of Man[45]

Who is man? What are we? Are we fundamentally good? Are we mere bodies? Are we just like animals? If we are just matter, then we are no different than bugs. It means nothing to squash human beings if you have such a view of man. Governments and leaders throughout history have had this view and have squashed many. In the twentieth century alone secular governments killed well over 100 million of their own citizens and thought nothing of it.

The dominant view today is that men are an accident that crawled out of the primordial ooze; men are merely grown-up worms. However, God declares all human beings have great value. They are important and special. Why? Man is created in the image of God (Genesis 1:26; James 3:9). This gives him value and worth. Men are equal in regards to their standing before God and the law, with certain God-given unalienable rights — life, liberty, and property. God Himself became a man (John 15). He could do so because man was made in God's image. Through the person of Christ, God paid the price to redeem mankind. Jesus' incarnation added to the great value of man.

The Christian idea of man says that each person has an important calling and destiny that contributes to God's overall plan in history. every individual has an important contribution to make in bringing life to men and nations, in training posterity, in advancing the economy, and in extending the kingdom of God. This understanding has made great impact in economics, invention, business, government, and the medical field.

The Christian idea of man motivated Joseph Lister to develop antiseptic surgery, which has saved millions and millions of lives in the past century and a half. This idea also influenced Florence Nightingale's work in establishing modern nursing. Cyrus McCormick's desire to elevate the common farmer and empower him to prosper helped motivate him to invent the reaper, which has done more to eliminate famine in the earth than any other action of man. The Christian faith and the high regard George Washington Carver had for individuals inspired him to discover many agricultural advancements that greatly benefited farmers in America and throughout the world.[46]

A society with a Christian view of man will seek to protect all life, not just those who are "important" or can contribute to the political fabric. This view breaks down class systems or castes.

While all men have great value, the Christian idea of man also reveals that man is sinful and in a fallen state. We are in need of a redeemer. We cannot save ourselves. We cannot live up to the standards of God.[47] We need the regenerating power of the Holy Spirit to work in us so that we might be delivered from the domain of darkness and born into the kingdom of light. Once we become a new creation we must grow in salvation — we must be sanctified in God's truth so we can go and extend His kingdom, His government, His truth in the nations. Biblical education is central in doing this.

Seeing man as sinful will affect how we live and conduct our societal affairs. One consequence is that we will not entrust man with too much power, because sinful man will tend to abuse power. John Adams said:

> To expect self-denial from men, when they have a majority in their favor, and consequently power to gratify themselves, is to disbelieve all history and universal experience; it is to disbelieve Revelation and the Word of God, which informs us, the heart is deceitful above all things, and desperately wicked…. There is no man so blind as not to see, that to talk of founding a government upon a supposition that nations and great bodies of men, left to themselves, will practice a course of self-denial, is either to babble like a new-born infant, or to deceive like an unprincipled impostor.[48]

John Adams

We seek to limit the power of our rulers in various ways: binding them down with a constitution; holding them accountable with frequent elections; dividing the legislative, executive, and judicial powers; and setting up checks and balances with-

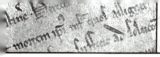

in these separate governing bodies. Thus, a people's view of man affects the form of civil government they adopt. It also affects their execution of justice, which should be swift but fair.

Without a Christian idea of man, society will see no difference between humans and animals. If man is just an animal, then his life is expendable. University of Texas biologist Eric Pianka was named the 2006 Distinguished Texas Scientist by the Texas Academy of Science. In his acceptance speech he reflected the humanistic view of man held by most of academia today, declaring "We're no better than bacteria!" He said that the planet is in danger from too many people and to alleviate the problem the human population must be reduced by 90 percent. War and famine are not killing enough people; disease is a better mechanism, but AIDS and other diseases are not working fast enough. What is needed, according to this "distinguished" scientist, is to release an airborne variety of the Ebola virus. This Central African virus kills rapidly by liquefying the internal organs. He estimates such action would have his desired results of killing about 90% of those who plague the world.[49]

Such an absurd idea follows logically from seeing man as a mere accident of nature. With regard to value, to those with a pagan view of man, a bacteria is a rat is a dog is a man. They see no difference, and believe we should think nothing of eliminating any men who are seen as a threat to the future of the world. Adhering to such a view of man is why Hitler, Stalin, Mao, and other pagan thinkers could wipe out tens of millions of their own citizens without any second thought. But if we believe what modern intellectuals teach, how can we condemn such tyrants? The Christian idea of man has protected life and advanced society, but today we are systematically destroying that concept.

Man Is a Moral Being.

Christian individuals have a transformed nature. Those who are redeemed through Christ are a new creation (2 Corinthians 5:17), having a new heart and new desires. Regenerated Christians no longer seek only the temporary pleasures of sin, but they seek to please their loving Father and the great Creator. No longer do they desire to live solely according to their own selfishness, but they seek to obey His commands and live in accordance with His righteous standard.

Jesus taught that if we love Him we will keep his commandments (John 14:15). We do so not to seek right standing with God by our good works, for no one can obey all His righteous standards. We are not justified by our works but by His grace through faith. Rather we obey from a spirit of gratitude. In the process we are sanctified, set apart, and made holy by His Spirit as we follow His precepts.

Obedience brings blessings. One of the most repeated messages in the Bible declares if we obey God and His Word, we will be blessed (Deuteronomy 5:29; 28:1-

12). If we disobey Him we will go backward (Jeremiah 7:23-24). The good news is that God wants to bless His people; however, He cannot violate His righteous standards and bless those who live in disobedience.

Consider what the loving God has done to bless us: through the atoning work of Christ, God initiated a New Covenant with His people. In this Covenant He gives repentant man a new heart. He takes out our heart of stone and replaces it with a heart of flesh (Hebrews 8:10; Jeremiah 31:33). In addition to giving us a new nature, He also fills us with the Holy Spirit to empower us to love and follow God, and obey His moral standards. This inward obedience produces great blessings, not only to the individual, but also to society.

The nature of the New Covenant is reflected in the statue of *Morality* on the Forefathers Monument in that she has the Ten Commandments in her left hand and the scroll of revelation in her right hand, both being necessary to build a free nation. In the New Covenant, God's Word is written upon our hearts. We are empowered from within to live in accordance with God's revealed Word as summarized by the Ten Commandments. The niches in the base of *Morality's* throne bear engravings of the *Evangelist* writing the Gospel and of *Prophecy*. This Gospel is first written within the heart, which will then flow out and affect all spheres of life.

As we mature as Christians we become more like Him in character and thought. We gradually display more of His holiness and character, seeking to be honest, loving, kind, pure, self-governed, and industrious. This Christian character or morality is essential for a free nation. Only a nation of regenerated men will remain a nation of free men. The statue representing *Morality* has no eyes for she is looking inward, indicating there must first be internal liberty within before there can be external liberty in society.

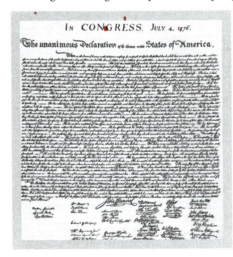

The Declaration recognizes truth emanating from our Creator as well as God-given, not government granted, rights.

This does not mean that the entire population must be Christian before a nation can obtain a measure of freedom, prosperity, virtue, and justice; but as the citizens gradually change within, this will have a gradual impact within the nation at large. Certainly the percentage of the population that is Christian determines in part their impact upon a nation, but this is not the

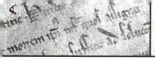
only factor. A people's worldview, character, and understanding of the call to transform the culture also have a great effect on the degree to which a nation experiences positive transformation.

Self-Evident Truths

A Christian people have their conscience awakened to God, which is essential for a people to see truth, to tell right from wrong, and to discern good and evil. The second paragraph of the Declaration of Independence begins with the famous phrase, "We hold these truths to be self-evident, that all men are created equal, that they are endowed by their Creator with certain unalienable Rights, that among these are Life, Liberty and the pursuit of Happiness." But are these truths self-evident? Were all men equal in the sight of Pharaoh or Caesar? Did Hitler believe all men have equal right to life and liberty? No, they obviously did not, as seen from the myriad people they enslaved and murdered. Is it self-evident to the modern Darwinian materialist, who believes only in a world of matter, devoid of any god of transcendent moral truth? It is not if he is consistent with his foundational presuppositions.

Understanding the American founding principle that all men have a right to life, liberty, and property is only self-evident to a Christian people, or to non-believers who have been thoroughly influenced by a biblical culture. This is who the American Founders were, primarily a Christian people, with a few biblical thinking theists, who by and large reflected Christian virtue.

Christian Character Is Essential for Freedom.

No nation can long endure without virtue or morality in the people. A loss of principles and manners is the greatest threat to a free people and will cause its downfall more surely than any foreign enemy. Samuel Adams, the Father of the American Revolution, said, "While the people are virtuous they cannot be subdued; but when once they lose their virtue they will be ready to surrender their liberties to the first external or internal invader."[50] He went on to say that the greatest security from enslavement in a country is virtue or morality among the people.

A lack of morality in the people threatens ev-

Samuel Adams

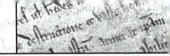

eryone's fundamental rights. People of character will desire to observe the law and will not willfully take the life, liberty or property of others. Consequently, people will not live in fear of other citizens. Less government will be required in a virtuous nation. Since fewer people will violate the law, a large police force and judicial system will not be needed. Law-making bodies will also have less to do because prohibitive laws will be at a minimum, as citizens will restrain themselves.

In a virtuous nation the rulers will be moral. This produces greater freedom because the rulers will not usurp individual rights through bad legislation. They will not steal from people through fiat money, excessive or graduated taxes, or other means. Consequently, citizens will not live in fear of civil government.

What is virtue or character? Virtue has been defined as conformity to a standard of right, and also a voluntary obedience to truth. Character is a convictional belief that results in consistent behavior.

Character literally means "to stamp and engrave through pressure." This sums up nicely what God is doing in our lives. God's plan is to make each person like Himself. Paul writes in Romans 8:29 that God has predestined that we, as His children, are to be conformed into the image of Christ. He is building His character within us, or you might say He is stamping and engraving upon us His image. He is doing this so that we might be examples of Him to the world and, also, that we may be able to fulfill His purpose for our lives.

History has shown that virtue in a people is the basis of happiness in a society and is absolutely necessary for a state to long remain free. As human nature is corrupted, the foundations of freedom are easily destroyed.

Some of the characteristics of virtuous citizens include:

- They will place a concern for the common good above self-interest.
- They will vigorously participate in local, regional, and national government, and will seek to correct wrong conduct in public officials.
- If necessary, they will risk their life, fortune, and honor for their country.
- They will perform their duties and seek right conduct in public and private life.

A free market economy depends on the people being virtuous because such a people:

- will not steal from their employers or others. Theft increases the cost of goods and services for everyone.
- will have a strong work ethic and be productive. Diligent labor will cause the economy to grow.
- will respect contracts.
- will save and invest to acquire a greater return later.
- will have a concern for their posterity and will seek to pass on a greater estate than they received.
- will not waste public resources and will be good stewards of the environment.

In contrast, a lack of character in the people can produce a stagnant or declining economy, corrupt laws, a lack of smooth transition from one political leader or party to another, a corrupt military that may take control of the government, and increased power in civil government to attempt to solve the many problems that result from the lack of character in the people.

A virtuous people will be vigilant to work to establish a free nation and then also to maintain it. Eternal vigilance is the price to maintain liberty. People of character will be eternally vigilant to secure their rights and demand that their government's power remain limited.[51]

The Founders understood only a moral people can be free. John Adams said while President in 1798:

The Power and Form of Free Governments

> [W]e have no government armed with power capable of contending with human passions unbridled by morality and religion. Avarice, ambition, revenge, or gallantry, would break the strongest cords of our Constitution as a whale goes through a net. Our Constitution was made only for a moral and religious people. It is wholly inadequate to the government of any other.[52]

Only a moral and religious people can supply the power necessary to support the form of our government. The figure to the right represents the power and form of the American republic. The pillars are the framework of our constitutional republic, and include decentralization of government, constitutionalism, separation of powers, an independent judiciary, trial by jury, civilian control of police and military, a free market, and election of representatives.[53] Americans desperately need to understand these ideas that are embedded in our unique form of government. However, it is more important to understand the power of our constitutional republic – the internal principles and ideas that must be a part of the thinking and action of the citizens.[54] Without this internal power, the form has no support. It will not work properly. Those internal principles include self-government, Christian union, individuality, property, education, and Christian character. Faith is at the foundation of this power, since all the principles of liberty flow from Christianity. Morality is that first principle that flows from faith in God and His Word.

The Founders of America saw that our virtue was rooted in Christianity. In 1838 the Legislature of New York said:

> Our Government depends for its being on the virtue of the people,— on that virtue that has its foundation in the morality of the Christian religion; and

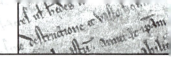
that religion is the common and prevailing faith of the people.[55]

The Founders not only taught the value of morality and Christian character, but they also lived it. They were great examples in word and deed.

George Washington: a Man of Christian Character

Throughout his military career, George Washington sought to impress a profound reverence for God upon the soldiers under his command. When he assumed command of the Continental Army in 1775, one of his first orders was to prohibit his men from swearing or using profanity, considering this one of the vilest of sins. No one ever wished to cross the General as William Johnson relates in this incident:

> On a certain occasion he had invited a number of officers to dine with him. While at table one of them uttered an oath. General Washington dropped his knife and fork in a moment, and in his deep undertone, and characteristic dignity and deliberation, said, "I thought that we all supposed ourselves gentlemen." He then resumed his knife and fork and went on as before. The remark struck like an electric shock, and, as was intended, did execution, as his observations in such cases were apt to do. No person swore at the table after that. When dinner was over, the officer referred to said to a companion that if the General had given him a blow over the head with his sword, he could have borne it, but that the home thrust which he received was too much — it was too much for a gentleman![56]

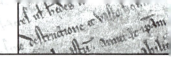
George Washington

Years later, as Washington was disbanding the army at the end of the Revolution, he wrote a letter to the governors of all the states on June 8, 1783, giving his advice on what needed to be done to assure the success of the newly formed nation. He ended his letter:

> I now make it my earnest prayer, that God would have you, and the State over which you preside, in his holy protection . . . that he would most graciously be pleased to dispose us all to do justice, to love mercy, and to demean ourselves with that charity, humility, and pacific temper of mind, which were the characteristics of the Divine Author of our blessed religion, and without an humble imitation of whose example in these things, we can never hope to be a happy nation.[57]

His advice to the governors? Imitate Jesus Christ and His character. Washington himself reflected the Divine Author of his blessed religion in many ways. One example is seen in his response to the attempt to make him king.

After the war ended, many people were looking for a way to deal with the problems the new nation faced. Members of the military were especially aware of the weaknesses of the Congress to handle the difficulties since many of them had not received the payment promised to them. A group of officers proposed making Washington king as the best means of averting national collapse. The people loved him

Washington praying at the meeting of the First Continental Congress in September 1774.

and the officers would support him, and both knew he would act in a benevolent manner. Colonel Lewis Nicola presented this idea to Washington in a letter in the spring of 1782. Washington's reply reveals his character:

Sir, With a mixture of great surprise and astonishment, I have read with attention the sentiments you have submitted to my perusal. Be assured, Sir, no occurrence in the course of the war has given me more painful sensations, than your information of their being such ideas existing in the army, as you have expressed, and I must view with abhorrence and reprehend with severity. . . .

The first thing Washington did was to rebuke those who suggested the idea of making him king, reminding them that they fought the war to get rid of kings, not to set up new kings. He went on to say:

I am much at loss to conceive what part of my conduct could have given encouragement to an address, which to me seems big with greatest mischiefs, that can befall my country. If I am not deceived in the knowledge of my self, you could not have found a person to whom your schemes are more disagreeable.[58]

Washington then looked into his own heart, pondering if he had in any way said or done anything that would make them think he would want to be king, for he thought he was against the idea more than anyone. The Father of our Country was displaying humility, which the Bible says is an essential quality for those who govern.[59]

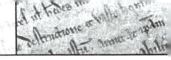

Ten months after Washington wrote to Colonel Nicola urging him to consider a constitutional means of resolving the problems facing them, a circular letter began appearing among the army calling for a military revolt. To avert national turmoil, Washington met with his officers on March 15, 1783, to hear their grievances and help them. He let them know, however, that he strongly opposed any civil discord. After talking at length, the officers were still sullen and silent. His plea had failed to persuade them. Finally, he reached into his pocket and pulled out a letter. He said there were congressmen anxious to help, and he wanted to read a letter describing what was being planned. He held up the letter and tried to read the small writing. Biographer James Flexner writes:

> The officers stirred impatiently in their seats, and then suddenly every heart missed a beat. Something was the matter with His Excellency. He seemed unable to read the paper. He paused in bewilderment. He fumbled in his waistcoat pocket. And then he pulled out something that only his intimates had seen him wear. A pair of glasses. He explained, "Gentlemen, you will permit me to put on my spectacles, for I have not only grown gray but almost blind in the service of my country."

After he was elected the first President, George Washington took the oath of office with his hand on the Bible. He added "so help me God," which has since become part of the official oath.

This simple statement achieved what all Washington's rhetoric and all his arguments had been unable to achieve. The officers were instantly in tears, and from behind the shining drops, their eyes looked with love at the commander who had led them all so far and long.

Washington quietly finished reading the congressman's letter, walked out of the hall, mounted his horse, and disappeared from the view of those who were staring from the window.[60]

All voted to support Washington for a peaceful, constructive approach to solve their problems (with one abstention). Historians point to this speech as pivotal. Jefferson wrote of Washington a year later:

> The moderation and virtue of a single character have probably prevented this revolution from being closed, as most others have been, by a subversion of that liberty it was intended to establish.[61]

We can easily see how the character of the Father of our Country helped to assure our survival and success. Both our leaders and citizens must practice "private and public Virtue," which according to John Adams, "is the only Foundation of Republics."[62] To our Founders, Christianity was the source of this foundational virtue, hence any attack upon Christianity was an attack upon our freedom. Signer of the Declaration, Charles Carroll wrote:

> Without morals a republic cannot subsist any length of time; they therefore who are decrying the Christian religion whose morality is so sublime and pure . . . are undermining the solid foundation of morals, the best security for the duration of free governments.[63]

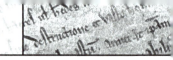

Review Questions

- Compare and contrast the Christian idea of man and the pagan idea of man.

- How does the sinful nature of man effect government? What can men do to limit the negative effects of sinful men in government?

- What affect does Christian character have upon the public life of a nation?

- How does the character of citizens affect the economy in a nation?

- Christian principles have produced the power and form of free nations. What kind of power and form do the religions of Islam, Hinduism, Shintoism, atheism, and humanism produce? Historically, how much freedom, prosperity, justice, and virtue have existed in nations where these religions have predominated?

- Give an example of how the Christian character of George Washington affected the nation of America. How do you think modern leaders would have responded if they were in Washington's place?

Law

All nations have a religious foundation. They are built upon a set of ideas and principles, ultimately rooted in a people's faith or in whom or what they consider to be sovereign. The laws of a nation reflect these ideas. Hence, law is the working religion of a people. Law emanates from what a people consider to be right and true. Thus, when a society institutes laws, they are encoding what they consider to be truth, which reveals whom they consider to be sovereign. From a biblical perspective, law and truth are related. A humanistic perspective denies any connection of truth to law.

The Christian Idea of Truth (Law)

How do we know what we know? What is the basis for what we consider true and right? For Christians, the basis of truth is found in God's Word. What the Bible proclaims is truth. Jesus prayed to the Father: "Your word is truth" (John 17:17). His Word is not just true, but it is truth. Truth is what Jesus teaches, and He taught that men must obey all the Scripture (Matthew 5:17-19). The Bible is God's Word and the source of Truth to all men. The degree to which men and nations have applied God's Word to all of life, is the degree to which they have prospered, lived in liberty, and been blessed.

Jesus declared that the Word of God is truth.

A Christian worldview proclaims that truth objectively exists. Right and wrong are absolutes that we can know. The secularist has a much different view of truth. From a humanistic perspective no absolute truth is possible. All so-called

 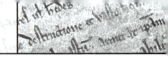

truths are relative. The relativist says: "Whatever I want to believe, I may believe. Whatever I think is true is true for me, and whatever you think is true is true for you. If you believe in a God as the source of truth, that's okay, but I don't believe in God or absolute truth; and you shouldn't force your view on me or on society."

Relativism has become the predominant view of those in academia, the media, and western governments. But such a view remains completely illogical. A simple question reveals the absurdity of relativism. When someone says "there is no absolute truth," merely ask, "Are you sure?" If they answer no, they have jettisoned their epistemology, acknowledging that they do not know for certain that no absolutes exist. If they answer yes, then they have affirmed the reality of absolutes. They are absolutely sure there are no absolutes.

After someone admits absolutes exist, the next question is the source of those absolutes. For Christians, God is the source through the Bible. For humanists, man, either as an individual or corporate body through the state, must represent truth to society.

Belief in the certainty of no absolutes remains illogical. It contradicts itself. One who believes this is like the man who built his house on the sand — it cannot stand up under the pressure of storms (see Matthew 7:24-27). If a worldview is built on this presupposition, it will fall apart when most needed.

A Christian worldview teaches absolute truth. God is right about everything, and He reveals in His Word the truth that man needs to know. Relativists condemn Christians as narrow-minded and bigoted for believing in right and wrong. They say, "You should not see things as right and wrong. It is **wrong** to do this."

In reality they are saying they do not want to face the Creator God — Who is the source of all right and wrong — and His standard of righteous living. They want to live life on their own terms. Hence, their theology, or worldview, follows their morality.

Truth emanates from an ultimate authority, from the Creator of all things. Truth is not what leaders or a majority declare to be true. That rulers or groups declare something to be true, does not make it so. Remember, James Otis said government cannot make 2 plus 2, 5, even if they declare such by law. Abraham Lincoln once posed the question, "How many legs does a dog have if you call the tail a leg?" Of course, the answer is four, but according to today's post-modernist relativistic thought, the answer could easily be five.

A pagan view of truth has captured the thinking of most of the world. Relativism is the dominant view of Americans today, even those Americans who claim to be Christians, as revealed in a poll conducted by the Barna Group in the spring of 2002. In a survey of adults and teenagers, people were asked if they believed moral absolutes are unchanging, or that moral truth is relative; only 6% said it is absolute. Among born-again Christians 32% of adults and 9% of teens expressed a belief in absolute truth. The number one answer as to what people believe is the basis for moral decisions, was doing whatever feels right (believed by 31% of

adults and 38% of teens).

Early Americans, who were mostly Christians, held to the Christian idea of truth. Their laws and constitutions reflected that worldview. They believed fixed law applies to everyone and is always true. God reveals His law in nature (the laws of nature) and by special revelation in the Bible (the laws of nature's God). The phrase Jefferson used in the Declaration of Independence — "the laws of nature and of nature's God" — had a well established meaning.[64]

An early civics textbook, *First Lessons in Civil Government* (1846) by Andrew Young, reveals the Founders' biblical view of law:

> The will of the Creator is the law of nature which men are bound to obey. But mankind in their present imperfect state are not capable of discovering in all cases what the law of nature requires; it has therefore pleased Divine Providence to reveal his will to mankind, to instruct them in their duties to himself and to each other. This will is revealed in the Holy Scriptures, and is called the law of revelation, or the Divine law.[65]

This view is in great contrast to the secular or socialist view of law, as revealed in the French Declaration of Rights (1794): "the Law … is the expression of the general will…. [T]he rights of man rests on the national sovereignty. This sovereignty … resides essentially in the whole people."[66] To the humanist, man is the source of law, of right and wrong. But if whatever man declares to be lawful is the standard for society, then everyone's fundamental rights are threatened, for a majority, or ruling dictator, can declare anyone to be an outlaw. Tyrants have done this throughout history, and millions upon millions of people have been killed under this worldview.

> creases his own.
> § 16. But it may be asked, if the law of nature is the rule by which mankind ought to regulate their conduct, of what use are written laws? The will of the Creator is the law of nature which men are bound to obey. But mankind in their present imperfect state are not capable of discovering in all cases what the law of nature requires; it has therefore pleased Divine Providence to reveal his will to mankind, to instruct them in their duties to himself and to each other. This will is revealed in the Holy Scriptures, and is called the law of revelation, or the Divine law.

Young's textbook, First Lessons in Civil Government (1846),
presents a biblical view of law.

The Christian view of law proclaims that all men have God-given unalienable rights, and the Bible states what those rights are. No man can take them away. All men are subject to God's higher law, rulers as well as common people. No man is above the law, nor is man the source of law. Hence, the rule of law originated in the

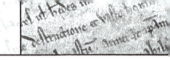

western Christian world where the Christian idea of law prevailed. This Christian view of law produced the unique nature of American constitutionalism and law.[67]

Who Is the Source of Law?

Who is the source of law of a society? This is a fundamental question each society should be asking, but few are. This is fundamental because the source of law of a society is the god of that society. Laws express the working religion of the state and its people. Laws express the will of the sovereign. Law is the word and will of a sovereign.

God's Law is His righteous standard, and it was originally the source of law in the United States. But over the last century or so in our nation man-centered evolutionary law has gradually been replacing God's absolute law. As we have changed law systems we have also changed gods. The removal of the Ten Commandments from court room walls and school room walls reflect this change. However, God's law was first removed from men's hearts.

The Founders' Christian view of law can easily be documented. It is attested to in many ways, including: 1) the political writings that shaped their worldview, 2) their own words on the nature of law, 3) the seminal constitutions, compacts, and charters of the colonies, 4) early laws written by the colonists, 5) documents in the early American republic, 6) court rulings, 7) the content of education in the schools, colleges, and textbooks.[68] Following is a brief summary of the belief of early Americans.

The Christian Foundation of Law in America

Dr. Donald Lutz conducted an exhaustive ten-year research of about 15,000 political documents of the Founders' Era (1760-1805). From 916 of these items he recorded every reference our Founders made to other sources. This list of 3154 citations reveals those writings and men that most shaped the political ideas of our Founders. By far, the most quoted source of their political ideas was the Bible, 34% of citations. The next most quoted sources were individuals who had a Christian view of law — Montesquieu (8.3%), Blackstone (7.9%), and Locke (2.9%).[69]

William Blackstone's view of law is representative of all three. He wrote that "Man, considered as a creature, must necessarily be subject to the laws of his creator," and according to him, these laws are revealed in nature and in the Holy Scriptures; "upon these two foundations, the law of nature and the law of revelation, depend all human laws; that is to say, no human laws should be suffered to contradict these."[70]

Nearly every Founder would agree with Blackstone, as expressed by James Wil-

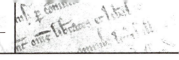

son, signer of the Declaration and the Constitution, and U.S. Supreme Court Justice:

> God … is the promulgator as well as the author of natural law.[71]
>
> All [laws], however, may be arranged in two different classes. 1) Divine. 2) Human…. But it should always be remembered that this law, natural or revealed, made for men or for nations, flows from the same Divine source: it is the law of God…. Human law must rest its authority ultimately upon the authority of that law which is Divine.[72]

William Blackstone

Rufus King, signer of the Constitution wrote: "[T]he … law established by the Creator … extends over the whole globe, is everywhere and at all times binding upon mankind…. [This] is the law of God by which he makes his way known to man and is paramount to all human control."[73]

The first laws written in America were *Laws Divine, Morall and Martiall, Etc.* written in Virginia from 1609 to 1612. The first ten laws were in essence a recounting of the Ten Commandments. The colonists were required to serve God, to attend divine services, to not speak against God or blaspheme God's holy name, and to not speak or act in any way that would "tend to the derision, or despight [open defiance] of Gods holy word upon paine of death."[74] Reading the over one hundred constitutions, compacts, and charters of early America reveal the same Christian foundations.[75]

Many of the early state constitutions required elected officials to take a Christian oath before they assumed office. In Maryland, the oath of office included "a declaration of a belief in the Christian religion."[76] The Constitution of Tennessee (1797) stated: "No person who denies the being of God, or a future state of rewards and punishments, shall hold any office in the civil department of this State."[77] They had such oaths because they believed only

The U.S. Constitution requires a Christian oath, acknowledges the Christian Sabbath, and is dated in the year of our Lord.

— 39 —

 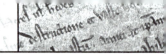

Christians could provide the power and form necessary for proper governing.

Early Americans clearly had a Christian view of law, but beginning in the mid to late nineteenth century this gradually began to change.[78] By the 1920s an evolutionary or relativistic view of law became predominant in many law schools. Many in the judicial system began to embrace this evolving view of law and rejected the Christian understanding of absolute law rooted in a higher power. For example Supreme Court justice Benjamin Cardozo (appointed in 1932) said:

> If there is any law which is back of the sovereignty of the state, and superior thereto, it is not law in such a sense as to concern the judge or lawyer, however much it concerns the statesmen or the moralist.[79]

Relativism began to affect judicial philosophy and constitutional interpretation, as reflected in the words of Charles Evans Hughes, Supreme Court Chief Justice from 1930 to 1941: "We are under a Constitution, but the Constitution is what the judges say it is."[80]

Most nations today look to man as the source of law. Thus, man is his own god. Statism is the general term we could use to describe the belief that man is the ultimate authority in the earth.[81] God forbids man being a law unto himself, where "every man [is] doing whatever is right in his own eyes" (Deuteronomy 12:8). He commands that we are not to have any other god or law or truth besides Him (Exodus 20:3). Statism has existed since the fall of man. It was dramatically displayed at Babel and strongly opposed by God (Genesis 11).

Choosing Godly Rulers

Since law is the working religion of a people, it is important to have good and godly laws. But in order to encode truth in society via good laws, people must first have truth (God's law) in their hearts. If godly laws leave the hearts of men, they will leave the society. Good laws are important, but good laws cannot be sustained unless men are good, both citizens and leaders. The founder of Pennsylvania, William Penn, wrote that "though good laws do well, good men do better."[82]

Therefore, we must participate in choosing good men to lead us. Paul wrote that civil leaders are to be ministers of God to you for good (Romans 13:4). Civil government cannot perform its biblical function of being a minister of good unless good people are involved. The Founders of America understood our duty to elect Christian men. John Jay, first Supreme Court Chief Justice, proclaimed: "Providence has given to our people the choice of their rulers, and it is the duty, as well as the privilege and interest of our Christian nation, to select and prefer Christians for their rulers."[83]

In his *Lectures on Revival*, Charles Finney listed numerous things that were necessary for revival to continue in our nation. One of those items was:

> "The Church must take right ground in regard to politics…. The time has come that Christians must vote for honest men, and take consistent ground in politics,… or the country will be ruined. God cannot sustain this free and blessed country, which we love and pray for, unless the Church will take right ground. Politics are a part of a religion in such a country as this, and Christians must do their duty to the country as a part of their duty to God…. He will bless or curse this nation, according to the course they [Christians] take [in politics]."[84]

Charles Finney

What constitutes a good leader? When Moses told the children of Israel to select from among them those who would govern them, he set forth a number of biblical qualifications. He said: "You shall select out of all the people, able men who fear God, men of truth, those who hate dishonest gain" (Exodus 18:21). "Choose wise and discerning and experienced men" (Deuteronomy 1:13). He put forth three general qualifications for governing officials: 1) Fear of God, 2) Christian Character, and 3) Biblical Worldview. We should seek to place such men in positions of leadership because the Bible says that, "When the righteous are in authority, the people rejoice, but when the wicked man rules, people groan" (Proverbs 29:2). Noah Webster summarized the effect of unprincipled men in office:

> Let it be impressed on your mind that God commands you to choose for yourselves rulers, "just men who rule in the fear of God." The preservation of a republican government depends on the faithful discharge of this duty; if the citizens neglect their duty and place unprincipled men in office, the government will soon be corrupted; laws will be made, not for the public good, so much as for selfish or local purposes; cor-

Noah Webster

rupt or incompetent men will be appointed to execute the laws; the public revenues will be squandered on unworthy men; and the rights of the citizens will be violated or disregarded. If a republican government fails to secure pub-

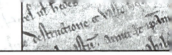

lic prosperity and happiness, it must be because the citizens neglect the divine commands, and elect bad men to make and administer the laws.[85]

The election of unprincipled men produces misery and tyranny, but godly rulers bring peace, prosperity, justice, and rejoicing. If we fulfill our duty and place godly men in office (who have knowledge, character, and faith) our future will be bright. According to 2 Samuel 23:3-4, "The God of Israel said … He who rules … in the fear of God, is as the light of the morning when the sun rises, a morning without clouds, when the tender grass springs out of the earth, through sunshine after rain."

Blueprint of God's Law

A blueprint is a set of plans detailing action to build. The Bible is a blueprint for all of life, personal and civil. The Bible is essential for discipling nations and for advancing the kingdom of God. For this reason God gave His law to Israel after He delivered them from bondage in Egypt and before He led them into the Promised Land to start a new nation. Through applying His law, Israel was transformed from a nation of slaves to a great nation, so great that Israel was known throughout the world. The Queen of Sheba came to see Israel for she had heard of her greatness.

God gave Israel two things that made her great and different than all the other nations. He gave them **His law** and **His presence** (Deuteronomy 4:5-8). Great nations will have God's presence and God's Law-Word. These are essential for His kingdom to come on earth. God's law was a template or blueprint with which to build a nation. It worked. Jesus said it is still a template (Matthew 5:17-19); it is for establishing and discipling a nation. These laws addressed all of life: not only matters of worship, but also, familial, civil, economic, and social affairs.

God's standards for living as revealed in His Word are not just for redeemed men but are for all men. God is the King over all the earth (Psalm 47:2, 7-8). Jesus is Lord of all. He is King of kings. God created individuals and established three divine institutions (family, church, state), all of which are to live according to the standards He has established in His Word. It is the duty of civil governments to take His Word as their law. Civil rulers are to be ministers of God's justice (Romans 13). His Word is the blueprint for all mankind, and for all spheres of life.

God's law speaks to all of life and gives practical means for building nations.[86] We are to see that every sphere of life reflects God's truth. His law is for this purpose. God's law transformed Israel from a nation of slaves to a great nation. His law contains practical principles for every sphere of life. As Israel lived according to these principles, the nation grew, prospered, and became free — they were blessed. Conversely, when Israel disobeyed they went backward.

God has a heart for nations. He wants people saved, but He also wants whole

 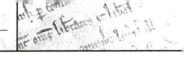

nations "saved." Nations throughout history have been changed and blessed to the degree they have applied all of His Word to all spheres of life. His Law-Word transformed Israel, but it also has transformed many other nations.

In using the Bible as a blueprint for building nations, we must remember that the New Covenant has modified the Old Covenant laws in various ways (for example, the ceremonial laws were fulfilled in Christ, and hence not applicable for us today, and the "holiness code" – those laws that set Israel apart as a unique physical nation – are not binding in the same way today.)

Building your life and society upon this blueprint will produce great blessing, the fruit of His Kingdom. In fact, the Bible teaches over and over again that if we obey Him and His Word we will be blessed, but if we disobey we will be cursed.[87]

His Word is not just personal. God's Word addresses every area of life. He gave it for the building of men and nations. Some of those areas include:

Biblical Blueprint: Addresses All of Life						
Worship	Personal Conduct	Family	Child Raising	Value of Man	Character in Society	Societal Structure
Health & Sanitation	Work and Rest	Social needs & Justice	Government & Law	Economics	Business	Liberty
Education	Crime and Punishment	Warfare	Philosophy	Arts and Media	Science & Technology	History & Literature

Self-Government

While correct law (that based upon God's higher law) is a foundation for good government, good government does not begin with external law. It begins with internal law and the ability for man to be self-governed.

All government begins in the heart of man with his ability (or inability) to direct, regulate, manage, and control his life. There are two spheres of government — internal and external. Internal government is self-government. External government occurs in the family, church, business, associations, and civil government. External spheres of government are a reflection of the degree of internal self-government a person or people possess. Internal government is causative to external government.

The power in a Christian society flows from the internal to the external, from the inside-out. All authority and power comes from God. It flows from Him into

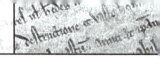

the heart and mind of man, and then out into the family, church, business, schools, and civil realm. This idea greatly affected the development of government in Amer-

Elias Boudinot

ica. President of the Continental Congress Elias Boudinot revealed a fundamental principle upon which America was founded:

> Another essential ingredient in the happiness we enjoy as a nation, and which arises from the principles of the revolution, is the right that every people have to govern themselves in such manner as they judge best calculated for the common benefit.[88]

This concept was new, because during most of history people lived under "ruler's law," where the rulers made the laws and the people had no voice in the matter. However, in America, the people made the laws, and everyone, including the rulers, was subject to them.

America's Founders understood that a people cannot govern themselves in civil affairs if they do not govern their own lives well. Robert C. Winthrop, Speaker of the United States House of Representatives from 1847-49, said in 1849:

> All societies of men must be governed in some way or other. The less they may have of stringent State Government, the more they must have of individual self-government. The less they rely on public law or physical force, the more they must rely on private moral restraint. Men, in a word, must necessarily be controlled either by a power within them, or by a power without them; either by the Word of God or by the strong arm of man; either by the Bible or the bayonet.[89]

Robert C. Winthrop

The basis of the ability for man to govern himself well is rooted in his being in subjection to a higher power. The Founders' firm commitment to God, as well as their commitment to govern their lives according to His laws as contained in the Bible, was the foundation for self-government in America. Examination of the scores of constitutions, compacts, and charters written in colonial America readily reveals that the source of their civil law was found in the Bible.

The Pilgrims wrote in their *General Laws* that "Laws ... are so far good and

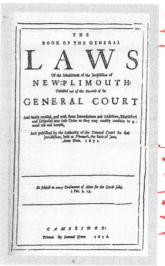

The Laws of the Pilgrims were derived from God's Law, and were reflective of early American law.

wholesome, as by how much they are derived from, and agreeable to the ancient Platform of God's Law."[90] In the Massachusetts Body of Liberties, written by Rev. Nathaniel Ward in 1641, the Pentateuch (the first five books of the Bible) was the basis for its criminal code, and "in case of the defect of a law in any perticular [sic] case" the standard was "the word of God."[91] Adopted January 14, 1639, the Fundamental Orders of Connecticut (the first written constitution in history that led to the formation of a new commonwealth) began with the inhabitants covenanting together under God "to maintain and preserve the liberty and purity of the gospel of our Lord Jesus which we now profess."[92] It gave the governor and magistrates "power to administer justice according to the Laws here established, and for want thereof according to the rule of the word of God."[93] The required oath of office ended with the elected official saying: "I . . . will further the execution of Justice according to the rule of Gods word; so helpe me God, in the name of the Lord Jesus Christ."[94]

Often the colonists would quote directly from the Scriptures and give references to justify their civil laws as seen, for example, in the laws of the Pilgrims.[95]

Self-government is limited apart from God; therefore, the ability to govern well is limited where the people and leaders do not seek to govern themselves and their nation under God. George Washington said, "It is impossible to govern the universe without the aid of a Supreme Being."[96]

The Christian idea of government led to the establishment of the American Christian Constitutional Federal Republic. It was unique in history and was only possible because the citizens were self-governed.

It is important to realize that the foundation for self-government is laid in the families of a nation. Families must begin early teaching the principle of self-government. One night, many years ago I was teaching my son, who was then about 5 years old, about self-government. I gave him a definition he could understand, telling him that "self-government is doing what you are supposed to do without anybody telling you." The next morning he woke me early, took me to his bedroom, pointed to his bed, which he had made up all by himself without anybody telling him to do so, and remarked: "Dad, I was being self-governed, wasn't I?" The transformation of nations begins with such small steps.

The power in a Christian society flows from the inside-out. The power in a pagan society flows from the outside-in, from the top-down. This top-down flow occurs because the people see the rulers as the source of power and authority — they are the ultimate authority in the earth. However, the state is not man's savior, nor the ultimate authority. Caesar thought he was, but Jesus made clear his authority was from God and was limited.[97] Most leaders throughout history have had this Caesar mentality, with most citizens agreeing. The spread of Christian ideas, especially after the Protestant Reformation, changed this in many nations, but unfortunately a majority of these nations are moving back toward a pagan view of government. Many people in the United States are embracing this idea as well. When trouble comes, who do people look to for help, provision, and salvation? Many first look to civil government, thinking the government owes them this provision. Since providing all things for the citizens is not the purpose of civil government, it will never do it effectively or efficiently.

Secularists have no savior, so they often look to government to be their savior — to bring peace, to establish a utopia, to meet needs, to provide material things, and so on. Christians have a Savior and do not need government for this. From a Christian perspective, civil government is a divine institution with a legitimate function, but it is very limited in what it is supposed to do. It is to protect the righteous, punish the evil doer, and administer God's justice in the civil realm that is under its sphere of authority.[98]

The Christian idea of government teaches that the state exists to serve man, not vice-versa; that government flows from the internal to the external, from the bottom-up; that government begins with self-government then flows to the family, church, and the civil realm.

God's Justice and Mercy

As mentioned before, when our Founding Fathers appealed to "the laws of nature and of nature's God" in the Declaration of Independence, they believed this to mean that God reveals His law (His truth) by general revelation in nature and the conscience of man (the laws of nature) and by special revelation in the Bible (the laws of nature's God). Thus, they would almost universally agree with these words of Noah Webster, the author of the first exhaustive English dictionary and the most influential educator of the nineteenth century:

> The moral principles and precepts contained in the Scriptures ought to form the basis of all our civil constitutions and laws. All the miseries and evils which men suffer from vice, crime, ambition, injustice, oppression, slavery, and war, proceed from their despising or neglecting the precepts contained in the Bible.[99]

God's Law-Word will provide justice to all members of society, because all people stand equal before His Law. Yet, the Scriptures reveal that God is not only just, but He is also merciful. This concept is reflected in the Forefathers Monument. The statue of Law has a copy of the law in his left hand, and his right hand is extended in mercy. The two carved reliefs underneath the throne where Law is seated represent Justice and Mercy. Our forefathers sought to administer civil justice while always having God's mercy in view. One example of this was displayed by Thomas McKean.

Thomas McKean

Like many of our Founders, Thomas McKean served in many capacities. He was a signer of the Declaration of Independence; he helped author the constitutions of Pennsylvania and Delaware, and served as governor of each of these states; he was a legal authority (writing *Commentaries on the Constitution of the United States of America*, 1792); and he served as Chief Justice of the Supreme Court of Pennsylvania. As Chief Justice he presided over a trial where John Roberts was sentenced to death for treason. After delivering the sentence McKean gave this advice to Roberts:

> You will probably have but a short time to live. Before you launch into eternity, it behooves you to improve the time that may be allowed you in this world: it behooves you most seriously to reflect upon your past conduct; to repent of your evil deeds; to be incessant in prayers to the great and merciful God to forgive your manifold transgressions and sins; to teach you to rely upon the merit and passion of a dear Redeemer, and thereby to avoid those regions of sorrow—those doleful shades where peace and rest can never dwell, where even hope cannot enter. It behooves you to seek the [fellowship], advice, and prayers of pious and good men; to be [persistent] at the Throne of Grace, and to learn the way that leadeth to happiness. May you, reflecting upon these things, and pursuing the will of the great Father of light and life, be received into [the] company and society of angels and archangels and the spirits of just men made perfect; and may you be qualified to enter into the joys of Heaven—joys unspeakable and full of glory![100]

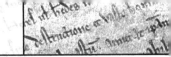

Review Questions

- What does it mean that "all nations have a religious foundation" and the "law is the working religion of a people"?

- Contrast and compare the Christian versus the humanistic view of truth.

- Why do you think so many "born again" Christians see truth as relative?

- Explain what is meant by the phrase in the Declaration of Independence, "the Laws of Nature and of Nature's God."

- Why is the answer to the question, "Who is the source of law in a society?" so important?

- What was William Blackstone's view of law?

- What is our biblical duty regarding those who govern us?

- Is the Bible more than just a personal handbook for knowing God? Give biblical evidence for your answer.

- What does it mean that the Bible is a blueprint for life?

- Summarize in a few sentences a biblical philosophy of government. Do you know any governing officials who hold to such a view? How can we produce more leaders who hold to such a perspective?

- Give a short definition of self-government.

- Contrast a pagan versus a Christian view of governance.

- What do you think would happen today if a judge gave the advice to a convicted criminal that Thomas McKean gave to John Roberts?

CHAPTER 5

Education

The Christian idea of man teaches us that all men have great value, but that men are sinful, in a fallen state, and in need of a redeemer. We cannot save ourselves. We need the regenerating power of the Holy Spirit to work in us, to translate us into the kingdom of God. Once we become a new creation we must grow in our salvation — we must be sanctified in His truth so we can extend His kingdom in the nations. Biblical education is central in accomplishing this.

All people must be educated so they can know the truth (God) themselves. In the fourth and fifth centuries, the church began to embrace a pagan philosophy of education, thinking only certain people can know and keep the truth (the Bible). These keepers of the truth (the clergy) would then tell the common person what that truth was. This practice led to bondage, as many people were cut off from the truth. The Protestant Reformation changed this. It sought to reclaim the Christian idea of education; that is, everyone should know the truth them-

One of the original rules of Harvard College: "Let every Student be plainly instructed, and earnestly pressed to consider well, the maine end of his life and studies is, to know God and Jesus Christ which is eternall life, (John 17:3), and therefore to lay Christ in the bottome, as the only foundation of all sound knowledge and Learning."

selves. Everyone should have access to the Bible, God's source of truth to mankind. This Christian idea motivated many people to translate the Bible into the common

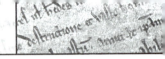

language of the people, both before and especially after the Reformation. In cases where a people group had no written language, Bible translators gave them one.

America's early settlers and our Founding Fathers were very much aware of the relation of education and liberty. They knew that a people cannot be both ignorant and free. Thomas Jefferson said it this way: "If a nation expects to be ignorant and free, in a state of civilization, it expects what never was and never will be."[101] Benjamin Franklin said that ignorance produces bondage: "A nation of well informed men who have been taught to know and prize the rights which God has given them cannot be enslaved. It is in the region of ignorance that tyranny begins."

America's Founders believed that all people must be educated in order to know the truth (God) for themselves. Everyone should have access to the Bible, God's source of truth to mankind. This Christian idea motivated the early settlers to start schools and colleges, and to also translate the Bible into the language of the Native Americans.

The Massachusetts school law of 1647, which provided directions for educating youth, begins, "It being one chief project of that old deluder, Satan, to keep men from the knowledge of the Scriptures."[102] One of the original rules of Harvard College, established in 1636, states: "Let every Student be plainly instructed, and earnestly pressed to consider well, the maine end of his life and studies is, to know God and Jesus Christ which is eternall life, (John 17:3), and therefore to lay Christ in the bottome, as the only foundation of all sound knowledge and Learning."[103] Puritan minister John Eliot worked for decades to give the Algonquin Indians a written language and then to publish the Bible in their language (1661-63). This was the first Bible printed in America.

Pilgrim Mother: "They brought up their families in sturdy virtue and a living faith in God, without which nations perish."

Education in America for the first few centuries was centered in the home because everyone believed it was the right and responsibility of parents to govern the education of their children. A statue to the Pilgrim Mother in Plymouth, Massachusetts, bears the inscription: "They brought up their families in sturdy virtue and a living faith in God, without which nations perish." The American home passed on the faith and virtue necessary for liberty. To our Founders, the most important aspect of education was to impart Christian character, to shape the inner man. Upon this foundation they taught a worldview deeply rooted in the Bible that provided instruction for all spheres of life. These ideas are reflected in the Forefathers Monument.

The statue of *Education* is holding an open book of knowledge (the Bible) implying its truth must be passed to all. Flanking her throne are two carved reliefs; one is *Youth* (the object of the parents instruction) and the other *Wisdom* (represented by a grand-father) pointing to the commands and an open Bible, with the world at his feet. The family, both parents and grandparents, were to teach the youth from a biblical perspective how the world works. *Education* is wearing a wreath of victory, which is obtained when children are well-instructed in the Lord.

All Education Is Religious

All education is religious. This is why state education is so dangerous; it passes on the predominant religion of those in control. Some people say education is neutral, and therefore religion must be kept separate from education, which in America today translates to mean that any mention of God or godly values must be extirpated from our public schools. But all education imparts a worldview and basic presuppositions about life which are rooted in religion. The issue is not keeping religion out of education (which is impossible); the issue is what religion forms the foundation of education.

Modern liberal, leftist, secularists decry any attempt to compel in matters of worship (and rightly so). However, the modern state compels everyone to be educated, and hence, is compelling in the arena of fundamental beliefs, in faith or religion. Throughout most of history, nations have controlled and compelled in the area of faith. Many people who came to America did so to escape this, and set an example that ended state-compelled worship.

In his Statute for Religious Freedom, Thomas Jefferson said to compel a man to support the "propagation of opinions which he disbelieves . . . is sinful and tyrannical." This was one argument used to end state established religion in early America. Throughout the nineteenth century this idea spread to many other nations in the western world. However, at about the same time the western world ended compelling worship, they adopted the practice of compelling in education.

While the modern humanist is appalled at forced worship, he does the same thing in the area of education, and since all education is religious, he is really compelling in the area of religion. We have need today for a Statute for Educational Freedom.

The foundational philosophy of education in a nation is of utmost importance because whoever controls the education of the nation controls the future of the nation. It has been said, the philosophy of the schoolroom in one generation will be the philosophy of government in the next.

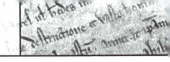

A Liberal Arts Education

Many Americans who go to college today receive a liberal arts education. In our primarily secular schools this means a liberal view of life and politics in the modern leftist, socialist sense of the word. They are trained in a worldview that is humanist, secular, and ungodly. Paul warns us to not be taken "captive through philosophy and empty deception, according to the tradition of men, according to the elementary principles of the world" (Colossians 2:8). A man-centered, worldly philosophy brings captivity. It leads men into bondage. In contrast, an education "according to Christ" brings liberty.

In times past, receiving a liberal arts education meant something good – it meant that you were educated to live in liberty. Education gave youth the character and ideas necessary to live free. It is not easy to live free. Liberty is not the default state of fallen man. Sinful man naturally devolves to a life of bondage. Early Americans understood this, so they not only taught their children at home, but also began to establish schools and colleges shortly after arriving in the wilderness. They wanted this nation to grow in liberty.

While Americans need a liberal arts education, they are unfortunately being educated to live socialistically. The Christian ideals and ideas upon which our nation was built are under assault. We are in a war today – not a war of guns and bullets, but a war of worldviews. One of our great enemies is statism (and its various relatives – secularism, socialism, humanism, and atheism).

Statism is the belief that the civil government (or man via civil government) is the ultimate authority in the earth, and as such is the source of law and morality. The state (and man as its head) defines what is right and wrong, what is lawful and unlawful, what is moral and immoral. The state becomes the de facto god of the society, or in the words of Roscoe Pound, President of Harvard Law School in the 1920s, "the state takes the place of Jehovah."[104]

Statists/humanists declare that man is god, there are no absolutes, and no such thing as truth exists. They are leading the great assault against God and truth today. This assault is evidenced in many ways – by the attempt to redefine the family; by the removal of prayer and the Bible from state schools; by the growing number of lawsuits brought against local or state governments or officials, as well as private organizations, who seek to mention God in the civil arena; by the attempt to remove God from government; and by the gradual replacing of biblical civil law with humanistic evolutionary law.

America's secular education is making a huge change in the thinking and action of many Americans, even those who are Christians. As mentioned previously, relativism has so permeated the worldview of Americans that only one-third of them believe moral absolutes exist, and among teenagers only six percent said moral truth is absolute. Surprisingly, this same percentage holds for those identifying themselves as born-again Christians. Only 32% of adults and 9% of teens expressed a belief in absolute truth. A decline of biblical thinking (and action) occurs when Christian parents fail to understand the great importance of education. Theologian Robert L. Dabney said:

> The education of children for God is the most important business done on earth. It is the one business for which the earth exists. To it all politics, all war, all literature, all money-making, ought to be subordinated; and every parent especially ought to feel, every hour of the day, that, next to making his own calling and election sure, this is the end for which he is kept alive by God – this is his task on earth.[105]

Noah Webster wrote: "The education of youth [is] an employment of more consequence than making laws and preaching the gospel, because it lays the foundation on which both law and gospel rest for success."[106]

Is this true? Its truth depends upon how you define education. While it is not true for modern statist education, it is true from a biblical perspective, because education is a key component of preaching the Gospel. Jesus said we disciple nations by teaching all He commanded. Discipling believers, especially our children, is a central command of the Scriptures. The biblical education of early America produced men and women of character with a worldview that gave birth to this free nation. Without biblical education there would be no America, no godly law, and no freedom to propagate the Gospel. Nor would we have the economic prosperity to pay for the spread of the Gospel throughout the world. Biblical education produced a free and prosperous America, and only biblical education can preserve a free and prosperous nation.

How have we come to this point of decay in America? Princeton Seminary Professor (1906-29) and a founder of Westminster Seminary in Philadelphia (1929) John Gresham Machen states it clearly: "If liberty is not maintained with regard to education, there is no use trying to maintain it in any other sphere. If you give the bureaucrats the children, you might just as well give them everything else."

We have given our children to secularists to train and disciple them, which would be like the children of Israel in times past giving their children to the Philistines to educate them. When we teach our youth they are merely animals (grown up worms evolved from bacteria) and that morality is based upon the ever-shifting views of a selfish people, we should not be surprised when they act like animals and throw off any moral constraints. After all, Jesus taught that we will be like our teachers (Luke 6:40).

Whoever controls the children in a society controls the future. The Marxists and communists of the twentieth century understood this and sought to control education whenever they went into a nation. God has given the responsibility of educating children primarily to the parents, not to the state.

The problem we have in America today is that we have rendered unto Caesar

(civil government) the things that are God's, contrary to Christ's command to render unto God the things that are God's. In particular, and with devastating consequences, we have given Caesar control of our children and control of our property (not to mention control of health, welfare, retirement, and much more). Statism has become the golden calf of America and much of the modern world.

What is the solution to America's problem? It is restoring biblical education to America.

Biblical Education

The Bible has much to say about education. Parents and grandparents bear the duty to teach their children and grandchildren all of the Word of God, using all opportunities as they walk through life (Deuteronomy 6:4-7). After all, Jesus told us that we disciple men and nations through teaching all of His Word (Matthew 28:18-20).

Education is a sowing and reaping process. The Bible tells us much about the seed principle. The parable of the sower and the soils (Mark 4) shows that the kingdom of God is like a seed. When we repent and submit ourselves to Christ we are instantly converted, but the establishment of God's character and kingdom within us is a gradual process. Like the growth of a plant or tree, a seed is planted; nourishment, care, and sunlight are provided; eventually a mature plant comes forth bearing fruit (we must remember the pruning process, also). This same principle applies in establishing God's truth in the nations of the world. A gradual process must occur. Christian education forms the core of that process.

What would be necessary for us to restore true liberal arts education to our nation? What does the education that produces liberty look like? What are the components of biblical or kingdom education? First such education must look far different than most education in the world today. The following represent a few general components of Kingdom education.

1) Education is primarily the responsibility of the family, who can delegate aspects of it to others.

Biblical education must be centered in the home. Parents have the right and responsibility to govern the education of their children. They bear the responsibility to train their children in both biblical character and worldview (Ephesians 6:1-4; Proverbs 1:8; 22:6). Parents should disciple their children. As they are faithful to do this, they will have an impact, not only on their children's lives, but on society at large, at times affecting nations. Consider one such example.

From an early age, Susanna would pray daily for God to guide her and make her life count. Born the twenty-fifth of 25 children to a minister and his wife, she loved God from her youth and had a burning desire to live her life for Him. As a young woman she dreamed of starting a fire that would burn all of London, all of the United Kingdom, and all over the world.

Susanna was always looking for an opportunity to fulfill that dream and was always asking God what He would have her do. How should she start that fire? Should she become a missionary, a teacher? Or did God have another plan for her? At a young age she married a minister and, like her mother, began having children—nineteen in all. She devoted most of her time and effort to being a good wife and mother.

Even in the midst of hardship after hardship, she continued to pour herself into her children and inspire them for good. When her children were around five or six-years-old she would set aside one whole day to teach them how to read. She taught the alphabet phonetically and then had her children read the Bible.

She never traveled throughout the world or directly started a spiritual fire in London or elsewhere. But Susanna's dream did become a reality in her thirteenth and seventeenth born children, Charles and John Wesley, who spread the Gospel throughout the world, giving birth to the Methodist movement. Their education, which was centered in the home, still impacts the world today.

Susanna's life gives meaning to the saying, "You can count how many seeds are in an apple, but you cannot count how many apples are in a seed." The potential for an entire forest resides in one seed. God wants His seed (His Truth), not the seed of secular humanism, to be planted in those who will bear fruit in our nation.

God's seed gave birth to America and passed on the heritage of liberty to the generations. Biblical education laid a foundation for America's liberty, prosperity, virtue, and justice. Early American education followed the pattern given to the covenant nation of Israel. First it was centered in the home where the seed of transformation is developed. The Founding Fathers were primarily educated at home. One third of the men who gave us the Declaration and Constitution had no, or very little, formal schooling; they were home-schooled and trained to be self-taught. Such was the case for the Father of our Country, George Washington. Others started their education at home and then supplemented this with tutors or at schools (which were mostly in someone's home). Most of these tutors in early America were ministers, since they were the best educated. Thomas Jefferson, James Madison, and Noah Webster were a few Founders who had such education. Only one in four of the Founders went to college, and these colleges were thoroughly Christian.

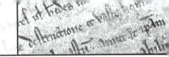

The Education of John Quincy Adams

The education of America's sixth president, John Quincy Adams, provides a great example. Adams father and mother, John and Abigail, taught him at home until around age eleven. As a 10-year-old, John Quincy knew French and Latin, read the writings of Charles Rollins and other difficult works, and helped manage the farm with his mother while his father was away serving the nation. Letters from John Quincy to his father at this time reveal the literacy level and reasoning skills his parents imparted to him. In one letter he wrote, "I wish, sir, you would give me some instructions with regard to my time, and advise me how to proportion my studies and my play, in writing, and I will keep them by me and endeavor to follow them."[107]

In a letter to his father on June 2, 1777, at age ten, John Quincy wrote: "Sir, If you will be so good as to favor me with a blank-book I will transcribe the most remarkable occurrences I meet with in my reading, which will serve to fix them upon my mind."[108]

At age eleven, John Quincy traveled with his father to France, yet Abigail used her letters to continue the education she had so well begun at their home in Braintree, Massachusetts. In June of 1778 she wrote:

> You are in possession of a naturally good understanding, and of spirits unbroken by adversity and untamed with care. Improve your understanding by acquiring useful knowledge and virtue, such as will render you an ornament to society, and honor to your country, and a blessing to your parents. Great learning and superior abilities, should you ever possess them, will be of little value and small estimation, unless virtue, honor, truth, and integrity are added to them. Adhere to those religious sentiments and principles which were early instilled into your mind, and remember, that you are accountable to your Maker for all your words and actions.[109]

In the same letter she encouraged John Quincy to pay attention to the development of his conduct by heeding the instruction of his parents; "for, dear as you are to me, I would much rather you should have found your grave in the ocean you have crossed . . . than see you an immoral, profligate, or graceless child."

This home-centered, morality based education that taught biblical methods of reasoning enabled John to go on to a remarkable career. When he was 14, he received a United States Congressional diplomatic appointment as secretary to the ambassador of the court of Catherine the Great in

John Quincy Adams

Russia. He served as foreign ambassador to England, France, Holland, Prussia, and Russia. He was a U.S. Senator, Secretary of State, and the sixth President, after which he served 18 years in the U.S. House of Representatives, during which time he was a leader in the antislavery movement. Biblical education produced this man who served his country and the cause of God.

Following the biblical model, home education can be supplemented by tutors and schools. For ancient Israel, the Levites provided these schools. In early America the first schools were started by Christians, and ministers were usually the teachers. These schools were started by the church to teach people to read the Bible. Making provision for everyone to be able to read the Bible was the primary impetus for common schools, which were established in the 1640s in Massachusetts. The Connecticut School Laws of 1650 began like that of Massachusetts (quoted previously): "It being one chief project of that old deluder, Satan, to keep men from the knowledge of the Scriptures."[110] A 1690 law declared: "This [legislature] observing that … there are many persons unable to read the English tongue and thereby incapable to read the holy Word of God or the good laws of this colony … it is ordered that all parents and masters shall cause their respective children and servants, as they are capable, to be taught to read distinctly the English tongue."[111] They understood that the devil wants to keep people ignorant, because if they are ignorant he can keep them in bondage.

Colleges were started to train ministers in a knowledge of the Bible. The first college, Harvard, was started in 1636 by the Puritans of New England, not long after they began to carve out a home in the wilderness, because they wanted "to advance learning, and perpetuate it to posterity, dreading to leave an illiterate ministry to the churches, when our present ministers shall lie in the dust."[112] As stated previously, one of the original rules of Harvard was for every student "to lay Christ in the bottome, as the only foundation of all sound knowledge and Learning."[113]

Yale University was started in 1701. The Regulations at Yale College in 1745 began,

> 1. All scholars shall live religious, godly, and blameless lives according to the rules of God's Word, diligently reading the Holy Scriptures, the fountain of

Yale University, like most of the early colleges, was started as a Christian educational institution.

light and truth; and constantly attend upon all the duties of religion, both in public and secret.[114]

The motto of Princeton University, which was started by Presbyterians in 1746 as a product of the First Great Awakening, was "Under God's Power She Flourishes."

In 1754, Rev. Samuel Johnson was chosen as the first President of Columbia College (called King's College up until 1784). In that year he composed an advertisement announcing the opening of the college. It stated:

> The chief Thing that is aimed at in this College is, to teach and engage the Children to know God in Jesus Christ, and to love and serve him, in all Sobriety, Godliness and Righteousness of Life, with a perfect Heart, and a willing Mind; and to train them up in all virtuous Habits, and all such useful Knowledge as may render them creditable to their Families and Friends.[115]

The biblical model followed by early Americans was: education was centered in the home where the parents discipled their children; home instruction was often supplemented by tutors and Christian schools; then young adults were apprenticed by their parents or others to learn vocational skills; a few went on to higher education at colleges. All were given the tools for self-study. This training helped them to fulfill their unique calling or vocation, where each contributed to the advancement of the liberty and prosperity of the nation.

They understood the idea of biblical vocation; that is, that God gives us talents and skills that we are to use to advance His purposes in the earth through every aspect of our life, especially in our work. Jesus taught this idea in Luke 19:11-27 telling us to "Occupy till I come" or "Do business with this (minas – representing our talents, skills, and abilities) until I come back" (v. 13). We are to work as partners with Him to take dominion over the earth (Genesis 1:26-28) by using the talents He has given us. Our work is a vital part of God's plan for us and the nations. We occupy through our occupation. We are to fulfill our biblical duties in every sphere of life whether the family, church, media, government, marketplace, education, and science.[116]

This model of education used in early America produced a people that gave the world a new and unique nation, the most free and prosperous the world has ever seen. Biblical education produces good fruit.

2) The philosophy, methodology, and content of education should be biblical.

The first thing we can do to restore biblical education to the nation is for families to assume the responsibility to govern the education of their children. A second component of biblical education is that all aspects of education – the philosophy (why), methodology (how), and content (what) – should be biblical.[117]

A biblical ideology motivated early Americans to teach their children at home, start schools and colleges, and make provision for those unable to obtain an education at home. The concept of education for all is a Christian idea and developed first in Christian civilization. Our system of state education is based

Columbia College: "The chief Thing that is aimed at in this College is, to teach and engage the Children to know God in Jesus Christ, and to love and serve him."

upon this idea of education for all; unfortunately, the way we attempt to provide universal education does not follow the biblical model. It is state controlled and mandated; it teaches a humanistic philosophy of life and denies the very existence of truth.

The Bible was the central text for early American education. John Locke observed in 1690 that children learned to read by following "the ordinary road of Hornbook, Primer, Psalter, Testament and Bible." Hornbooks were the most widely used tool for teaching reading in seventeenth century America. A hornbook was a flat piece of wood with a handle, upon which a sheet of printed paper was attached and covered with transparent animal horn to protect it. A typical hornbook had the alphabet, the vowels, a list of syllables, the invocation of the Trinity, and the Lord's Prayer. Some had a pictured alphabet.

Another important educational book was the *New England Primer*, which was first published in Boston around 1690 by devout Protestant Benjamin Harris. It was the most prominent schoolbook for about 100 years, and was frequently reprinted through the 1800s. It sold over 3 million copies in 150 years. The rhyming alphabet is its most characteristic feature.

From a 1777 Primer, the alphabet was taught with this rhyme:

A In Adam's Fall
    We sinned all.
B Heaven to find
    The Bible Mind.
C Christ crucify'd
    For sinners dy'd.
D The Deluge drown'd
    The Earth around.

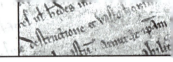

E Elijah hid
    By Ravens fed.
F The judgment made
    Felix afraid.
G As runs the Glass,
    Our Life doth pass
H My Book and Heart
    Must never part....[118]

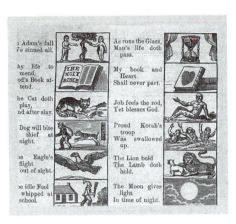

New England Primer. This edition of the Primer differed somewhat from the 1777 version but still used Biblical imagery.

The Primer's Christian character is easy to see. The book underwent various modifications over the years.

Noah Webster's Blue Backed Speller was first published in 1783 and sold over 100 million copies during the next century. It was the most influential textbook of the era and was written to instill into the minds of the youth "the first rudiments of the language and some just ideas of religion, morals, and domestic economy." Its premise was that "God's word, contained in the Bible, has furnished all necessary rules to direct our conduct." It included a moral catechism, large portions of the Sermon on the Mount, a paraphrase of the Genesis account of creation, and numerous moral stories. Students would read such things as:

Noah Webster's Blue Backed Speller

"God will forgive those who repent of their sins, and live a holy life."

"Examine the Scriptures daily and carefully, and set an example of good works."

"Those who enjoy the light of the gospel, and neglect to observe its precepts, are more criminal than the heathen."[119]

Noah Webster also produced the monumental work, *An American Dictionary of the English Language*. Webster spent over 20 years working on this first exhaustive dictionary in the English language. First published in 1828, Webster's Dictionary gave biblical defini-

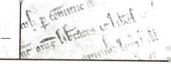

tions and used thousands of Scriptural references. In contrast, dictionaries today, even those bearing Webster's name, give humanistic definitions and indoctrinate youth in a non-biblical worldview.

Consider, for example, the word *immoral*. In his original 1828 dictionary, under the definition for immoral, Noah Webster writes: "Every action is immoral which contravenes any divine precept, or which is contrary to the duties men owe to each other."[120] To Webster, divine precept was the standard to judge immorality. Today, the standard is quite different, as reflected in the definition of immoral in modern dictionaries. *Webster's New World Dictionary* defines immoral as "not in conformity with accepted principles of right and wrong behavior."[121] The standard for immoral behavior today has become what the consensus of the population thinks. Man, rather than God, has been declared the judge of right and wrong conduct. Man becomes his own god when we embrace relativism.

Other prominent textbooks from early America, like McGuffey's *Readers*, Murray's *Reader*, Butler's *General History*, and Young's *Civil Government* were thoroughly Christian as well.

3) Biblical education advances God's kingdom with good fruit.

A primary purpose of education is to build Christian character, to shape people both internally and externally. Noah Webster gave a biblical definition for education: "Education comprehends all that series of instruction and discipline which is intended to enlighten the understanding, correct the temper, form the manners and habits of youth, and fit them for usefulness in their future stations."[122] The focus of education should firstly be the inner man. The fruit of education, according to Webster, is the same fruit that the Word of God will produce within an individual. Paul writes that "all Scripture is inspired by God and profitable for teaching, for reproof, for correction, for training in righteousness; that the man of God may be adequate, equipped for every good work" (2 Timothy 3:16). Webster's definition for education coincides with the fruit of the Word of God. Biblical educa-

A Colonial Hornbook, The Lord's Prayer was the first reading lesson.

tion will build the total man (inside and out) and prepare him to fulfill his destiny ("fit them for usefulness in their future stations").

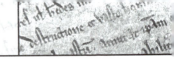

A central purpose of education is to build godly character. Whoever controls education in a nation controls the formation of character. Whoever controls the character of the people controls the form of government. America began as a constitutional republic because the Christian character necessary to support such a government was formed in Americans in the homes and churches. Rosalie Slater writes that "as we let go the control of education, we let go the control of character, and we declined from a republic into a socialistic democracy."[123]

Biblical education will not only affect individual lives but will also impact all of life. It is a primary way we will accomplish our godly mission to bring His kingdom to earth[124] and to disciple the nations.[125] Biblical education brings God's kingdom on earth. State education brings man's kingdom on earth.

Christian education gave birth to America. Almost everyone was biblically literate and knew principles of liberty. Thus, these people could effect a Christian revolution and give birth to the American Christian Constitutional Federal Republic. Education in biblical truth produced a free society with little crime. The crime that existed was a concern for the Founders, but they knew how to most effectively deal with it. Benjamin Rush wrote in 1806 that:

> the only means of establishing and perpetuating our republican forms of government, … is, the universal education of our youth in the principles of Christianity by the means of the bible. For this Divine book, above all others, favors that equality among mankind, that respect for just laws, and those sober and frugal virtues, which constitute the soul of republicanism.[126]

G. K. Chesterton said that "Education is simply the soul of a society as it passes from one generation to another. Whatever the soul is like, it will have to be passed on somehow, consciously or unconsciously…. It is…the transfer of a way of life." What way of life are we transferring today?

The Protestant reformer Martin Luther recognized the great power of education. He said:

> I am afraid that schools will prove to be the great gates of hell unless they diligently labor in explaining the Holy Scriptures, engraving them in the hearts of youth. I advise no one to place his child where the scriptures do not reign paramount. Every institution in which men are not increasingly occupied with the Word of God must become corrupt.[127]

Martin Luther

Theologian A.A. Hodge was even more direct:

> I am as sure as I am of the fact of Christ's reign that a comprehensive and centralized system of national education separated from religion, as is now

commonly proposed, will prove the most appalling enginery for the propagation of anti-Christian and atheistic unbelief, and of anti-social, nihilistic ethics, individual, social, and political, which this sin-rent world has ever seen.[128]

The home is primarily where the transfer of a way of life occurs. The ability to affect society can grow exponentially with each succeeding generation, as evidenced by Jonathan and Sarah Edwards. Jonathan Edwards was a leader in the First Great Awakening and was one of America's greatest theologians. He and his wife faithfully trained their eleven children in accordance with their biblical duty. Their children, in turn, passed on to future generations the vision for advancing liberty and building up their nation. A study was done of 1400 descendants of Jonathan and Sarah. Of these, 13 were college presidents, 65 were professors, 100 lawyers, 30 judges, 66 physicians, and 80 holders of public office including 3 senators, 3

Jonathan Edwards

governors, and a vice president of the United States.[129] Their training not only benefited their children, but thousands of their descendants, and the nation at large. The seeds we plant today through the education of our children (and others) have impact beyond measure in the future. Remember the great potential that comes from even a single seed.

Biblical education will produce kingdom fruit. As stated earlier, a primary purpose of education is to build Christian character, to shape the man both internally and externally. Biblical education will not only affect individual lives, but it will also impact all spheres of life.

John Witherspoon was a Kingdom educator who trained young men to be "Kingdom men." He was "the man who shaped the men who shaped America." Witherspoon was a Presbyterian minister who came from Scotland in 1768 to serve as President of the College of New Jersey. During Witherspoon's tenure there were 478 graduates of what became Princeton University. Of these, at least 86 became active in civil government and included: one president (James Madison), one vice-president (Aaron Burr), 10 cabinet officers, 21 senators, 39 congressmen, 12 governors, a Supreme Court justice (Brockholst Livingston), and one attorney general of

Rev. John Witherspoon trained the men who gave birth to the nation.

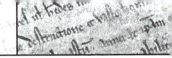

the United States (William Bradford).[130]

Nearly one-fifth of the signers of the Declaration of Independence, one-sixth of the delegates of the Constitutional Convention, and one-fifth of the first Congress under the Constitution were graduates of the College of New Jersey.[131]

Here was a man who literally discipled his nation. Those today with a vision for biblical education, and an understanding of the components of kingdom education, may, likewise, have an opportunity to disciple the nations.

The history of America shows that biblical education is central to the advancement of liberty and prosperity in history. Biblical education will produce kingdom fruit. Christian ideas have transformed the world.

4) Christian education will pass the baton to future generations.

Psalm 78:1-7 reveals to us as parents and educators that we are to pass on to our posterity all of the vision, mission, principles, character, and truth that God has made known to this generation. We are to do this in such a way that they will then, in turn, teach their children, who will teach their children, "that they may arise and tell them to their children, that they should put their confidence in God and not forget the works of God" (verses 6-7).

We are in a race — not a hundred yard dash but a relay race. We will not win the race by merely running fast. We must pass the baton (that is, find faithful men who will teach others, 2 Timothy 2:2). Our generation was not given the baton, but had to grope around and find it in the weeds. After finding it we had to learn what the race was all about, where the track was, how to run, and how to pass the baton. We also must train our posterity to run in the race, how to receive the baton, and how to pass it to the next generation. We can do great things for God in this generation, but if we fail in this, we have failed to fulfill God's purpose for this generation.

Biblical education is the means of passing the baton (the kingdom) to the next generation and equipping them to pass it to their posterity. The extent to which we educate in a kingdom manner determines, the extent to which His kingdom will come on earth. Establishing biblical education in the nations is, therefore, of utmost importance.

The Story of Korea

The people of North Korea have lived in bondage for over 60 years, with no freedom and little material wealth. How have they been kept in such bondage for so long?

The people living in the Korean peninsula had a common history up until the end of World War II. They embraced the same religion and cultural influences. Christianity was first introduced to Korea toward the end of the nineteenth century when missionaries from the United States carried the Gospel to them. In 1907 a great revival swept throughout the land. Three years later the Japanese invaded the country and began to persecute the people, especially those who were Christians. Many Christians fled to the countryside and established many "prayer mountains," where they hid out in the many hills and small mountains throughout the nation. Many of these prayer mountains remain today.

At the end of World War II, a decision was made for the defeated Japanese troops south of the 38th parallel to surrender to the Americans, while those north of this line surrendered to the Russians. Under the Americans, South Korea gained freedom, while communism grew in the North. The Korean War started in 1950 when communist forces from the North invaded the South. It ended a few years later with the permanent division of the nation along the 38th parallel, the North governed by communists, the South by those embracing liberty. Under the free South, Christianity flourished and many churches were started, some growing to enormous size. The largest church in the world is in Seoul, South Korea – there are 750,000 members in the church started by Dr. Paul Yonggi Cho. The largest Presbyterian church in the world is also in Seoul, with 70,000 members.

These Christians carried their faith into all spheres of life. They started many Christian schools and colleges, including a Christian law school. They started many businesses, seeking to build them upon biblical principles. They became involved in government, having such an influence that today about 40% of the national legislature is Christian. The economy has grown greatly and liberty has flourished.

This is in great contrast to North Korea. During the time of great advancement and change in the South, the North has barely survived under the oppression of the communist dictators. The people cannot produce enough

A satellite picture of the Korean peninsula at night

food to feed themselves. They have no freedom of any kind –religious, civil, political or economic.

The contrast between North and South Korea is astonishing; it is as different as day and night. A satellite picture of the Korean peninsula at night (on previous page) clearly reveals the stark contrast. In this image South Korea is lit up from lights all over the nation (which shows just one aspect of her great prosperity), but the North is in complete darkness as they do not have enough electricity to power the nation, nor the prosperity to buy all that is necessary to light the nation. What has made the difference? Liberty. Liberty is the primary reason for the great disparity between these two nations. Liberty is the cause of progress for mankind. Liberty causes more cultivation, more invention, more labor, more wealth.

Liberty produces prosperity. Liberty is the most important factor in why nations prosper. The amount of natural resources is not primary for prosperity; the amount of liberty is. Yet, even more important is to understand the source of liberty. Where does liberty originate? From Christianity. Christianity produces liberty, which in turn produces prosperity.

So how then has North Korea been kept in such darkness and bondage? They certainly have not lived in liberty, because Christianity has been kept from the people. Why have they not risen up and thrown off the tyrant, especially with modern means of communication? A pastor from South Korea asked this question many years ago and secretly took numerous trips into the North to find an answer. He discovered that when children are still infants the government takes them out of the home and puts them into government schools to "train" (rather indoctrinate) them. They are taught the philosophy of the communist government – that society is of first importance and citizens must sacrifice for the good of all — which translates for the prosperity of the party leaders. Government leaders are the supreme voice. Remember, whoever controls the children controls the future, and pagan thinkers want to control the future, so they seek to control education. Indoctrination through state schools is why the North still lives in darkness today and shows the power of education in shaping the future course of nations.

Renovating the Age

God has called us to transform the nations. The Father of the American Revolution, Samuel Adams, declared that education in the principles of the Christian religion is the means of renovating our age. He wrote in a letter October 4, 1790,

Samuel Adams

to John Adams, then vice-president of the United States:

> Let divines [ministers] and philosophers, statesmen and patriots, unite their endeavors to renovate the age, by impressing the minds of men with the importance of educating their little boys and girls, of inculcating in the minds of youth the fear and love of the Deity and universal philanthropy, and, in subordination to these great principles, the love of their country; of instructing them in the art of self-government, without which they never can act a wise part in the government of societies, great or small; in short, of leading them in the study and practice of the exalted virtues of the Christian system.[132]

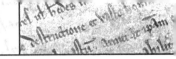

Review Questions

- Why is biblical education so important?

- People today say we must keep religion out of education, that it must remain neutral regarding religion. Do you believe this is true? Why or why not?

- How does modern state education violate biblical principles?

- What are the implications for America today of the statement, "whoever controls the children in a society controls the future"?

- Why is education like the principle of sowing and reaping?

- Who is primarily responsible for the education of children according to the Bible. Give Scriptural support for your answer.

- Give one observation regarding the education of John Quincy Adams.

- What did education look like in early America?

- What is the biblical purpose of education?

- Read Noah Webster's definition of education. List the four goals of education given in his definition. How are these four goals being achieved in your life through your education?

- What do you think about the quotes of Luther and Hodge on education?

- What lesson(s) can we learn from the story of Korea over the last century?

Chapter 6

Liberty

The fruit of a people with biblical faith, morality, law, and education is liberty. The Forefathers Monument tells us that Christianity produces liberty. After all, Jesus came to liberate man: "It was for freedom that Christ came to set us free."[133] In what could be called Jesus' inaugural address (Luke 4:18-19), He tells us that He was sent to proclaim release to the captives and to set at liberty those who are oppressed. Jesus manifested the kingdom of God by liberating man — physically, mentally, and spiritually — and casting out Satan and his cohorts, who seek only to destroy and bring man into bondage.

Jesus came to liberate mankind.

Jesus gave us His Spirit so that we might live free because, "Where the Spirit of the Lord is, there is liberty" (2 Corinthians 3:17). When the Spirit of the Lord comes into the heart of a man, that man is liberated. Likewise, when the Spirit of the Lord comes into a nation, that nation is liberated. The degree to which the Spirit of the Lord is infused into a society (through its people, laws, and institutions) is the degree to which that society will experience liberty in every realm (personal, political, civil, religious, and economic). Spiritual freedom ultimately produces political freedom. External political slavery reflects internal spiritual bondage.

Jesus came to set us free, both internally and externally. He gave us internal freedom from the bondage of sin as well as external freedom from the fruit of sin in the earth. He came to give us both personal and civil freedom. He came to not only bring internal personal salvation, but also external political freedom. Christ Jesus provided God's pathway to liberty for man, which is from the internal to the external.

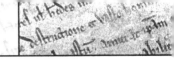

In Acts 1:6 Jesus' disciples asked Him when the kingdom of God would be restored. They were thinking of an external kingdom. They thought the Messiah would set up such a kingdom and deliver them from external bondage. How did Jesus respond to this question? He did not deny that the kingdom would be manifested externally on the earth. He said that times and epochs would follow that would contribute to bringing God's rule and reign on the earth (see Acts 1:7-8). We can look back over the centuries and see those times and epochs.

Since the time of Christ there has been no end to the increase of His government or kingdom in the earth (Luke 1:33) — it has grown steadily. But Jesus did correct their wrong understanding of how the kingdom would come. He said it would first be birthed within man's heart (the kingdom of God is within you[134]) which would then flow out from him and affect every sphere of life.

God's plan is to bring liberty to man — internal and external, spiritual and physical, personal and civil liberty. God is the author of liberty, all liberty. Engraved on the memorial in Washington, DC, honoring Thomas Jefferson are these words: "God who gave us life gave us liberty. Can the liberties of a nation be secure when we have removed a conviction that these liberties are the gift of God?" Our Founders knew, in the words of Jefferson's pastor Rev. Charles Clay, that "the sacred cause of liberty [is] the cause of God."[135] John Dickinson, a signer of the Constitution, wrote, "Our cause . . . is nothing less, than to maintain the Liberty with which heav'n itself hath made us free."[136]

David Ramsay

Historian of the American Revolution, David Ramsay, said: "There can be no political happiness, without liberty; there can be no liberty without morality; and there can be no morality, without religion."[137] When our Founders spoke of religion, they meant Christianity, for Christianity was true religion to them. Noah Webster wrote in his United States history textbook:

> Almost all the civil liberty now enjoyed in the world owes its origin to the principles of the Christian religion. . . The religion which has introduced civil liberty, is the religion of Christ and his apostles, which enjoins humility, piety, and benevolence; which acknowledges in every person a brother, or a sister, and a citizen with equal rights. This is genuine Christianity, and to this we owe our free constitutions of government.[138]

We need to understand the great liberty that God desires us to have. Lack of knowledge of the value and source of our liberty has caused many people today, including many Christians, to give up their liberty for a little security and care. Like Esau, these people have traded their birthright for a bowl of pottage.

Through Christ's liberating work, we can be freed to direct our own affairs under God. Even God Himself does not seek to control us from without, but desires that we desire to obey Him from within. His kingdom is birthed within us, where we consent to live in it. God does judge the acts of every man, but He does not control all the actions of men. Jesus gave to the state what it can take by force — money (via taxes), material things, and even His physical life (for a time) — but He never gave His freedom, His self-determination to accomplish His purpose, or His belief in His Father.

Many have given to Caesar the control of their lives (or at least part of their lives) thinking that government or leaders should control them and/or provide for them. We are not to render to Caesar our liberty, our self-determination, or our care. We become slaves if we do so. God created man and desires redeemed man to live free under Him, to act and make choices, to labor and be productive, to take dominion. He delegated to us the responsibility to govern our destiny, our children, and our property.

Engraved on the Jefferson Memorial are his words: "God who gave us life gave us liberty. Can the liberties of a nation be secure when we have removed a conviction that these liberties are the gift of God?"

Throughout history many people have resigned themselves to the idea that their lot in life is already determined and they can do little about it. Two examples include the Hindu caste system and the feudal system where some were peasants and laborers, some lords, some knights. People in these instances surrender to the idea that other people or circumstances govern who they are, what they will do, and where they will be. The Christian idea of man and the Christian idea of history declare something different. God says we can change things. If society contains evil, then we can and should change it. If something is wrong in our life, we can change it by God's grace. We can be changed, and we can change society because we have access to God, His truth, and His liberty. He tells us to continually grow into His image.

God wants us to live free under Him, directing our own affairs, in covenant with others, fulfilling His purposes for our lives. Others, via government or force, are not to direct our lives or tell us everything to do (from how to educate our children to what food to eat, to how to spend our money, or how to support the poor). We are not to give to the state control of our lives, liberty, or property; nor are we to look to government to provide our needs, manage our affairs, or fulfill our

 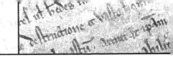

responsibilities.

God does not intend for earthly authorities to control us. We are to govern ourselves under God and His standard of truth. We should seek to change the mentality of letting others govern. Civil government is supposed to restrict unlawful behavior of men who would take or threaten the life, liberty, and property of others. It wields the sword for this reason (Romans 13:4). It controls evil men, but not those who do what is right.

Freedom to choose is one key way we resemble God. As we choose what pleases Him, we bring Him glory. When evil governments (or other evil men) deprive us of the ability to make free choices, a part of our God-likeness is suppressed. Thus people will pay almost any price for freedom. Patrick Henry's cry, "Give me liberty or give me death!" resonates deep in the heart of all men created in God's image.[139]

What is liberty?

Understanding that our liberty comes from God enables us to know what true liberty is. In considering the nature of liberty, Abraham Lincoln observed that liberty for the sheep is different than liberty for the wolf. For sheep, liberty is being free from the fear of being eaten by the wolf. Yet liberty for the wolf is being able to eat the sheep. For many people today, liberty is being free to do whatever they feel like doing, as long as they do not harm others. However, true liberty is not doing whatever I want to do, but doing what God wants me to do. Before God supernaturally transforms us by faith in Christ into a new Creature with a new nature that desires to please the Creator, we are not free to choose the path of life. Our choices lead to death. Once God liberates us from within, we have the freedom to follow the Lord and obey Him. This path of liberty must begin internally and will gradually flow out to bring liberty to families, businesses, communities, and nations. God's pathway to liberty starts from the internal and goes to the external. It begins with Christ the redeemer.

As has been stated already, the Founders of America believed that Christianity produced liberty. This belief arose from their biblical worldview and from their knowledge of history. Signer of the Declaration Samuel Adams stated, "Religion and good morals are the only solid foundations of public liberty and happiness."[140] Our Founders believed that the foundation of free societies was not just faith in any god or religion. It was specifically the Christian religion and faith in the only true God. That truth comes through His Word, the Bible. As Noah Webster wrote, "The Christian religion, in its purity, is the basis or rather the source of all genuine freedom in government."[141] John Adams declared:

> The general principles on which the fathers achieved independence were
> … the general principles of Christianity.… I will avow that I then believed,

and now believe, that those general principles of Christianity are as eternal and immutable as the existence and attributes of God; and that those principles of liberty are as unalterable as human nature.[142]

In fact, the story of America's independence reveals that Christianity is the source of our great liberty.

America's Liberty and Independence: Founded on the Christian Faith

The story of America's independence reveals there would be no liberty without Christianity. Though this story starts centuries before, we will begin in the year 1765 and look briefly at some of the events that resulted in our becoming a nation — and in so doing see the central role that Christianity played.

To pay for the debt of the French and Indian War, England imposed a tax

Patrick Henry: "If this be treason, make the most of it."

upon the colonists through the Stamp Act. The colonists were not opposed to paying for their defense, but they were opposed to the idea of the Parliament being able to tax them without their consent, or the consent of their representatives, for this violated the principle of property.[143] One man who led the opposition to the Stamp Act was Patrick Henry in Virginia.

In May, 1765, Patrick Henry was elected to the House of Burgesses from Louisa County. The topic of foremost concern for the Virginia legislature was the newly passed Stamp Act. Though Henry was a novice at the assembly, when he found no one willing to oppose the tax he felt compelled to take action, so he wrote down some resolutions on his own. He would later write of the events: "Upon offering them to the house, violent debates ensued. Many threats were uttered, and much abuse cast on me, by the party for submission."[144]

During the debates on his resolutions, Patrick Henry spoke out boldly against the Stamp Act saying that only the legislatures of the colonies had the right to tax the American people. On the floor of the House of Burgesses he went on to say:

"Caesar had his Brutus; Charles the First, his Cromwell; and George the Third . . ."

"Treason! Treason!" shouted the Speaker of the House.

"Treason! Treason!" echoed from every part of the room.

Without faltering for an instant, and fixing on the Speaker an eye that flashed fire, the orator added—

". . . may profit by their example. If this be treason, make the most of it."[145]

In his autobiography, Jefferson said of Henry's speech:

> I attended the debate at the door of the lobby of the House of Burgesses, and heard the splendid display of Mr. Henry's talents as a popular orator. They were great indeed; such as I have never heard from any other man. He appeared to me to speak as Homer wrote.[146]

Henry explained the outcome:

> After a long and warm contest, the resolutions passed by a very small majority, perhaps of one or two only. The alarm spread throughout America with astonishing quickness, and the ministerial party were overwhelmed. The great point of resistance to British taxation was universally established in the colonies. This brought on the war, which finally separated the two countries, and gave independence to ours. Whether this will prove a blessing or a curse, will depend upon the use our people make of the blessings which a gracious God hath bestowed on us. If they are wise, they will be great and happy. If they are of a contrary character, they will be miserable. — Righteousness alone can exalt them as a nation. Reader! whoever thou art, remember this; and in thy sphere, practice virtue thyself, and encourage it in others.[147]

Patrick Henry

Henry wrote on his copies of the resolutions that "they formed the first opposition to the stamp act, and the scheme of taxing America by the British parliament."[148] Numerous leaders in America attributed to Henry the leading role in the great revolution. William Wirt Henry writes:

> America was filled with Mr. Henry's fame, and he was recognized on both

sides of the Atlantic as the man who rang the alarm bell which had aroused the continent. His wonderful powers of oratory engaged the attention and excited the admiration of men, and the more so as they were not considered the result of laborious training, but as the direct gift of Heaven. Long before the British poet applied the description to him, he was recognized as—the forest-born Demosthenes, Whose thunder shook the Philip of the seas.[149]

Patrick Henry "was hailed as the leader raised up by Providence for the occasion."[150]

The Boston Tea Party

A

DISCOURSE

On "the good News from a far Country."

Deliver'd *July* 24th.
MDCCLXVI.
A Day of Thanks-giving to Almighty GOD, throughout the Province of the *Maſſachuſetts-Bay* in *New-England*, on Occaſion of the REPEAL of the STAMP-ACT :

Dr. Charles Chauncy's sermon delivered on July 24, 1766, in response to the repeal of the Stamp Act.

Due to the efforts of Henry and other patriots, the Stamp Act was repealed. The response of the colony of Massachusetts was to proclaim a Day of Prayer and Thanksgiving. Dr. Charles Chauncy was chosen to deliver a sermon to commemorate the glorious event. He chose his text from Proverbs 25:25. The title page of his printed sermon read: "A Discourse on 'the good News from a far Country.' Deliver'd July 24th. MDCCLXVI. A Day of Thanksgiving to Almighty God, throughout the Province of the Massachusetts-Bay in New-England, on Occasion of the Repeal of the STAMP-ACT."[151]

Proclamations for days of prayer and thanksgiving like that of Massachusetts, with corresponding sermons, were not unusual. Civil governments on the state and local level had proclaimed over 1000 days of prayer and thanksgiving or prayer and fasting during the 150 years of colonization.[152] Americans would continue these regular public proclamations throughout the Revolutionary War, the establishment of the constitutional republic, and for well over 100 years. Various states, and at times the national government, continue this practice to today.

The Stamp Act was repealed, but the belief of the English government to tax the colonies without their consent continued with the Townsend Act in 1767 and the Tea Act in 1773. With a tax on tea, the colonists refused to buy English tea. Consequently, it began to pile up in warehouses in England. Merchants petitioned

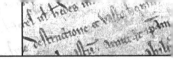

the Parliament to do something about this. Parliament's response was to vote to subsidize the tea and make it cheap, thinking the colonists would then buy it. Benjamin Franklin said:

> They have no idea that any people can act from any other principle but that of interest; and they believe that three pence on a pound of tea, of which one does not perhaps drink ten pounds in a year, is sufficient to overcome all the patriotism of an American.[153]

Unfortunately, this may be enough to overcome the patriotism of many Americans today, though thankfully not then. Our Founders were men of principle. They reasoned and acted from principles that were rooted in the Bible. It was not money but principles that motivated the colonists. The attempt of England to tax them without their consent violated the principle of property. The Americans refused to buy the tea even though it was cheap.

When King George III decided to send the tea and make the colonists purchase it, patriots in the major shipping ports held town meetings to decide what

to do when the tea arrived. Ships were turned back at four cities, but one docked in Boston. The patriots put a guard at the docks to prevent the tea from being unloaded. Almost 7000 people gathered at the Old South Meeting House to hear from Mr. Rotch, the owner of the ships. He explained that if he attempted to sail from Boston without unloading the tea, his life and business would be in danger, for the British said they would confiscate his ships unless the tea was unloaded by a certain date. The colonists decided, therefore, that in order to protect Mr. Rotch, they must accept the tea, but they wouldn't have to drink it! By accepting the shipment

Benjamin Franklin

they were agreeing to pay for it, but they would make a radical sacrifice in order to protest this injustice before the eyes of the world. Thus ensued the "Boston Tea Party." To protect the individuals involved, the men disguised themselves as Indians. Richard Frothingham records the incident:

> The party in disguise ... whooping like Indians, went on board the vessels, and, warning their offi-cers and those of the custom-house to keep out of the way, unlaid the hatches, hoisted the chests of tea on deck, cut them open, and

Boston Tea Party

hove the tea overboard. They proved quiet and systematic workers. No one interfered with them. No other property was injured; no person was harmed; no tea was allowed to be carried away; and the silence of the crowd on shore was such that the breaking of the chests was distinctly heard by them. "The whole," [Governor] Hutchinson wrote, "was done with very little tumult."[154]

Boston Port Bill

When King George and the English government got word of what the colonists had done, they responded by passing the Boston Port Bill, which closed the port of Boston and was intended to shut down all commerce on June 1st and starve the townspeople into submission. Committees of Correspondence spread the news by letter throughout all the colonies. The colonies began to respond. Massachusetts, Connecticut and Virginia called for days of fasting and prayer. Thomas Jefferson penned the resolve in Virginia "to implore the divine interposition … to give us one heart and one mind firmly to oppose, by all just and proper means, every injury to American rights."[155] Frothingham writes of the day the Port Act went into effect:

> The day was widely observed as a day of fasting and prayer. The manifestations of sympathy were general. Business was suspended. Bells were muffled, and tolled from morning to night; flags were kept at halfmast; streets were dressed in mourning; public buildings and shops were draped in black; large congregations filled the churches.
>
> In Virginia the members of the House of Burgesses assembled at their place of meeting; went in procession, with the speaker at their head, to the church and listened to a discourse. "Never," a lady wrote, "since my residence

> *Ordered,* therefore, that the Members of this Houſe do attend in their Places at the Hour of ten in the Forenoon, on the ſaid 1ſt Day of *June* next, in Order to proceed with the Speaker and the Mace to the Church in this City for the Purpoſes aforeſaid ; and that the Reverend Mr. *Price* be appointed to read Prayers, and the Reverend Mr. *Gwatkin* to preach a Sermon ſuitable to the Occaſion.
>
> *Ordered,* that this Order be forthwith printed and publiſhed.
>
> *By the* HOUSE *of* BURGESSES.
>
> GEORGE WYTHE, C. H. B.

In the proclamation authored by Jefferson, the Members of the House set apart June 1 "as a Day of Fasting, Humiliation and Prayer" and ordered the Members of the Virginia House to attend church to pray and hear a sermon.

in Virginia have I seen so large a congregation as was this day assembled to hear divine service." The preacher selected for his text the words: "be strong and of good courage, fear not, nor be afraid of them; for the Lord thy God, He it is that doth go with thee. He will not fail thee nor forsake thee." "The people," Jefferson says, "met generally, with anxiety and alarm in their countenances; and the effect of the day, through the whole colony, was like a shock of electricity, arousing every man and placing him erect and solidly on his centre." These words describe the effect of the Port Act throughout the thirteen colonies.[156]

The colonies responded with material support as well, obtained, not by governmental decree but, more significantly, by individual action. A grassroots movement of zealous workers went door to door to gather patriotic offerings. These gifts were sent to Boston accompanied with letters of support. Out of the diversity of the colonies, a deep Christian unity was being revealed on a national level. John Adams spoke of the miraculous nature of this union: "Thirteen clocks were made to strike together, a perfection of mechanism which no artist had ever before effected."[157]

Members of the House gathered with a large assembly at Bruton Parish Church in Williamsburg to observe the Day of Prayer.

Here we see an excellent historical example of the principle of Christian union. The external union of the colonies came about due to an internal unity of ideas and principles that had been sown in the hearts of the American people by the families and churches. Our national motto reflects this Christian union: *E Pluribus Unum* (one from the many).

The First Continental Congress

Further evidence of our national unity and union was found in the convening of the first Continental Congress in September, 1774. One of the first acts of the Congress that met in Carpenters Hall in Philadelphia was to pass the following resolution: "Resolved, That the reverend Mr. Duché be desired to open the Congress tomorrow morning with prayers, at the Carpenter's Hall at nine o'clock." *The Journal of the Proceeding of Congress* records for September 7, 1774:

Agreeable to the resolve of yesterday, the meet-

Our national motto, E Pluribus Unum, reflects the principle of Christian union.

ing was opened with prayers by the reverend Mr. Duché. Voted, That the thanks of the Congress be given to Mr. Duché, by Mr. Cushing and Mr. Ward, for performing divine service, and for the excellent prayer, which he composed and delivered on the occasion.[158]

John Adams wrote to his wife, Abigail, of Rev. Duché's prayer at Congress:

> [N]ext Morning he appeared ... and read several Prayers, in the established Form; and then read the Collect for the seventh day of September, which was the Thirty fifth Psalm.—You must remember this was the next Morning after we heard the horrible Rumour, of the Cannonade of Boston.—I never saw a greater Effect upon an Audience. It seemed as if Heaven had ordained that Psalm to be read on that Morning.
>
> After this Mr. Duché, unexpected to every Body struck out into an extemporary Prayer, which filled the Bosom of every Man present. I must confess I never heard a better Prayer or one, so well pronounced. Episcopalian as he is, Dr. Cooper himself never prayed with such fervour, such Ardor, such Earnestness and Pathos, and in Language so elegant and sublime —for America, for the Congress, for The Province of Massachusetts Bay, and especially the Town of Boston, It has had an excellent Effect upon every Body here.[159]

Delegate Silas Deane wrote that "Mr. Duché . . . prayed with-out book about ten minutes so pertinently, with such fervency, purity, and sublimity of style and sentiment . . . that even Quakers shed tears."[160] Deane declared that Duché's prayer "was worth riding one hundred mile to hear."[161]

George Washington, Patrick Henry, and members of the First Continental Congress join with Rev. Jacob Duché in prayer.

The Battle of Lexington

About seven months after the first Continental Congress met in Philadelphia, Paul Revere set out on his famous ride to warn the colonists, and in particular two leaders of the "rebellion," Samuel Adams and John Hancock, that the British were coming. He knew precisely where to find them – at the home of Rev. Jonas Clark in Lexington. Rev. Clark had for some time been teaching his church and prominent men of Massachusetts

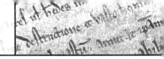

biblical ideas of liberty. He had also prepared his parishioners to defend themselves if necessary. After being warned that British troops were on the way he was asked if the people of Lexington would fight. He replied, "I have trained them for this very hour." The shot that was heard around the world took place on the morning of April 19, 1775. Fighting began on the lawn of Rev. Clark's church, and his parishioners were the ones who died that day. Upon seeing them slain he declared, "From this day will be dated the liberty of the world!"[162]

Statue of Jonathan Trumbull in the U.S. Capitol.

About one month before the Battle of Lexington, the Governor of Connecticut had considered what he and his state could do regarding the growing conflict between England and the Colonies. Jonathan Trumbull was an ordained minister who had early in his career left the pulpit ministry to serve in the civil ministry. As Governor of Connecticut during the entire Revolutionary War, he provided great support to General Washington, who called him Brother Jonathan. In March 1775 his determined course of action was to call upon the colony to observe a

> Day of public Fasting and Prayer ... that God would graciously pour out his Holy Spirit on us, to bring us to a thorough repentance and effectual reformation; . . . That He would restore, preserve and secure the liberties of this, and all the other American Colonies, and make this land a mountain of Holiness and habitation of Righteousness forever. . . . That God would preserve and confirm the Union of the Colonies in the pursuit and practice of that Religion and virtue which will honour Him.[163]

Governor Trumbull recognized they needed God's help in those trying times, and so he proclaimed a Day of Prayer and Fasting. What day had he selected for them to be praying? "Wednesday, the nineteenth Day of April."[164] Thus, on the day that fighting began that eventually led to the independence of America and a new era of liberty in the world, God had an entire colony praying. This

Gov. Trumbull's Prayer Proclamation.

did not happen by mere chance, but was one of many providential events that occurred during the war. What an awesome example of God's hand in history!

In response to the battle at Lexington and Concord, England declared Massachusetts would be put under martial law. The response of the Continental Congress was to proclaim the first colony-wide day of fasting and prayer to be observed on July 20, 1775, the day martial law was to go into effect. In the proclamation they appealed to "the Great Governor of the World" who "frequently influences the minds of men to serve the wise and gracious purposes of His providential government." They "recommended to Christians of all denominations to assemble for public . . . Humiliation, Fasting and Prayer."[165] A vast majority of the three million inhabitants of America observed this day of fasting and prayer.

The Price the Signers Paid

Fighting had begun, but it would be 14 months before the colonists declared their independence. They still considered themselves British and sought all means possible to end the conflict without a total break from England. By July 1776 the delegates to the Congress had come to agree it was time to declare independene.

Who were these men who risked so much for posterity? Today they are presented as a bunch of self-serving atheists, secularists, or at best deists.

Proclamation for the first colony-wide Day of Fasting and Prayer, issued by the Continental Congress on June 12, 1775, John Hancock, President.

But in reality they were almost all Christians. In fact, all but two or three of the signers were orthodox Christians, and 29 of them held seminary degrees.[166] Reading their voluminous writings, including their last will and testaments, reveal their strong faith. Here are just a few of their words.

Robert Treat Paine plainly expressed his faith in his will: "I am constrained to express my adoration of the Supreme Being, the Author of my existence, in full belief of His providential goodness and His forgiving mercy revealed to the world through Jesus Christ, through Whom I hope for never-ending happiness in a future state."[167] In his will Samuel Adams said, "I rely upon the merits of Jesus Christ for a pardon of all my sins."[168]

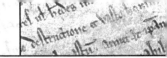

Charles Carroll wrote: "On the mercy of my Redeemer I rely for salvation, and on His merits; not on the works that I have done in obedience to His precepts."[169] Roger Sherman, who also signed the United States Constitution, stated:

> I believe that there is one only living and true God, existing in three persons, the Father, the Son, and the Holy Ghost. . . . that the Scriptures of the Old and New Testaments are a revelation from God. . . . that God did send His own Son to become man, die in the room and stead of sinners, and thus to lay a foundation for the offer of pardon and salvation to all mankind so as all may be saved who are willing to accept the Gospel offer.[170]

Benjamin Rush declared: "My only hope of salvation is in the infinite, transcendent love of God manifested to the world by the death of His Son upon the cross. Nothing but His blood will wash away my sins. I rely exclusively upon it. Come, Lord Jesus! Come quickly!"[171]

Roger Sherman

The men who signed the Declaration of Independence were not thinking they would be famous, but rather, they would most likely be killed for their action. After signing the document with unusually large writing, the President of the Continental Congress, John Hancock, declared: "His majesty can now read my name without glasses. And he can also double the price on my head."[172] Then he went on to say at that tense moment, "we must be unanimous; there must be no pulling different ways; we must all hang together." Benjamin Franklin responded in his characteristic wit, "Yes, we must indeed all hang together, or most assuredly we shall all hang separately!"[173]

Many years later, after observing the celebration of the 4th of July in Philadelphia, Benjamin Rush wrote to his friend John Adams that the celebrants had not mentioned the great price paid by the signers:

> Scarcely a word was said of the solicitude and labors and fears and sorrows and sleepless nights of the men who projected, proposed, defended, and subscribed the Declaration of Independence. . . . Do you

John Hancock

recollect the pensive and awful silence which pervaded the house when we were called up, one after another, to the table of the President of Congress to subscribe what was believed by many at that time to be our own death warrants? The silence and the gloom of the morning was interrupted, I well recollect, only for a moment by Colonel Harrison of Virginia, who said to Mr. Gerry at the table: "I shall have a great advantage over you, Mr. Gerry, when we are all hung for what we are now doing. From the size and weight of my body I shall die in a few minutes, but from the lightness of your body you will dance in the air an hour or two before you are dead." The speech procured a transient smile, but it was soon succeeded by the solemnity with which the whole business was conducted.[174]

Elbridge Gerry

Death was a very real possibility, and so the fifty-six men who signed the Declaration did so only after much thought and consideration. After all, they had more to lose than anyone in the colonies. They were the brightest minds, had the greatest talents, many had great wealth, and most had families they loved dearly. In signing that document they were not considering it as an avenue for fame, glory, or future advancement. They all knew they would be identified above all others by the British as the leaders of the "rebellion," and, consequently, those most likely to suffer retribution. They knew that "history was strewn with the bones and blood of freedom fighters."[175] And they were up against the greatest military power on earth, and so faced a very real chance of losing everything.

They all suffered in some way. Virtually all the men had greater wealth before taking up the cause of liberty than afterwards. T.R. Fehrenbach writes:

> Nine Signers died of wounds or hardships during the Revolutionary War. Five were captured or imprisoned, in some cases with brutal treatment. The wives, sons, and daughters of others were killed, jailed, mistreated, persecuted, or left penniless. One was driven from his wife's deathbed and lost all his children. The houses of twelve Signers were burned to the ground. Seventeen lost everything they owned. Every Signer was proscribed as a traitor; every one was hunted. Most were driven into flight; most were at one time or another barred from their families or homes. Most were offered immunity, freedom, rewards, their property, or the lives and release of loved ones to break their pledged word or to take the King's protection. Their fortunes were forfeit, but their honor was not. No Signer defected, or changed his stand, throughout the darkest hours. Their honor, like the nation, remained intact.[176]

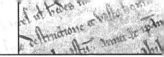

These men died and most have been forgotten by Americans today. It is sad that we have forgotten these Founders of America, but it is tragic that we have forgotten the high price they paid for liberty—that liberty which we possess today, but may lose if we forget its great cost.

Since our liberty and happiness are a result of faith and morality, we must cry out to God, seek to obey Him, and imitate His Son. John Adams wrote that the day of Independence

> will be the most memorable epocha in the history of America.—I am apt to believe that it will be celebrated, by succeeding generations ... as the day of deliverance, by solemn acts of devotion to God Almighty, ... from one end of this continent to the other, from this time forward forever more.[177]

All but two or three of the signers of the Declaration were Christians. They all sacrificed much to purchase liberty for posterity.

On July 8, 1776, the Liberty Bell rang out from the State House in Philadelphia, calling together the assembly of the citizens to hear the first public reading of the Declaration of Independence, which had been approved four days before. Its ringing led the celebration that followed.

A scripture was engraved on that bell, Leviticus 25:10 — "Proclaim Liberty throughout all the land, unto all the inhabitants thereof. Lev. XXV, X." This verse was very appropriate because it speaks of the jubilee year of liberty, where debts were forgiven, land was returned to the original owners, and enslaved Israelites were set free. With the birth of America, a new era of liberty was beginning in the world. As Rev. Clark observed, "From this day will be dated the liberty of the world!"[178]

God's liberty could be proclaimed, and eventually secured, because the people had been prepared from within to support freedom. A foundation of religion, morality, and biblical truth had been established in their lives.

Concerning the observance of American independence, President of the Continental Congress Elias Boudinot said:

> Let us ... unite our endeavors this day to remember with reverential gratitude to our Supreme Benefactor all the wonderful things He has done for us, in a miraculous deliverance from a second Egypt – another house of bondage. This day is kept as a day of joy and gladness, because of the great things the Lord has done for us, when we were delivered from the threatening power of an invading foe. Who knows but the country for which we have fought and

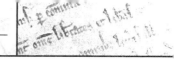

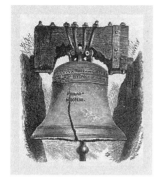

Leviticus 25:10 is engraved on the Liberty Bell.

bled may hereafter become a theater of greater events than have yet been known to mankind? May these invigorating prospects lead us to the exercise of every virtue, religious, moral, and political. And may these great principles, in the end, become instrumental in bringing about that happy state of the world when from every human breast, joined by the grand chorus of the skies, shall arise, with the profoundest reverence, that divinely celestial anthem of universal praise, "Glory to God in the highest; peace on earth; good will towards men."[179]

We must understand and value the great liberty that God desires us to have. Lack of knowledge of the source of our liberty has caused many people today, including many Christians, to give up their liberty for a little security and care. The freedom our Forefathers gave us can only be preserved if we are willing to defend it at all costs. The seated statue *Liberty* has a sword in his hand, prepared to protect the family and protect liberty. Eternal vigilance is the price of liberty; and it is necessary to overcome *Tyranny* (depicted in one carved relief below the *Liberty* statue) and preserve *Peace* (depicted in another).

Most Americans today have forgotten the source of, and price paid for, our liberty. We have abandoned the principles necessary to live free. We have put aside the matrix of liberty presented to us in the Forefathers Monument. We have failed to acknowledge God Almighty as the giver of life and liberty. Consequently, we have begun to lose our liberty, our happiness, and all the fruit that comes from obeying the King of all nations. Let us cry out as our Founders did for God to once again deliver us from a house of bondage and use this nation as a "theater of greater events than have yet been known to mankind."[180]

Review Questions

- Explain the relationship of liberty and Christianity.

- What is biblical liberty? How should liberty be measured in a nation; that is, how can we determine how much liberty people have in the nation where they live?

- Relate the story of the Boston Tea Party. Your answer should contain information dealing with who, what, where, when, why, and how the event occurred.

- How did England respond to the Tea Party? How did this affect the town of Boston?

- How did the colonies respond to what England did to Boston?

- Give examples of the role prayer played in the events leading up to the Revolutionary War.

- The signers of the Declaration paid a great price to guide our nation through obtaining independence. Describe some of their sacrifices. Why do you think they were willing to make these sacrifices?

SECTION TWO

The Story of Liberty

CHAPTER 7

The Chain of Liberty: Preparation of the Seed of the American Republic

Providential History

Providence is a theological term meaning God's superintending care over His creation. It signifies the overruling power of God that governs in the affairs of men. Since God is the author of history, He is carrying out His plan through it. Any account of America, or any country, that ignores God is not true history. He is Sovereign over His creation and "His Story" in the earth. He is at work in significant and seemingly insignificant events to accomplish His purposes. This providential view of history was held by the vast majority of people who founded this nation.

According to Rev. S.W. Foljambe history is "the autobiography of Him 'who worketh all things after the counsel of His will' (Eph. 1:11) and who is graciously timing all events after the counsel of His Christ, and the Kingdom of God on earth. It is His-Story."[181] History is the outworking of God's plan and purposes for mankind. To understand the history of America, one must understand God's plan from the beginning. Hence, America's history begins at Creation, which is where Noah Webster started his textbook on United States history.

Failure to teach a providential view of history has been one of the leading factors in the secularization of America and the erosion of liberty. Providential history reveals God's plan for the liberation of men and nations, and when people are ignorant of this, they slip deeper into bondage.

God has been unfolding His plan in a systematic, purposeful way. The story of liberty in history is like a chain. The Chain of Liberty is the sequence of events in the

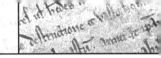

lives of men and nations that form links or stepping stones bringing forth internal and external liberty. A brief highlight of the Chain of Liberty follows.

The Chain of Liberty

In this and the following chapters we will highlight some of the links on the Chain of Liberty.[182] In so doing we give a framework to better understand America's place in God's plan, as well as a better understanding of how our destiny fits into God's plan.

Creation

God created humans, male and female, in His image, placed man in the Garden and gave them a mandate to "bring forth fruit and multiply, and fill the earth, and subdue it, and rule over" it (Genesis 1:26-28, Geneva). From the beginning, God established the family as the primary institution for fulfilling this dominion mandate.

God created man with the capacity to govern himself and to fulfill all of God's commands.

Garden of Eden by Thomas Cole

The test of man's self-government was his ability, without any type of external restraints, to resist eating of the forbidden tree. He had to internally govern himself to succeed (Genesis 2:16-17).

Fall

Through Adam and Eve's failure to exercise self-control, sin entered into the world and made it difficult for any man to govern himself. At this time no civil government yet existed. The dominion mandate to Adam did not include the responsibility for ruling over other men. Therefore, when Cain did not control his anger and jealousy, he violently slew his brother. At this time God personally handled matters of justice and protection of life, liberty, and property (Genesis 4:1-16).

Flood

Our sin brought continual evil thoughts in our hearts, which resulted in the earth being filled with violence. God saw the end result would be all people destroying one another (Genesis 6:5-13); therefore, He decided to intervene and bring a flood to destroy all but one righteous family. When God brings Noah through the flood to a new earth, He re-establishes the dominion mandate but now delegates to humans the responsibility for governing other people in order to protect human life (Genesis 9:5-7). He does this by instituting capital punishment—the backbone of civil government – stating that "whoever sheds man's blood, by man his blood shall be shed (Genesis 9:6).

Civil government, then, is a divine institution, as is the family and the church. All three were established by God with clear purposes and responsibilities revealed in the Bible. According to Paul and Peter, the purpose of government is to protect the life, liberty and property of all individuals, by punishing evildoers and encouraging the righteous (Romans 13:1-4; 1 Peter 2:13-14). When governing rulers fail to do this, then they themselves are resisting the ordinances of God and become illegitimate authorities. Such rulers should be resisted and replaced. The main functions, therefore, of the family, church and civil government are procreation, propagation and protection respectively.

Babel

The tendency of fallen man is to centralize power. Nowhere in Scripture is civil government said to have responsibility to be provider or savior for men by the centralization of its powers; yet early on men began to pervert the purpose of civil government in this way. The men at Babel began to congregate together rather than spread out and "fill the earth." They wanted to make a name for themselves and save themselves through the state as their *counterfeit* messiah. Babel was the first public expression of humanism where sovereignty was placed in a man or a collection of men rather than God (Genesis 11:1-8). In order to prevent centralized, one-world government, God made diverse languages, which are an effective deterrent to this day.

Babel

Hebrew Republic

Moses and God's comandments

Around 2200 B.C. God called Abraham out of his pagan culture to establish a new nation, from which a seed would come forth who would bless all the families of the earth (Genesis 12:1-3). By around 1500 B.C. the descendants of Abraham had been living as slaves in Egypt for many generations. God then raised up Moses to deliver the children of Israel from bondage and lead them into the Promised Land. Over time these slaves became a great nation, known throughout the world. How did this occur? God gave Israel two things that none of the other nations had. He gave them His law and His presence (Deuteronomy 4:5-8). God's Law-Word was a blueprint to build a nation. It worked, producing blessing and liberty when Israel obeyed God (Deuteronomy 5:29); though, as God warned, they declined when they disobeyed (Jeremiah 7:23-24). Jesus said God's Word is still a blueprint (Matthew 5:17-19) to build free, prosperous, just, and charitable nations. The Founders of America sought to follow this example.

When God gave Moses the Law around 1500 B.C. to be interpreted by judges and prophets in Israel, the first representative republic on earth was established. From the beginning, God's purpose was not limited to Israel, but He desired that these laws and their blessings might be exported to all nations which had perverted God's plan of civil government into pagan centralized monarchy. God established in Israel a decentralized, representative government where every group of 10, 50, 100 and 1,000 families could choose or elect someone to be their judge or ruler (Deut. 1:13-17; Exod. 18:12-26). All of their civil laws were based upon God's higher fixed law, not majorities. This makes it a republic, not a democracy.

Kings and Centralized Government

By 1120 B.C., however, as Israel backslid from God and failed to govern themselves or their families via God's Word, there arose very poor and corrupt leadership under their judges (1 Samuel 8:19-20). The people asked for a king, which God warned would lead to bad consequences, but the people were tired of governing themselves and wanted to be like all the other nations (with top-down government), so God gave them a king. Pagan monarchy was effective in keeping order but at the high price of oppression, taxation and the loss of much liberty (1 Samuel 8:10-20).

Israel, however, conformed to this pagan form of civil government where dominion was turned into domination. From this point forward until the establishment of the American Republic—almost 3000 years—the entire world would know nothing of full external liberty for the individual man.

Greece and Rome

Toward the latter centuries of the pre-Christian era and into the first centuries after Christ, Greece and Rome attempted to establish civil liberty within their empires. Their pagan attempts provide us with an example of the best man can do apart from God and His truth. While obtaining a degree of liberty, at least for citizens, they fell far short of what God intended.

The Greek and Roman governments were never as democratic as the Hebrew because of their belief in the inequality of men. The ideas of democracy and freedom were only extended to certain classes, and all others were denied basic rights. Such tyranny eventually produced conflicts in society that led to chaos and disorder. Greek and Roman contributions to democratic ideas were therefore more theoretical than actual, but were helpful to later generations who learned from their mistakes. The fundamental flaws of their attempts at democracy were rooted in their belief that man was naturally unequal and that only one or a privileged few were competent to govern the rest.

The pagan and Christian ideas of man and government are contrasted well by historian Richard Frothingham. Of this pagan view that dominated the world at this time in history, he wrote:

> At that time, social order rested on the assumed natural inequality of men. The individual was regarded as of value only as he formed apart of the political fabric, and was able to contribute to its uses, as though it were the end of his being to aggrandize the State. This was the pagan idea of man. The wisest philosophers of antiquity could not rise above it. Its influence imbued the pagan world;... especially the idea that man was made for the State, the office of which, or of a divine right vested in one, or in a privileged few, was to fashion the thought and control the action of the many.[183]

Jesus Introduces the Christian Idea of Man and Government

With the coming of Jesus Christ and His death on the cross for the sins of the world, man's ability to govern himself internally was restored. The Law of God was no longer only external, but now could be written on men's hearts and interpreted not by prophets and judges, but by the Spirit within them.

In addition to this internal liberty, Christ also proposed principles for external civil liberty. As the church propagated these principles throughout the pagan world, the Christian idea of man and government became clear. As Frothingham states:

> Christianity then appeared with its central doctrine, that man was created in the Divine image, and destined for immortality; pronouncing that, in the eye of God, all men are equal. This asserted for the individual an independent value. It occasioned the great inference, that man is superior to the State, which ought to be fashioned for his use,… that the state ought to exist for man; that justice, protection, and the common good, ought to be the aim of government.[184]

Why did Jesus come into the world? There are many answers to this question. He came to seek and to save those who are lost, He came to destroy the works of the devil, and He came to establish the Kingdom of God, to name a few.

We have seen how man lost his ability to be self-governed when he disobeyed God. This led to external governmental tyranny. Christ also came to restore to man the potential of being self-governing under God. As man begins to be self-governed, all external governments will be positively affected. Jesus came to not only bring internal salvation, but also external political freedom.

Jesus Christ

After Jesus had risen from the dead and before He ascended into heaven, He gathered His disciples together, at which time they asked Him, "Lord, is it at this time You are restoring the kingdom to Israel?" (Acts 1:6-8). Jesus' disciples were speaking of an external kingdom. For centuries the Hebrew people had read the prophecies of Scripture declaring a Messiah would come and set up His throne and deliver the people from bondage.

While Jesus walked on the earth, many of His followers thought He would set up His reign in their day. They even tried to make Him king. His disciples did not understand how His kingdom was going to come. While they had not seen it established during Jesus' ministry on earth, they thought surely now that He had risen from the dead, He would restore the kingdom.

Jesus did not deny that an external expression of the kingdom would come. In fact, He said that times and epochs would follow (which we can look back upon today) that would contribute to the establishment of the kingdom and the extension of liberty (both external and internal) "to the remotest part of the earth." The "power" for this external establishment of liberty is the "Spirit of the Lord;" therefore, Jesus emphasized the receiving of this "power" through the outpouring of the Holy Spirit. He knew the inevitable result of internal liberty would be external liberty.

God's Pathway to Liberty

God's pathway to liberty flows from the internal to the external. God's desire is for an external expression of His kingdom on earth. Yet, it must first begin in the heart of man – the kingdom of God is within you (Luke 17:20-21) – and then it will naturally express itself externally in all aspects of society: family, occupation, community, business, civil society.

As previously mentioned, the Bible reveals that "where the Spirit of the Lord is, there is liberty" (2 Corinthians 3:17). When the Spirit of the Lord comes into the heart of a man, that man is liberated. Likewise, when the Spirit of the Lord comes into a nation, that nation is liberated. The degree to which the Spirit of the Lord is infused into a society is the degree to which that society will experience liberty in every realm. Christ came to set us free (Galatians 5:1, 3). Spiritual freedom or liberty ultimately produces political freedom. External political slavery reflects internal spiritual bondage.

Jesus not only liberated us internally, but He also taught principles of civil liberty, including:

- God created and is sovereign over civil government (John 19:11).
- Government is due the taxes and services of its citizens (Mt. 17:24-27; Mt. 22:17-21).
- Government jurisdiction is limited (Mt. 22:17-21).
- Individuals have inherent value (Mt. 6:26; Mt. 9:12; Mt. 10:31; Mt. 22:17-21).
- Mosaic law is applicable today (Mt. 5:17-38; Mt. 15:4; Mt. 19:7-19; Jn. 8:1-7).
- Government is to serve all men equally (Luke 22:25-26; Jn. 4:7-9; Mt. 20:25-26).
- Social change is to be gradual and democratic, internal to external (Mt. 19:3-8; Mt. 28:19; Acts 1:6-8; Luke 19:11-17).
- Political and legal means can be used to achieve social justice (Luke 19:11-17; Mt. 12:18-21; Luke 18:2-8; Mt. 23:23).
- Governmental injustice is to be resisted through protest, flight, and force in self-defense (Luke 10:11; Mt. 10:17-23; Luke 22:35-38; Mt. 26:51-52; Luke 12:58; Mt. 27:14; Luke 18:1-5; Luke 10:10-11; Luke 13:31-32; Mt. 3:1-4; Mk. 11:15-16).
- Military strength can be used to maintain peace (Luke 11:21-22; Luke 14:31; Luke 22:36-38).

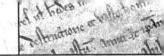

Early Church

As the early church applied the principles Jesus taught, they not only affected multitudes of lives, but also turned the entire known world upside down. Paganism was being overthrown throughout Europe as Christianity rapidly spread. By 500 A.D. about 25 percent of the known world had become Christian and over 40 percent had been evangelized.[185]

However, as the centuries went on, the church gradually lost its virtue and biblical knowledge. Thus it embraced elements of the pagan philosophy of government and education. The clergy thought that only they could understand God's Word and, therefore, they must tell the common people what God required of them, instead of allowing every person to be self-governed and learn for themselves.

Instead of sowing the truth in the hearts of the people and allowing the inevitable fruit to grow, the clergy simply tried to externally dictate to the people what they thought God commanded (and what they thought was often quite contrary to the Bible).

Constantine Unites the Church and State

Roman Emperor Constantine's conversion to Christianity around 312 A.D. helped end persecution of Christians and bring peace to the church. His desire to make his empire Christian was worthy, yet not understanding God's method of gradualism, he superficially united the church and state and set up a national church, declaring all citizens in his empire must be Christians. His noble yet ignorant attempt, accompanied by the centralization of power in the church via the papal system beginning around the

Constantine's conversion by
Peter Paul Rubens

seventh century, hindered the work of God for centuries. The result became an era we call the dark ages. It was dark primarily due to the light of God's Word being hidden from the common man. Great examples of light in the darkness did occur, the most notable in Ireland.

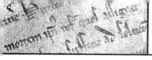

Patrick Transformed Ireland

When Patrick, in response to the call of God, went to Ireland around 432 A.D. it was a pagan land. When he died 28 years later the nation had been completely transformed. Historian Seumas MacManus writes:

> All histories of all countries probably could not disclose to the most conscientious searcher another instance of such radical change in a whole nation's character being wrought within the lifespan of one man.[186]

Saint Patrick

A complete transformation of Ireland came about from the time before and after Patrick. The people before Patrick were worshiping idols and "were carrying the ruthless law of the sword far over sea and land" enslaving those they encountered. After Patrick, the worship of the living God was predominant throughout the nation and the Irish people "left the conquering sword to be eaten by rust, while they went far and wide again over sea and land, bearing now to the nations—both neighbouring and far off—the healing balm of Christ's gentle words."[187]

Patrick worked at all levels to establish God's Word as a blueprint for every sphere of life: he saw untold thousands converted; he founded 700 churches; he trained and set in place church leadership — 700 bishops and 3000 ministers; he set up training centers to educate thousands; he transformed civil government, working with kings to establish godly laws — he wrote *Liber Ex Lege Moisi*, which were extracts from the law of Moses used as the basis for civil law in Ireland.

He not only transformed Ireland, but the fruit of Patrick's work transformed a continent. Many great reformers came out of Patrick's churches and training centers. Carrying Christianity, Ireland's sons "became the teachers of whole nations, the counsellors of kings and emperors."[188]

The apostle to the Picts, Columba, was a product of Patrick's Ireland. He did much to impact nations: Columba founded about 30 monasteries or Christian training centers in Ireland; in 562 he left Ireland and founded a monastery and school at Iona; his disciples carried the Gospel first to the Picts of Scotland and then to the Britons and the Saxons of England; people from all over came to Columba's schools. All of the British Isles and much of Europe were transformed through Columba and those going out from his schools.

In the centuries that followed, western European culture was transformed by Irish Celtic Christianity. A few highlights include: Columba began to disciple Scotland around 563 A.D.; Columbanus started to disciple France, Switzerland, Germany, Austria and Italy (590); Aiden began to disciple England (634); Ina established Celtic/Anglo-Saxon Law code in Wessex (693). The Irish saved civilization by planting the seeds of God's kingdom. The fruit of Patrick's work in Ireland transformed a continent.

John Wycliffe

While the fruit of Patrick's work kept the Christian faith alive and advancing in some nations for centuries, the centralized Roman Church grew in a form of godliness but kept the life and truth of God's Word hidden from the common man. The leaders of the established church were like the blind leading the blind into the ditch. The result was tyranny, both in church and state, which was the norm when God raised up John Wycliffe, a Catholic clergyman, who said that "Scripture must become the common property of all." His translation of the Bible into English in 1382 was the catalyst for a revival that was so great that up to half of the population of England "ranged themselves on the side of the Lollards" (the followers of Wycliffe).[189] His work affected many on mainland Europe, and laid the foundation for the Protestant Reformation of the sixteenth century.

John Wycliffe

Wycliffe and his followers were persecuted by the authorities, some even being put to death. John Hus was one of these, being burned at the stake in 1415. As prevalent error in the church began to be addressed, the church leaders showed their appreciation by trying to eradicate this movement they considered heretical. Over the decades, they were able to eradicate most of the effects of Wycliffe's work and drive his followers underground, but the seeds of truth had been planted, that would later spring forth and produce a Reformation that no man could stop.

In 1425, hoping to remove all the traces of Wycliffe's "treachery," the church ordered his bones exhumed and burned along with some 200 books he had written. His ashes were then cast into the little river Swift, "the little river conveyed Wycliffe's remains into the Avon, the Avon into the Severn, the Severn into the narrow seas, they to the main ocean. And thus the ashes of Wycliffe are the emblem of his doctrine, which now is dispersed all the world over."[190] With John Wycliffe, the "Morn-

ing Star of the Reformation," the first rays of the light of God's Word began to shine forth in the darkness.

Printing Press

The authorities could stop the reform started by Wycliffe because there was no way to mass produce God's Word. All copies of the Bible were made by hand, which caused them to be rare (taking more than one year for one person to produce one copy) and expensive. The invention of the moveable-type printing press around the year 1455 by Johann Gutenberg assured that the light of the truth would never be put out by any civil or ecclesiastical government. The first complete book printed by Gutenberg was the Bible, of which he said: "Through it [the press] God will spread His Word. A spring of pure truth shall flow from it! Like a new star, it shall scatter the darkness of ignorance, and cause a light heretofore unknown to shine among men."

Gutenberg Bible on display in the Library of Congress

In the next century as the Reformation broke forth, the use of the printing press was instrumental in spreading the knowledge of liberty. Within 10 years of the invention of the press the total number of books increased from 50,000 to 10 million. Charles Coffin wrote: "Through the energizing influence of the printing press, emperors, kings, and despots have seen their power gradually waning, and the people becoming their masters."[191]

Christopher Columbus

Most Americans know that in "1492 Columbus sailed the ocean blue," and in so doing opened up the New World to colonization from Europe. But few know what motivated Columbus to seek to fulfill his vision of reaching the east by sailing west. He clearly reveals this in a book he wrote after his third voyage entitled Book of Prophecies, which contains hundreds of prophetic Scriptures regarding the restoration of Jerusalem and the propagation of the Gospel that he – Christopher, "the Christ bearer" – believed he was fulfilling. Also in his Prophecies are various letters

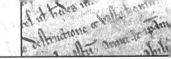

he wrote regarding his life work, including one to the King and Queen of Spain, Ferdinand and Isabella, who financed his voyage, in which he said:

> I have seen and put in study to look into all the Scriptures, cosmography, histories, chronicles and philosophy and other arts, which our Lord opened to my understanding (I could sense his hand upon me), so that it became clear that it was feasible to navigate from here to the Indies.... All those who heard about my enterprise rejected it with laughter, scoffing at me.... Who doubts that this illumination was from the Holy Spirit? I attest that he [the Spirit], with marvelous rays of light, consoled me through the holy and sacred Scriptures...
>
> For the execution of the enterprise of the Indies, neither reason, nor mathematics, nor world maps were profitable to me; rather the prophecy of Isaiah.... No one should be afraid to take on any enterprise in the name of our Savior, if it is right and if the purpose is purely for his holy service.[192]

Columbus' choice of names for lands he discovered also reveals his Christian faith. A painting of the "Landing of Columbus" on display in the Rotunda of the U.S. Capitol shows Columbus on the small island in what is today the Bahamas where he first landed in October 1492. After coming ashore, he knelt, kissed the ground and led the men in prayer, thanking God for his success. He then arose, drew his sword, and took possession of the island for Spain christening it "San Salvador" meaning Holy Savior. He named one island he discovered Trinidad, after the Holy Trinity.

Columbus said it was the Lord who inspired him in his life work.

While God used Christopher Columbus to open up the New World to European colonization, it was not Columbus or Spain that colonized what would become the United States. Columbus, Spain, and the various papal nations of Europe adhered to religious and civil ideas of tyranny. God desired a different seed to plant the nation of America. So during the sixteenth century, while colonies were planted in Central and South America, historian B.F. Morris writes that "God held this vast land in reserve, as the great field on which the experiment was to be made in favor of a civil and religious liberty. He suffered not the foot of Spaniard, or Portuguese, or Frenchman, or Englishman to come upon it until the changes had been wrought in Europe which would make it certain that it would always be a land of religious freedom."[193] Those changes are what we call the Protestant Reformation.

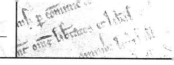

The Protestant Reformation

The focal point of the Protestant Reformation was the Bible being translated and made available in the common languages of the people. People began to read the Bible, and when they did these things happened: 1) Individuals were transformed; 2) The church began to be changed, putting off corruption; 3) The state was gradually reformed. The fruit of the Reformation was revival of individuals, restoration of the church, and reformation of all society.

God uses individuals to change nations and the course of history. Some of those people God used in the Protestant Reformation included Martin Luther, John Calvin, William Tyndale, and John Knox.

Martin Luther

Martin Luther was God's instrument to awaken the conscience of man. His act of nailing his 95 theses on the church door at Wittenberg in 1517 is often referred to as a beginning point of the Protestant Reformation. Yet he was influenced by the words and actions of previous reformers, like Wycliffe and Hus. Luther's defense at the Diet of Worms in 1521 reveals that which characterized his life:

> "I am," he pleaded, "but a mere man, and not God; I shall therefore defend myself as Christ did, who said, 'If I have spoken evil, bear witness of the evil'. . . . For this reason, by the mercy of God I conjure you, most serene Emperor, and you, most illustrious electors and princes, and all men of every degree, to prove from the writings of the prophets and apostles that I have erred. As soon as I am convinced of this, I will retract every error, and will be the first to lay hold of my books, and throw them into the fire. . . . I cannot submit my faith either to the Pope or to the councils, because it is clear as the day that they have frequently erred and

Martin Luther

> contradicted each other. Unless, therefore, I am convinced by the testimony of Scripture, or by the clear reasoning, unless I am persuaded by means of the passages I have quoted, and unless my conscience is thus bound by the Word of God, I cannot and will not retract; for it is unsafe and injurious to act against one's own conscience. Here I stand, I can do no other: may God help me! Amen.[194]

His life, and those of the reformers, can be summed up in the Latin phrase, *sola scriptura*, "Scripture alone." He translated the first Bible into German in 1534. This book, rather than the decree of pope or king, was to be the basis of the reformers' thoughts and actions. It was Luther who brought forth out of darkness the great truth that we are justified by faith.

John Calvin

John Calvin (1509-1564) was a French Protestant whose influence in "religion, theology, politics, sociology and economics goes far beyond that of any other reformer."[195] Calvin's *Institutes of the Christian Religion*, completed when he was 26 years old, has been called "the single most influential book on theology in church history." "No writing of the Reformation era was more feared by Roman Catholics, more zealously fought against and more hostilely pursued, than Calvin's *Institutes*."[196] Historian of the Reformation J.H. Merle D'Aubigne summarized his ideas:

John Calvin

> The liberty which the Truth brings is not for individuals only: it affects the whole of society. Calvin's work of renovation, in particular, which was doubtless first of all an internal work, was afterwards destined to exercise a great influence over nations.[197]

In fact, Calvin's writings had a great impact on at least five governments.[198] The vast majority of those who settled America were Calvinists, in that Calvin's ideas were central in shaping their thought and actions. These ideas affected all areas of life — personal religious belief, civil and religious liberty, the structure of government, and economic development. His ethic of work and frugality provided the theological energy for the age of economic growth. His writings provided the foundation for individual enterprise and Christian capitalism. As the biblical foundation has left Western capitalism in recent times, there has been a rise in materialism and other ungodly extremes. Besides a spiritual revival, we also need an economic revival. The latter will follow the former, if it is complete, embracing ideas as Calvin presented.

The city of Geneva became a model of reform, and the Protestant university Calvin established there served to train many leaders from throughout Europe (including French Huguenots, Puritan leaders from England, and John Knox of Scotland). So many graduates became martyrs that Calvin's university was called the "school of death."

He, as other reformers, was not perfect. As these men were coming out of spiritual darkness, they reflected the shortcomings of the age. Thus, Calvin could be a terrifying opponent.

D'Aubigne observed the great influence Calvin had upon the United States:

> Lastly, Calvin was the founder of the greatest of republics. The *pilgrims* who left their country in the reign of James I and, landing on the barren shores of New England, founded populous and mighty colonies, are his sons, his direct and legitimate sons; and that American nation which we have seen growing so rapidly boasts as its father the humble reformer on the shores of the Leman.[199]

William Tyndale

God's chief instrument in bringing the Reformation in England was William Tyndale. Much of Tyndale's life was spent fulfilling his vision: "If God preserves my life, I will cause a boy that driveth a plow to know more of the Scriptures than the pope."[200] During 12 years in exile from England, he translated the Bible from the original languages with the idea of making it available to the common man. His New Testament was published in 1525 and his Old Testament about eleven years later. His work served as the basis for other English translations that would follow (including the King James Version), and, in fact, formed the foundation of the modern English language.

William Tyndale

In 1536 Tyndale was burned at the stake. What was his crime? He was declared a heretic for giving the English people the Bible in their own language and desiring them to read the Word of God for themselves. On the day of his death, Tyndale calmly stated: "I call God to record that I have never altered, against the voice of my conscience, one syllable of his Word. Nor would I this day, if all the pleasures, honors, and riches of the earth might be given to me."[201]

Before he was strangled and burned at the stake he prayed for King Henry VIII who had persecuted and put to death many reformers and caused Tyndale to flee his country. As he was being fastened to the stake he cried out with these final words: "Lord, open the king of England's eyes!" Although his life was extinguished,

the flames of liberty would burn brighter than ever, for the Word of God would be spread to people throughout England. And, in answer to Tyndale's prayer, He would even use the pagan King Henry VIII.

Henry VIII

When Henry VIII became king of England in 1509, Roman Catholicism was the established religion, not only in England, but in all of Western Europe. The government of the church reached beyond its biblical sphere of jurisdiction by exercising control in all areas of life. When the pope denied Henry permission to divorce his wife, Catherine of Aragon, in order to marry Anne Boleyn, Henry decided he would not only go on and divorce Catherine, but he would also divorce himself and his country from the Catholic Church, and in its place set up his own national church (around 1534). Henry wanted "to emancipate England from Romish domination" in order that the Church of England would succeed. He saw the "Holy Scriptures as the most powerful engine to destroy the papal system" and so shortly after Tyndale's death he "authorized the sale and the reading of the Bible throughout the kingdom."[202]

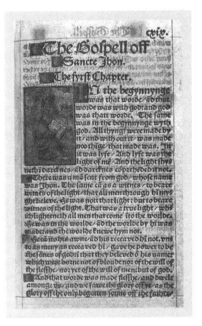

A page from the book of John from the Tyndale Bible.

During Tyndale's life many copies of his New Testament were circulated throughout England, but only in secret for the king had banned Tyndale's work. But now after his death, the king put his approval on the Matthew Bible (the revised to be called The Great Bible promoted by Henry VIII in 1539), which was in reality Tyndale's work under another name, and he ordered it placed in all the churches throughout England. Many people began to flock to the churches to hear the Bible read to them.

God was using Henry, who was not a godly man, to fulfill His purposes. Henry's actions toward Tyndale and other reformers reveal that his split from Rome had nothing to do with godly reform, but only selfish desires; yet, God who governs in

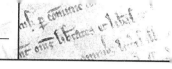

the affairs of men, used this historical event to accomplish His will. As the Word of God spread throughout the land, many people cried out with Tyndale, "We know that this Word is from God, as we know that fire burns; not because anyone has told us, but because a Divine fire consumes our hearts."[203]

While Henry broke from Roman Catholicism, there was still no freedom for individuals to worship God. Due to Tyndale's translation of the Bible, people throughout England were being awakened, yet the climate of Henry's England did not permit reform to flourish. Many saw that the Church of England needed reform as much as the Catholic Church, but little external reform occurred under Henry.

Puritans and Separatists in England

After Henry died his son Edward VI became king in 1547. Edward's protectorates, who governed the nation because Edward was a child, wanted further reform in the Church of England, so they encouraged the Puritan movement. Puritans were those desiring to purify the church of its errors and ungodliness. Freedom for these reformers was short-lived, as Edward died in 1553 and Mary became queen. She not only sought to stop the Puritan movement, but to once again make England a Catholic nation. Her persecution of the reformers was so great, where hundreds were put to death, she earned the name "Bloody Mary." Thousands of Puritans fled England, but God was at work be-

The Spanish Armada was sent to bring England back into the Holy Roman Empire. After it was miraculously defeated, England and Holland proclaimed public days of prayer and thanksgiving. Holland minted a coin showing on one side a ship fleeing and a ship sinking, and on the other side four men praying with the words, "Man purposeth; God disposeth, 1588."

cause many of them found refuge in Geneva and came under the biblical influence of John Calvin. While there, they learned ideas of religious and civil liberty, and also produced the Geneva Bible, the most influential Bible for generations. It was the first English Bible divided into chapter and verse, and therefore a good study Bible, and was also portable and relatively affordable. The Pilgrims and Puritans carried the Geneva Bible with them when they settled America.

 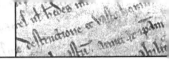

Mercifully, Mary died in 1558, and Elizabeth became queen. Promised toleration the Puritans returned to England, but when they began to seek more reform than Elizabeth desired, she issued her *Articles of Religion* in 1562 prohibiting further purifying of the church. At this point some of the Puritans gave up hope of ever seeing the Church of England transformed so they separated themselves and started their own churches. Thus, the "Separatist" movement was born around 1580. This movement continued to grow throughout Elizabeth's long reign, although there were attempts from within England and from other nations to stop it. (Philip II of Spain sent the Spanish Armada partly for this purpose.) The Pilgrims who first sailed to America in 1620 were English separatists.

At Elizabeth's death in 1603, James I came to the throne. Intense persecution of Separatists under James' policies caused many of them to flee the country, a large number going to Holland. This providential chain of events helped prepare those people who were to be "stepping stones" for the founding of a new nation—one birthed by God.

Fruit of the Protestant Reformation

The fruit of the Protestant Reformation is still impacting the world after nearly five centuries. One of its most immediate positive effects was shaping the new nation of America. The people who gave birth to the original thirteen colonies were a product of the Protestant Reformation. Many of them had been driven from Europe as they sought to live out their new-found faith. The Pilgrims, Puritans, and pioneers who settled America were a product of the Bible. This book first began to become available to commoners in their language (German, English, French, etc.) as a result of the Protestant reformers. The Bible was by far the single most important book in the birth, growth, and development of the United States. In fact, without God and the Bible there would be no America as we know it today.[204]

The fruit of this revival impacted individuals. Multitudes put away sin, destroyed personal and social idols, and turned to the worship of God. It impacted the church as well. New theological ideas were recovered – *Sola scriptura* ("by Scripture alone"), *Sola fide* ("by faith alone"), *Sola gratia* ("by grace alone"), *Solus Christus* or *Solo Christo* ("Christ alone" or "through Christ alone"), *Soli Deo gloria* ("glory to God alone") – and many new churches and church denominations came into being that were built upon these ideas. It also impacted the society at large.

As people began to read and study the Bible, its comprehensive worldview began to govern the thoughts and actions of men. Liberty began to advance, not only personal liberty, but also religious, civil, political, and economic liberty. A profusion of civil documents of liberty began to come forth in the seventeenth and eighteenth centuries (such as the Mayflower Compact, the English Petition of Rights, the Fundamental Orders of Connecticut, the Massachusetts Body of Liberties, the English

Bill of Rights, the Frame of Government of Pennsylvania, the Declaration of Independence, and the United States Constitution).[205] These were only possible due to the Bible translations in the prior two centuries.

New ideas of religious freedom, representative government, individual enterprise, jurisdictional authority, limited government, and private property began to shape America and influence some European nations. A new era of liberty and prosperity began to come into the world.

 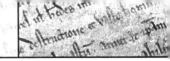
Review Questions

- What is a providential view of history?
- How did Satan get Adam and Eve to disobey God – what internal change had to happen to them before the external action occurred? You will need to read more about this incident in the first few chapters of Genesis.
- What internal change happened to Adam and Eve after they took the forbidden fruit? How did this change affect all of their descendants? What did God have to do in order to keep their descendants from destroying themselves?
- What do you think of the idea of the state as a "counterfeit" messiah? Why would pagan man be looking for a savior?
- What was the first republic in mankind's history, and what are some key components of this republic?
- Compare and contrast the pagan and Christian idea of man and government.
- Explain in more detail three of the principles of civil liberty that Jesus taught.
- How did the early church turn the world upside down?
- Who was Patrick and what influence did he have?
- What are some events that preceded and were essential for the Protestant Reformation?
- What difference do you think it would have made for America if Spain or France or Portugal had been allowed by God to colonize America?
- Why would someone say that John Calvin was a founder of America, even though he lived long before our revolution?
- Why would the Pope and some kings make studying the Bible illegal? Why would civil and religious leaders authorize the killing of heretics like William Tyndale?
- How did God use non-Christian leaders in sixteenth century England to advance His purposes? Include in your answer how the Puritan and Separatist movements were born.
- What is some of the fruit of the Protestant Reformation?

CHAPTER 8

The Pilgrims: Planting the Seed of the American Republic

Eight paintings hang in the United States Capitol Rotunda. One of those is the *Embarkation of the Pilgrims at Delft Haven, Holland, July 22nd, 1620* painted by Robert W. Weir in 1843. Before leaving Holland to plant a new colony in America, the Pilgrims set aside a day of fasting and prayer to cry out to God. This painting shows Pastor Robinson, Governor Carver, William Bradford, Miles Standish, and others in prayer. In the center of the painting, Elder William Brewster has an open Bible on his lap upon which are written the words: "The New Testament of our Lord and Savior Jesus Christ." This is the Geneva Bible. It was produced in 1560 by English reformers who had fled to Geneva to escape persecution in their home country. It was of great importance because it was the first English Bible divided into chapter and verse, it was relatively portable and affordable, and it contained many marginal notes address-

Embarkation of the Pilgrims at Delft Haven, Holland, July 22nd, 1620 – painted by Robert W. Weir in 1843

ing relevant topics, including governmental tyranny.

On the sail of the small ship can be seen the phrase, "God with Us," which marks well the entire lifestyle of these men and women who have been called the "Parents of our Republic." From their earliest years in England through the establishment of the Plymouth Colony, their words and actions reveal their entire life was centered in God and doing His will. William Bradford, governor of Plymouth Colony for 33 years, relates how in their early years in Scrooby, England, these people's lives "became enlightened by the Word of God and had their ignorance and sins discovered unto them, and began by His grace to reform their lives."[206] But this enlightening brought much persecution from the religious system of England and after some years of enduring evil, the Pilgrims "shook off this yoke of antichristian bondage, and as the Lord's free people joined themselves (by a covenant of the Lord) into a church estate, in the fellowship of the gospel, to walk in all His ways ... whatsoever it should cost them, the Lord assisting them."[207]

This desire to worship God freely was costly. They were exiled to Holland where they encountered persecutions, poverty, and much hard work, but by God's grace and their Christian character they were able to overcome the difficulties.

After 12 years in Holland they decided to sail to the new land of America. Their decision was prompted by a desire to find a home where they could more freely worship God and that was more conducive to raising godly children. They were also motivated, in the words of Bradford, by "a great hope and inward zeal ... of laying some good foundation, or at least to make some way thereunto, for the propagating and advancing the gospel of the kingdom of Christ in those remote parts of the world; yea, though they should be but even as stepping stones unto others for the performing of so great a work."[208]

When the Mayflower set sail in 1620, it bore more than just 102 Pilgrims and strangers. The Pilgrims carried with them Bible-based principles that were to become the seeds of the greatest and freest nation the world has ever known.

After 66 days at sea the Mayflower reached America. The Pilgrims intended to settle just north of the Virginia Colony but were providentially blown off course to a region that was outside the jurisdiction of the Virginia Company. Being unable to sail southward due to the weather, they put ashore at Cape Cod, and after some searching found a cleared and deserted location to settle. Had they arrived here some years earlier they would have been met by the Patuxet Indian tribe and, as one of the fiercest in the area, would have most likely wel-

Signing of the Mayflower Compact

comed the Pilgrims with many arrows, but in 1617 a plague had mysteriously wiped them out. The neighboring tribes were afraid to come near the place for fear that some great supernatural spirit had destroyed them, which left the area open for the Pilgrims.

Being out from under the authority of the Virginia Company caused some of the non-separatists to talk mutinously of abusing their liberty once they went shore, so before leaving the ship the Pilgrims drew up their own governmental compact which states:

> Having undertaken for the glory of God and advancement of the Christian faith, and the honour of our king and country, a voyage to plant the first colony in the Northern parts of Virginia, do by these presents solemnly and mutually in the presence of God, and one of another, covenant and combine ourselves together into a civil body politic.[209]

This document, the Mayflower Compact, placed the Pilgrim's civil government on a firm Christian base and was the beginning of American constitutional government.

Upon arriving on shore the Pilgrims fell to their knees and blessed and thanked God and confirmed their reliance upon Him. That first winter one half of their number died. The next spring when the Mayflower returned to Europe, however, not one went back. They had not come for personal convenience or reward, but that they might walk in liberty with their God and be even as stepping stones for others to do the same.

Of Plymouth Plantation

Because the Pilgrims were stepping stones, many others came and planted seeds of the American Christian Constitutional Republic. Every American should know their story and their great example of Christian character, but few do. The best way to learn their story is from their own words. William Bradford records their history in "Of Plimoth Plantation." The following excerpts are from his original manuscript, written in 1647. (The text is from *Bradford's History "Of Plimoth Plantation"* from the Original Manuscript printed by order of the General Court of Massachusetts by Wright & Potter Printing Co., State Printers, in 1898. The spelling and some punctuation have been modernized.) The story starts in the early 1600s in England when many people who had been converted began to be persecuted as they lived out their new-found faith.

 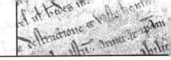

"Of Plimoth Plantation" by William Bradford

When as by the travail and diligence of some godly and zealous preachers, and God's blessing on their labors, as in other places of the land, so in the North parts, many became enlightened by the Word of God, and had their ignorance and sins discovered unto them, and began by His grace to reform their lives, and make conscience of their ways, the work of God was no sooner manifest in them, but presently they were both scoffed and scorned by the profane multitude; and the ministers urged with the yoke of subscription, or else must be silenced...

So many, therefore, of these professors as saw the evil of these things in these parts, and whose hearts the Lord had touched with heavenly zeal for His truth, they shook off this yoke of antichristian bondage, and as the Lord's free people joined themselves (by a covenant of the Lord) into a church estate, in the fellowship of the gospel, to walk in all His ways made known, or to be made known unto them, according to their best endeavors, whatsoever it should cost them, the Lord assisting them. And that it cost them something this ensuing history will declare....

Of their Departure into Holland and their Troubles thereabout, with some of the many difficulties they found and met withal. Anno 1608

Being thus constrained to leave their native soil and country, their lands and livings, and all their friends and familiar acquaintance, it was much, and thought marvelous by many. But to go into a country they knew not (but by hearsay), where they must learn a new language and get their livings they knew not how, it being a dear place and subject to the miseries of war, it was by many thought an adventure almost desperate; a case intolerable and a misery worse than death. Especially seeing they were not acquainted with trades nor traffic (by which that country doth subsist) but had only been used to a plain country life and the innocent trade of husbandry. But these things did not dismay them (though they did sometimes trouble them) for their desires were set on the ways of God and to enjoy His ordinances; but they rested on His providence, and knew Whom they had believed. Yet this was not all, for though they could not stay, yet were they not suffered to go; but the ports and havens were shut against them, so as they were fain to seek secret means of conveyance, and to bribe and fee the mariners, and give extraordinary rates for their passages. And yet were they often times betrayed (many of them), and both they and their goods intercepted and surprised, and thereby put to great trouble and charge, of which I will give an instance or two and omit the rest.

There was a large company of them purposed to get passage at Boston in Lincolnshire, and for that end had hired a ship wholly to themselves and made agreement with the master to be ready at a certain day, and take them and their goods in at a convenient place, where they accordingly would all attend in readiness. So after long waiting and large expenses, though he kept not day with them, yet he came at length and took them in, in the night. But when he had them and their goods aboard, he betrayed them, having beforehand complotted with the searchers and other officers so to do; who took them, and put them into open boats, and there rifled and ransacked them, searching to their shirts for money, yea even the women further than became modesty; and then carried them back into the town and made them a spectacle and wonder to the multitude which came flocking on all sides to behold them. Being thus first, by the catchpoll officers rifled and stripped of their money, books and much other goods, they were presented to the magistrates, and messengers sent to inform the Lords of the Council of them; and so they were committed to ward. Indeed the magistrates used them courteously and showed them what favor they could; but could not deliver them till order came from the Council table. But the issue was that after a month's imprisonment the greatest part were dismissed and sent to the places from whence they came; but 7 of the principal were still kept in prison and bound over to the Assizes.

The next spring after, there was another attempt made by some of these and others to get over at another place. And it so fell out that they light of a Dutchman at Hull, having a ship of his own belonging to Zealand; they made agreement with him, and acquainted him with their condition, hoping to find more faithfulness in him than in the former of their own nation. He bade them not fear, for he would do well enough. He was by appointment to take them in between Grimsby and Hull, where was a large common a good way distant from any town. Now against the prefixed time, the women and children, with the goods, were sent to the place in a small bark which they had hired for that end; and the men were to meet them by land. But it so fell out that they were there a day before the ship came, and the sea being rough and the women very sick, prevailed with the seamen to put into a creek hard by, where they lay on ground at low water. The next morning the ship came but they were fast and could not stir until about noon. In the meantime, the shipmaster, perceiving how the matter was, sent his boat to be getting the men aboard whom he saw ready, walking about the shore. But after the first boatful was got aboard and she was ready to go for more,

A Dutch Ship

the master espied a great company, both horse and foot, with bills and guns and other weapons; for the country was raised to take them. The Dutchman seeing that, swore his country's oath, "sacremente," and having the wind fair, weighed his an-

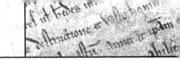

chor, hoisted sails, and away.

But the poor men which were got aboard were in great distress for their wives and children which they saw thus to be taken, and were left destitute of their helps; and themselves also, not having a cloth to shift them with, more than they had on their backs, and some scarce a penny about them, all they had being aboard the bark. It drew tears from their eyes, and anything they had they would have given to have been ashore again; but all in vain, there was no remedy, they must thus sadly part. And afterward endured a fearful storm at sea, being 14 days or more before they arrived at their port; in 7 whereof they neither saw sun, moon nor stars, and were driven near the coast of Norway; the mariners themselves often despairing of life, and once with shrieks and cries gave over all, as if the ship had been foundered in the sea, and they sinking without recovery. But when man's hope and help wholly failed, the Lord's power and mercy appeared in their recovery; for the ship rose again and gave the mariners courage again to manage her. And if modesty would suffer me, I might declare with what fervent prayers they cried unto the Lord in this great distress (especially some of them) even without any great distraction, when the water ran into their mouths and ears and the mariners cried out, "We sink, we sink!" they cried (if not with miraculous, yet with a great height or degree of divine faith), "Yet Lord Thou canst save! Yet Lord Thou canst save!" with such other expressions as I will forbear. Upon which the ship did not only recover, but shortly after the violence of the storm began to abate, and the Lord filled their afflicted minds with such comforts as everyone cannot understand, and in the end brought them to their desired haven, where the people came flocking, admiring their deliverance; the storm having been so long and sore, in which much hurt had been done, as the master's friends related unto him in their congratulations.

But to return to the others where we left. The rest of the men that were in greatest danger made shift to escape away before the troop could surprise them; those only staying that best might to be assistant unto the women. But pitiful it was to see the heavy case of these poor women in this distress; what weeping and crying on every side, some for their husbands that were carried away in the ship as is before related; others not knowing what should become of them and their little ones; others again melted in tears, seeing their poor little ones hanging about them, crying for fear and quaking with cold. Being thus apprehended, they were hurried from one place to another and from one justice to another, till in the end they knew not what to do with them; for to imprison so many women and innocent children for no other cause (many of them) but that they must go with their husbands, seemed to be unreasonable and all would cry out of them; and to send them home again was as difficult, for they alleged, as the truth was, they had no homes to go to, for they had either sold or otherwise disposed of their houses and livings. To be short, after they had been thus turmoiled a good while and conveyed from one constable to another, they were glad to be rid of them in the end upon any terms, for all were wearied and tired with them. Though in the meantime they (poor souls) endured misery enough; and thus in the end necessity forced a way for them.

But that I be not tedious in these things, I will omit the rest, though I might relate many other notable passages and troubles which they endured and underwent in these their wanderings and travels both at land and sea; but I haste to other things. Yet I may not omit the fruit that came hereby, for by these so public troubles in so many eminent places their cause became famous and occasioned many to look into the same; and their godly carriage and Christian behavior was such as left a deep impression in the minds of many. And though some few shrunk at these first conflicts and sharp beginnings (as it was no marvel) yet many more came on

Leyden, Holland

with fresh courage and greatly animated others. And in the end, notwithstanding all these storms of opposition, they all got over at length, some at one time and some at another, and some in one place and some in another, and met together again according to their desires, with no small rejoicing.

Of their settling in Holland, and their manner of living, and entertainment there

Being now come into the Low Countries, they saw many goodly and fortified cities, strongly walled and guarded with troops of armed men. Also, they heard a strange and uncouth language, and beheld the different manners and customs of the people, with their strange fashions and attires; all so far differing from that of their plain country villages (wherein they were bred and had so long lived) as it seemed they were come into a new world. But these were not the things they much looked on, or long took up their thoughts, for they had other work in hand and another kind of war to wage and maintain. For although they saw fair and beautiful cities, flowing with abundance of all sorts of wealth and riches, yet it was not long before they saw the grim and grisly face of poverty coming upon them like an armed man, with whom they must buckle and encounter, and from whom they could not fly. But they were armed with faith and patience against him and all his encounters; and though they were sometimes foiled, yet by God's assistance they prevailed and got the victory....

And when they had lived at Amsterdam about a year... they removed to Ley-

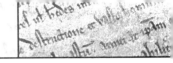

den, a fair and beautiful city and of a sweet situation, but made more famous by the university wherewith it is adorned, in which of late had been so many learned men…. And first, though many of them were poor, yet there was none so poor but if they were known to be of that congregation the Dutch (either bakers or others) would trust them in any reasonable matter when they wanted money. Because they had found by experience how careful they were to keep their word, and saw them so painful and diligent in their callings; yea, they would strive to get their custom and to employ them above others in their work, for their honesty and diligence….

Showing the reasons and causes of their removal

After they had lived in this city about some 11 or 12 years (which is the more observable being the whole time of that famous truce between that state and the Spaniards) and sundry of them were taken away by death and many others began to be well stricken in years (the grave mistress of Experience having taught them many things), those prudent governors with sundry of the sagest members began both deeply to apprehend their present dangers and wisely to foresee the future and think of timely remedy. In the agitation of their thoughts, and much discourse of things hereabout, at length they began to incline to this conclusion, of removal to some other place. Not out of any newfangledness or other such like giddy humor by which men are oftentimes transported to their great hurt and danger, but for sundry weighty and solid reasons, some of the chief of which I will here briefly touch.

The Pilgrims consistenly sought God in prayer.

And first, they saw and found by experience the hardness of the place and country to be such as few in comparison would come to them, and fewer that would bide it out, and continue with them…. Yea, some preferred and chose the prisons in England rather than this liberty in Holland with these afflictions. But it was thought that if a better and easier place of living could be had, it would draw many and take away these discouragements….

Secondly, they saw that though the people generally bore all these difficulties very cheerfully, and with a resolute courage, being in the best and strength of their years; yet old age began to steal on many of them, (and their great and continual labors, with other crosses and sorrows, hastened it before the time)....

Thirdly; ... many of their children, by these occasions and the great licentious-ness of youth in that country, and the manifold temptations of the place, were drawn away by evil examples into extravagant and dangerous courses, getting the reins off their necks and departing from their parents. Some became soldiers, others took upon them far voyages by sea, and others some worse courses tending to dissolute-ness and the danger of their souls, to the great grief of their parents and dishonor of God. So that they saw their posterity would be in danger to degenerate and be corrupted.

Lastly (and which was not least), a great hope and inward zeal they had of lay-ing some good foundation, or at least to make some way thereunto, for the propa-gating and advancing the gospel of the kingdom of Christ in those remote parts of the world; yea, though they should he but even as stepping-stones unto others for the performing of so great a work.

These and some other like reasons moved them to undertake this resolution of their removal; the which they afterward prosecuted with so great difficulties, as by the sequel will appear.

The place they had thoughts on was some of those vast and unpeopled coun-tries of America, which are fruitful and fit for habitation, being devoid of all civil inhabitants, where there are only savage and brutish men which range up and down, little otherwise than the wild beasts of the same. This proposition being made public and coming to the scanning of all, it raised many variable opinions amongst men and caused many fears and doubts amongst themselves.... For there they should be liable to famine and nakedness and the want, in a manner, of all things. The change of air, diet and drinking of water would infect their bodies with sore sicknesses and grievous diseases. And also those which should escape or overcome these difficul-ties should yet be in continual danger of the savage people, who are cruel, barbarous and most treacherous, being most furious in their rage and merciless where they overcome; not being content only to kill and take away life, but delight to torment men in the most bloody manner that may be; flaying some alive with the shells of fishes, cutting off the members and joints of others by piecemeal and broiling on the coals, eat the collops of their flesh in their sight whilst they live, with other cruelties horrible to be related.

And surely it could not be thought but the very hearing of these things could not but move the very bowels of men to grate within them and make the weak to quake and tremble. It was further objected that it would require greater sums of money to furnish such a voyage and to fit them with necessaries, than their con-sumed estates would amount to; and yet they must as well look to be seconded with supplies as presently to be transported.

Also many precedents of ill success and lamentable miseries befallen others in the like designs were easy to be found, and not forgotten to be alleged; besides their own experience, in their former troubles and hardships in their removal into Hol-

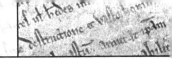

land, and how hard a thing it was for them to live in that strange place, though it was a neighbor country and a civil and rich commonwealth.

It was answered, that all great and honorable actions arc accompanied with great difficulties and must be both enterprised and overcome with answerable courages. It was granted the dangers were great, but not desperate. The difficulties were many, but not invincible. For though there were many of them likely, yet they were not certain. It might be sundry of the things feared might never befall; others by provident care and the use of good means might in a great measure be prevented; and all of them, through the help of God, by fortitude and patience, might either be borne or overcome....

[Next are two chapters dealing with their difficult legal and economic preparation.]

Of their departure from Leyden

At length, after much travail and these debates, all things were got ready and provided.... So being ready to depart, they had a day of solemn humiliation, their pastor taking his text from Ezra 8.21: "And there at the river, by Ahava, I proclaimed a fast, that we might humble ourselves before our God, and seek of him a right way for us, and for our children, and for all our substance." Upon which he spent a good part of the day very profitably and suitable to their present occasion. The rest of the time was spent in powering [pouring] out prayers to the Lord with great fervency, mixed with abundance of tears....

John Robinson (at right) prays with the Pilgrims as they leave Holland in 1620.

So they left that goodly and pleasant city which had been their resting place near 12 years; but they knew they were pilgrims [Heb. 11], and looked not much on those things, but lift up their eyes to the heavens, their dearest country, and quieted their spirits....

At their parting Mr. Robinson write a letter to the whole company; which though it hath already been printed, yet I thought good here likewise to insert it….

Loving Christian friends, I do heartily and in the Lord salute you all…. And first, as we are daily to renew our repentance with our God, especially for our sins known, and generally for our unknown trespasses…. sin being taken away by earnest repentance and the pardon thereof from the Lord, sealed up unto a man's conscience by His Spirit, great shall be his security and peace in all dangers, sweet his comforts in all distresses, with happy deliverance from all evil, whether in life or in death….

Lastly, whereas you are become a body politic, using amongst yourselves civil government, and are not furnished with any persons of special eminency above the rest, to be chosen by you into office, of government; let your wisdom and godliness appear, not only in choosing such persons as do entirely love and will promote the common good, but also in yielding unto them all due honor and obedience in their lawful administrations, not beholding in them the ordinariness of their persons, but God's ordinance for your good; not being like the foolish multitude who more honor the gay coat than either the virtuous mind of the man, or glorious ordinance of the Lord….

I do earnestly commend unto your care and conscience, joining therewith my daily incessant prayers unto the Lord, that He who hath made the heavens and the earth, the sea and all rivers of waters, and whose providence is over all His works, especially over all His dear children for good, would so guide and guard you in your ways. … John Robinson…

Of their voyage…and… safe arrival at Cape Cod

Sept. 6…. and now all being compact together in one ship, they put to sea again with a prosperous wind, which continued diverse days together, which was some encouragement unto them; yet according to the usual manner many were afflicted with sea-sickness. And I may not omit here a special work of God's providence. There was a proud and very profane young man, one of the sea-men, of a lusty,

When the Pilgrims arrived at shore "they fell upon their knees and blessed the God of heaven, who had brought them over the vast and furious ocean and delivered them from all the perils and miseries thereof."

able body, which made him the more haughty. He would always be contemning the poor people in their sickness, and cursing them daily with grievous execrations, and did not let [hesitate] to tell them, that he hoped to help to cast half of them over board before they came to their journey's end, and to make merry with what they had; and if he were by any gently reproved, he would curse and swear most bitterly. But it pleased God before they came half seas over, to smite this young man with a grievous disease, of which he died in a desperate manner, and so was himself the first that was thrown overboard. Thus his curses light on his own head; and it was an astonishment to all his fellows, for they noted it to be the just hand of God upon him.

After they had enjoyed fair winds and weather for a season, they were encountered many times with cross winds, and met with many fierce storms, with which the ship was shroudly [much] shaken, and her upper works made very leaky.... In sundry of these storms the winds were so fierce, and the seas so high, as they could not bear a knot of sail, but were forced to hull, for diverse days together.... [A]fter long beating at sea they fell with that land which is called Cape Cod; the which being made and certainly known to be it, they were not a little joyful....

Being thus arrived in a good harbor and brought safe to land, they fell upon their knees and blessed the God of heaven, who had brought them over the vast and furious ocean, and delivered them from all the perils and miseries thereof, again to set their feet on the firm and stable earth, their proper element. And no marvel if they were thus joyful....

But hear I cannot but stay and make a pause, and stand half amazed at this poor peoples present condition; and so I think will the reader too, when he well considers the same. Being thus passed the vast ocean, and a sea of troubles before in their preparation (as may be remembered by that which went before), they had now no friends to welcome them, nor inns to entertain or refresh their weatherbeaten bodies; no houses or much less towns to repair to, to seek for succour. It is recorded in Scripture [Acts 28] as a mercy to the Apostle and his shipwrecked company, that the barbarians showed them no small kindness in refreshing them, but these savage barbarians, when they met with them (as after will appear) were readier to fill their sides full of arrows than otherwise. And for the season it was winter, and they that know the winters of that country know them to be sharp and violent, and subject to cruel and fierce storms, dangerous to travel to known places, much more to search an unknown coast.

Besides, what could they see but a hideous and desolate wilderness, full of wild beasts and wild men – and what multitudes there might be of them they knew not. Neither could they, as it were, go up to the top of Pisgah to view from this wilderness a more goodly country to feed their hopes; for which way soever they turned their eyes (save upward to the heavens) they could have little solace or content in respect of any outward objects. For summer being done, all things stand upon them with a weatherbeaten face, and the whole country, full of woods and thickets, represented a wild and savage hue. If they looked behind them, there was the mighty ocean which they had passed and was now as a main bar and gulf to separate them from all the civil parts of the world. If it be said they had a ship to succour them, it is true; but what heard they daily from the master and company? But that with speed they should look out a place with their shallop, where they would be at some near distance; for the season was such as he would not stir from thence till a safe harbor was discovered by them, where they would be, and he might go without danger; and that victuals consumed apace but he must and would keep sufficient for themselves and their return. Yea, it was muttered by some that if they got not a place in time, they would turn them and their goods ashore and leave them. Let it also be considered what weak hopes of supply and succour they left behind them, that might bear up their minds in this sad condition and trials they were under; and they could not but be very small. It is true, indeed, the affections and love of their brethren at Leyden was cordial and entire towards them, but they had little power to help them or themselves; and how the case stood between them and the merchants at their coming away hath already been declared.

What could now sustain them but the Spirit of God and His grace? May not and ought not the children of these fathers rightly say: Our fathers were Englishmen which came over this great ocean, and were ready to perish in this wilderness [Deut. 26:5,7]; but they cried unto the Lord, and He heard their voice and looked on their adversity, etc. Let them therefore praise the Lord, because He is good: and His mercies endure forever [Psa. 107: 1,2,4,5,8]. Yea, let them which have been redeemed of the Lord, show how He hath delivered them from the hand of the oppressor. When they wandered in the desert wilderness out of the way, and found no city to dwell in, both hungry and thirsty, their soul was overwhelmed in them. Let them confess before the Lord His lovingkindness, and His wonderful works before the sons of men....

[The Mayflower Compact and Their First Winter]

I shall a little return back and begin with a combination made by them before they came ashore, being the first foundation of their government in this place; occasioned partly by the discontented and mutinous speeches that some of the strangers amongst them had let fall from them in the ship — That when they came ashore they would use their own liberty; for none had power to command them, the patent they had being for Virginia and not for New England, which belonged to another government, with which the Virginia Company had nothing to do. And partly that such an act by them done, this their condition considered, might be as firm as any patent, and in some respects more sure.

The form was as followeth.

In the name of God, Amen. We whose names are underwritten, the loyal subjects of our dread Sovereign Lord, King James, by the Grace of God, of Great Britain, France, and Ireland king, defender of the faith, etc., having undertaken, for the glory of God and advancement of the Christian faith and honour of our king and country, a voyage to plant the first colony in the Northern parts of Virginia, do by these presents solemnly and mutually in the presence of God, and one of another, covenant and combine ourselves together into a civil body politic, for our better ordering and preservation and furtherance of the ends aforesaid; and by virtue hereof to enact, constitute and frame such just and equal laws, ordinances, acts, constitutions and offices, from time to time, as shall be thought most meet and convenient for the general good of the Colony, unto which we promise all due submission and obedience. In witness whereof we have hereunder subscribed our names at Cape Cod, the 11th of November, in the year of the reign of our sovereign lord, King James, of England, France and Ireland the eighteenth, and of Scotland the fifty-fourth. Anno Domini 1620.

Mayflower Compact in the handwriting of William Bradford.

After this they chose, or rather confirmed, Mr. John Carver (a man godly and well approved amongst them) their Governor for that year. And after they had provided a place for their goods, or common store (which were long in unlading for want of boats, foulness of the winter weather and sickness of diverse) and begun some small cottages for their habitation; as time would admit, they met and consulted of laws and orders, both for their civil and military government as the necessity of their condition did require, still adding thereunto as urgent occasion in several times, and as cases did require.

In these hard and difficult beginnings they found some discontents and murmurings arise amongst some, and mutinous speeches and carriages in other; but they were soon quelled and overcome by the wisdom, patience, and just and equal carriage of things, by the Governor and better part, which clave faithfully together in the main.

 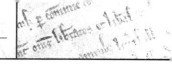

[The Starving Time]

But that which was most sad and lamentable was, that in 2 or 3 months' time half of their company died, especially in January and February, being the depth of winter, and wanting houses and other comforts; being infected with the scurvy and other diseases which this long voyage and their inaccommodate condition had brought upon them. So as there died some times 2 or 3 of a day in the foresaid time; that of 100 and odd persons, scarce 50 remained. And of these, in the time of most distress, there was but 6 or 7 sound persons, who, to their great commendations be it spoken, spared no pains, night nor day, but with abundance of toil and hazard of their own health, fetched them wood, made them fires, dressed them meat, made their beds, washed their loathsome clothes, clothed and unclothed them; in a word, did all the homely and necessary offices for them which dainty and queasy stomachs cannot endure to hear named; and all this willingly and cheerfully, without any grudging in the least, showing herein their true love unto their friends and brethren; a rare example and worthy to be remembered....

[Squanto: a special instrument sent of God]

But about the 16. of March a certain Indian came boldly amongst them, and spoke to them in broken English, which they could well understand but marveled at it.... His name was Samaset; he told them also of another Indian whose name was Squanto, a native of this place, who had been in England and could speak better English than himself. Being, after some time of entertainment and gifts, dismissed, a while after he came again, and 5 more with him...and made way for the coming of their great Sachem, called Massosoyt; who, about 4 or 5 days after, came with ... the aforesaid Squanto. With whom, after friendly entertainment, and some gifts given him, they made a peace with him, which hath now continued this 24 years....

After these things he returned to his place ... but Squanto continued with them, and was their interpreter, and was a special instrument sent of God for their good beyond their expectation. He directed them how to set their corn, where to fish, and to procure other commodities, and was their pilot to bring them to unknown places for their profit, and never left them till he died....

Afterwards they (as many as were able) began to plant their corn, in which service Squanto stood them in great stead, showing them both the manner how to set it, and after how to dress and tend it. Also he told them, except they got fish and set with it (in these old grounds) it would come to nothing. And he showed them that in the middle of April they should have store enough come up the brook, by which they began to build, and taught them how to take it, and where to get other provisions necessary for them. All which they found true by trial and experience....

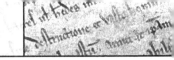

And thus they found the Lord to be with them in all their ways, and to bless their outgoings and incomings, for which let His holy name have the praise forever, to all posterity.[210]

(Various editions of *Bradford's History* are available at libraries and used bookstores if you wish to read more.)

The First Thanksgiving

Squanto not only taught the Pilgrims how to plant corn and catch fish, he also taught them to stalk deer, plant pumpkins, find berries, and catch beaver, whose pelts proved to be their economic deliverance. He was also helpful in securing a peace treaty between the Pilgrims and surrounding Indian tribes, which lasted over fifty years. In the words of William Bradford, "Squanto … was a special instrument sent of God for their good beyond their expectation."[211] His life story is amazing in itself.

In 1605, Squanto, a member of the Patuxet Indian tribe, was captured by an English explorer and taken to England. He remained there nine years, during which time he learned to speak English. In 1614, Captain John Smith took him back to New England, but shortly after this he was again taken captive and sold into slavery at a port in Spain. Providentially, some local friars bought and rescued him.

From Spain, he eventually went to England where he remained until 1619, when he obtained passage back to his home in New England. As Squanto went ashore at what was to become Plymouth, he found his entire tribe had been killed by a plague. He was the only survivor of the Patuxet tribe. Joining himself to a nearby tribe, he remained there until the spring of 1621 when he joined himself with the Pilgrims, determining to see them survive at the place where his tribe had not.[212]

Thanks to God, His instrument Squanto, and the character and determination of the Pilgrims, half of them had survived an unimaginably difficult first year. Moreover, they harvested a sufficient food supply for their second winter at Plymouth. Even though there was no surplus food, things looked much better than the preceding winter.

Governor Bradford appointed a day of thanksgiving and invited the nearby Wampanoag Indians (Squanto's adopted tribe) to celebrate and give thanks unto God with them. Chief Massasoit and ninety of his men came and feasted with the Pilgrims. They ate deer, turkey, fish, lobster, eels, vegetables, corn bread, herbs, berries, pies, and the Indians even taught the Pilgrims how to make popcorn. The Pilgrims and Indians also competed in running, wrestling, and shooting games. Massasoit enjoyed himself so much that he and his men stayed for three days.[213] It is easy to see where the American tradition of feasting at Thanksgiving began.

While many people today follow the Pilgrim's example of feasting at Thanksgiving, they too often ignore the entire reason that the Pilgrims set aside a special day – that was to give thanks to Almighty God and ackowledge their utter dependence upon Him for their existence. While many today take ease in having plenty, never seeing a need to cry out to God, the Pilgrims relied upon God in their lack and thanked Him in their abundance. Their trust was in God and not in their abundant provisions. This trust was seen even more fully in the two years following their first Thanksgiving.

The Pilgrims at church.

Shortly after their Thanksgiving celebration, thirty-five new persons unexpectedly arrived who planned to remain and live at Plymouth. The plantation was glad for this added strength, but when they found out they had no provisions it also brought a soberness. Yet their reliance was upon God, so they gladly shared their food, clothing, and homes. With the new additions, their food, even at half allowance for each person, would last six months at most.

Their provisions had almost completely run out when they spied a boat in May of 1622. They hoped the English Company who had sponsored their colonizing Plymouth had sent provisions; however, this boat not only did not bring any food (nor the hope of any), but seven more hungry people to stay in Plymouth. In their extreme hunger, as in times of plenty, they put their complete trust in God to provide.

No one starved to death, yet it would be over a year before famine was completely removed from their midst. During that time there were many days where they "had need to pray that God would give them their daily bread above all people in the world."[214]

That spring and summer of 1622 God miraculously fed them, even as the ravens fed Elijah in the wilderness. He provided because the Pilgrims had determined to walk in the way of their Lord Jesus. This was most evident in early summer when sixty "lusty" men (as Bradford called them) came to them for help. Even though these men showed no gratitude, the Pilgrims still gladly took care of them, for many were sick. They gave them housing and shared their meager provisions. This they did for almost the entire summer until the men left.

Like the year before, the harvest of 1622 proved insufficient to meet the Pil-

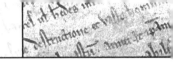

grims' needs. Outside help appeared doubtful, so the Pilgrims considered how they could produce a larger harvest. Through God's wisdom they chose to replace the collective farming they had practiced the two preceding years (being imposed upon them by their sponsoring company) with individual farming, assigning to every family a parcel of land.

Bradford wrote: "This had very good success, for it made all hands very industrious, so as much more corn was planted than other wise would have been by any means the Governor or any other could use... and gave far better content. The women now went willingly into the field, and took their little ones with them to set corn, which before would allege weakness and inability; whom to have compelled would have been thought great tyranny and oppression."[215] As they were freed from economic communism and entered into individual enterprise, abundance began to come upon these people.

The Pilgrims learned the hard way that communism does not work, even among a covenant community. Bradford wrote that "the experience that was had in this common course and condition, tried sundry years, and that amongst godly and sober men, may well evince the vanity of that conceit of Platos and other ancients, applauded by some of later times; – that the taking away of property, and bringing in community into a common wealth, would make them happy and flourishing; as if they were wiser than God."[216]

The Pilgrims' hard work, resulting from them being able to directly benefit from the fruit of their labors, caused them to plant about six times more crops than the previous year. While labor certainly increases our prosperity, there are other factors. God wanted the Pilgrims to never forget that it is the Lord that gives men the power to get substance or wealth (Deuteronomy 8:18).

The Pilgrims had great hopes for a large crop, yet as Bradford wrote, "the Lord seemed to blast, and take away the same, and to threaten further and more sore famine unto them, by a great drought which continued from the 3. week in May, till about the middle of July, without any rain and with great heat (for the most part) insomuch as the corn began to wither away."[217]

In response to this, "they set a part a solemn day of humiliation to seek the Lord by humble and fervent prayer, in this great distress. And he was pleased to give them a gracious and speedy answer, both to their own and the Indians admiration that lived amongst them. For all the morning, and greatest part of the day, it was clear weather and very hot, and not a cloud or any sign of rain to be seen, yet toward evening it began to overcast, and shortly after to rain, with such sweet and gentle showers, as gave them cause of rejoicing and blessing God. It came, without either wind, or thunder, or any violence, and by degrees in that abundance, as that the earth was thoroughly wet and soaked therewith. Which did so apparently revive and quicken the decayed corn and other fruits, as was wonderful to see, and made the Indians astonished to behold."[218]

An Indian named Hobamak who witnessed this event said to a Pilgrim: "Now

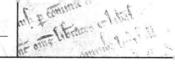

I see that the Englishman's God is a good God, for he hath heard you, and sent you rain, and that without storms and tempests and thunder, which usually we have with our rain, which breaks down our corn, but yours stands whole and good still; surely your God is a good God."[219]

Depiction of a Thanksgiving meal

The harvest of 1623 brought plenty to each person, with the more industrious having excess to sell to others. From the time they started a biblical economic system, no famine or general want ever again existed among them. That autumn of 1623, the Pilgrims again set apart a day of thanksgiving unto God.[220] They had much to give thanks for and knew Whom to acknowledge.

Each year when we celebrate Thanksgiving, let us remember the heritage of that day and why the Pilgrims set aside a day of thanksgiving. In the words of President Abraham Lincoln, proclaiming the second National Thanksgiving Day: this is "a day of thanksgiving and praise to Almighty God, the beneficent Creator and Ruler of the Universe."[221]

 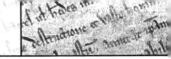
Review Questions

■ Who were the Pilgrims? What motivated them to come to America?

■ The excerpts from Bradford's history are divided by numerous headings. State the title of each section and relate one difficult thing the Pilgrims experienced in each section, and what kind of courage in God they showed in dealing with that particular difficulty.

■ The Pilgrims were on a divine mission from God and sought to act in a Christian manner in all things. Why do you think God allowed one half of their number to die during the first winter of their settlement in Plymouth?

■ How do you see God's providence in Squanto's relationship to the Pilgrims?

■ Do you think the Mayflower Compact was a Christian document? Why?

■ What economic lessons did the Pilgrims learn during their first years in America?

■ Many Americans today associate the Thanksgiving holiday with the Pilgrims. What important lessons can we learn from the Pilgrims and pass on to our posterity when we gather to celebrate this holiday each year?

CHAPTER 9

The Christian Colonization of America: Cultivating the Seed of Liberty

The Bible: Rock of Our Republic

The Pilgrims planted the seed of the Plymouth Colony in 1620. A few settlers had come before them (like those in Jamestown, Virginia, 1607), and many more would follow. The planting of all thirteen original colonies was dominated by the Christian faith. President Andrew Jackson summarized this truth, declaring of the Bible: "That book ... is the rock on which our Republic rests."[222] Early Americans would almost universally agree that the religious, social, educational, and political life of America was primarily shaped by the Bible.

Our states were colonized by people who desired to freely worship the God of the Bible; our schools were begun so that everyone would be able to read and understand the Bible for themselves; our universities were founded to train ministers who were knowledgeable of the Scriptures; our laws and constitutions were written based on biblical ideas; and our Founding Fathers overwhelmingly had a biblical worldview.

Most Americans today have not been taught

Geneva Bible Title Page

of the importance of the Bible in our history, even though many still recognize it. *Newsweek* magazine, on December 26, 1982, acknowledged that: "Now historians are discovering that the Bible, perhaps even more than the Constitution is our Founding document." That America's biblical foundation produced America's freedom, justice, and prosperity was common knowledge in the past.

In recent generations America has been shifting from a biblical foundation to a humanistic foundation, where the God of the Bible is being replaced by man as god. The result has been the decay of society and loss of liberty. Noah Webster wrote:

> The moral principles and precepts contained in the Scriptures ought to form the basis of all our civil constitutions and laws. All the miseries and evils which men suffer from vice, crime, ambition, injustice, oppression, slavery, and war, proceed from their despising or neglecting the precepts contained in the Bible.[223]

For the good of America we must once again restore the Bible to the central role it played in shaping this nation. To do this we must first understand that role. Following is a brief look at the central influence of the Bible in the colonization of America.

The Bible was the single most important influence in the lives of colonial Americans.

Educator Lawrence A. Cremin writes:

> Above all, the colonists were acquainted with the Bible itself, principally in the Geneva Version but increasingly in the King James Version. The Bible was read and recited, quoted and consulted, early committed to memory and constantly searched for meaning. Deemed universally relevant, it remained throughout the century the single most important cultural influence in the lives of Anglo-Americans. . . . Though the Bible had been richly valued for generations, it was not until the seventeenth century that it was widely read and studied. The message of Protestantism was that men could find in Scripture the means to salvation, the keys to good and evil, the rules by which to live, and the standards against which to measure the conduct of prince and pastor.[224]

New England of the 1700s was described by historian George Bancroft in this way:

> In the settlements which grew up in the interior, on the margin of the greenwood, the plain meeting-house of the congregation for public worship was

everywhere the central point; near it stood the public school. The snug farmhouses, owned as freehold, without quit-rents, were dotted along the way. In every hand was the Bible; every home was a house of prayer; all had been taught, many had comprehended, a methodical theory of the divine purpose in creation, and of the destiny of man.[225]

1) The People who settled America were people of the Book.

A majority of the settlers of America were a product of the Protestant Reformation. The major impetus of this reform was the Bible being translated into the common languages of the people. Throughout Europe the people read the Scriptures and began looking to them as the source of their faith and worldview. The Bible became the standard by which they judged not only their own actions but also that of priest and king, which brought many trials and persecutions and forced many to flee their native countries to America.

Many of those who had paved the way for the first settlers were inspired by the Scriptures as well. Composed in 1502 after his third voyage, Columbus' *Book of Prophecies* reveals he felt he was fulfilling a divine mission through his voyages. This work contains hundreds of prophetic passages of Scripture that Columbus related to his great enterprise.[226] The man most responsible for the English colonization of America was a minister, Richard Hakluyt. He said he was first inspired by the Scriptures to promote colonization. His chief motive was to extend God's Kingdom throughout the earth, writing:

> "Wee shall by plantinge there inlarge the glory of the gospel, and from England plante sincere religion, and provide a safe and a sure place to receave people from all partes of the worlde that are forced to flee for the truthe of Gods worde."[227]

Rev. Hakluyt was directly involved in the establishment of Jamestown. The following are a few examples of the role of the Bible and Christianity in Jamestown and a few of the other early settlements.

Carved relief in the Capitol Rotunda showing Pocahontas saving John Smith's life

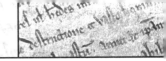

Jamestown

Jamestown was the first permanent English settlement in America. One of the first acts of the settlers after they landed in Virginia in April of 1607 was to erect a wooden cross on the shore at Cape Henry. It was at the foot of this cross that Reverend Robert Hunt led the 149 men of the Virginia Company in prayer, thanking God for their safe journey and recommitting themselves to God's plan and purpose for this New World. The Virginia Charter of 1606 reveals that part of their reason for coming to America was to propagate the "Christian Religion to such People, as yet live in Darkness and miserable Ignorance of the true knowledge and worship of God."[228]

Many Native Americans became Christians. The most well known is Pocahontas, who, before her conversion, providentially saved John Smith's life and helped preserve Jamestown as a settlement. She was later brought into the knowledge of the saving grace of Jesus Christ by the ministry of Rev. Alexander Whitaker and others. A painting in the U.S. Capitol Rotunda records her baptism and reminds us of one primary reason why many individuals originally came to America.

The Baptism of Pocahontas in the U.S. Capitol Rotunda

Pilgrims

As we saw in the last chapter, the Pilgrims were enlightened by the Word of God and sought to live according to its precepts. Pastor to the Pilgrims, John Robinson, wrote in his farewell letter:

> I charge you, before God and his blessed angels, that you follow me no farther than you have seen me follow the Lord Jesus Christ. The Lord has more truth yet to break forth out of his holy word. I cannot sufficiently bewail the condition of the reformed churches, who are come to a period in religion, and will go at present no farther than the instruments of their reformation. Luther and Calvin were great and shining lights in their times, yet they penetrated not into the whole counsel of God. I beseech you, remember it – 'tis an article of

your church covenant – that you be ready to receive whatever truth shall be made known to you from the written word of God.[229]

Puritans

The early settlers of Salem, Massachusetts were typical of the many Puritans who came to America. One reason they came was to "wynne the natives to the Christian faith."[230] During their voyage from England they "constantly served God, morning and evening, by reading and expounding a chapter in the Bible, singing and prayer."[231]

The First Charter of Massachusetts (1629) states the desire that all the inhabitants would "be so religiously, peaceably, and civilly governed, as their good life and orderly conversation may win and incite the natives of country to the knowledge and obedience of the only true God and Savior of mankind, and the Christian faith, which in Our royal intention and the adventurers' free profession, is the principal end of this plantation."[232]

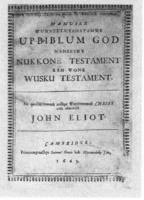

Title page of John Eliot's Algonquin Bible

The center of the seal of the colony of Massachusetts Bay shows an Indian speaking the words, "Come Over And Help Us."[233] The work of John Eliot, "Apostle to the Indians," and Daniel Gookin, a civil magistrate and superintendent to the Indians, shows how many of the early settlers desired to bring the gospel to the native Americans, and in so doing fulfill the prophetic words on the seal. These two men worked for over 40 years to evangelize and civilize the Algonquin Indians of Massachusetts. Eliot constantly traveled to various Indian villages and taught them the gospel. When many began to be converted he set up "Praying Towns" where these Christian Indians could live out their new life in Christ and learn how to separate themselves from their pagan way of life. In these towns, which came to number fourteen, the Indians were self-governed and self-supporting. Twenty-four of these Christian Indians became ministers in order to carry on the work of the gos-

The seal of Massachusetts Bay, with the words of an Indian saying, "Come Over and Help Us," is at the top of this 1676 broadside of a Proclamation for a Day of Prayer and Thanksgiving.

pel among their own people. Hundreds attended schools and some attended Harvard College.

Eliot believed that the Indians needed the Bible in their own language in order to truly grow in the complete liberty of the gospel, both internally and externally, both personally and civilly. Therefore, after learning the native Indian language, he developed a written language for the Algonquin tongue, as none existed. He then worked for twelve years on translating the Bible, while continuing his pastoral duties in the church in Roxbury and regularly traveling to minister to the Indians. He completed the work in 1658. The Algonquin Bible was first published in 1661-1663 with funds primarily contributed by Englishmen. This was the first Bible printed in America.

Many of the early schools and colleges in the colonies were started to not only train ministers, but also to evangelize and educate Indians. For example, the College of William and Mary was started mainly due to the efforts of Rev. James Blair in order, according to its charter of 1691, "that the Church of Virginia may be furnished with a seminary of ministers of the Gospel, and that the youth may be piously educated in good letters and manners, and that the Christian religion may be propagated among the Western Indians to the glory Almighty God."[234] Brafferton Hall was built specifically for Indian students. Dartmouth began in 1770 when Congregational pastor Eleazar Wheelock (1711-79) secured a charter from the governor of New Hampshire in March, 1770, to establish a college to train young men for missionary service among the Indians. Its Latin motto means: "the voice of one crying in the wilderness." The first students met in a log cabin, and when weather permitted Dr. Wheelock held morning and evening prayers in the open air.[235]

Connecticut and Rhode Island Started by Ministers

Rev. Thomas Hooker was instrumental in the beginning of Connecticut when he led about 100 members of his church from Newtown, Massachusetts, into the Connecticut Valley in 1636. He was instrumental in writing its founding document. Adopted January 14, 1639, the Fundamental Orders of Connecticut began with the inhabitants covenanting together under God "to maintain and preserve the liberty and purity of the gospel of our Lord Jesus which we now profess."[236]

Rev. Roger Williams founded Rhode Island in 1636, naming the first town Providence, "in a sense of God's merciful providence unto me in my distress." The Charter of Rhode Island (1663)

Roger Williams meeting with Indians in Rhode Island.

mentioned their intentions of "godlie edifieing themselves, and one another, in the holie Christian ffaith
and worshipp" and their desire for the "conversione of
the poore ignorant Indian natives."[237]

Seal of Rhode Island Colony

Scotch-Irish Presbyterians

Many Scotch-Irish Presbyterians settled on the
western frontiers of Pennsylvania, Maryland, Virginia,
and North Carolina. At every place they "had their pas-
tor, and trained their children in Bible truth, in the catechism, obedience to parents,
— a wholesome doctrine practically enforced by all the colonists, — and reverence
for the Sabbath and its sacred duties."[238]

Pennsylvania

When Quaker minister William Penn was given the land between New York
and Maryland in 1681 he said that "my God that has given it to me ... will, I believe,
bless and make it the seed of a nation."[239] In 1682 the Great Law of Pennsylvania was

Quaker minister William Penn

enacted revealing the desire of Penn and the inhabitants of the colony to establish "laws as shall best preserve true Christian and civil liberty, in opposition
to all unchristian, licentious, and unjust practices,
(whereby God may have his due, Caesar his due, and
the people their due)."[240]

Thomas Jefferson called Penn "the greatest law-
giver the world has produced." Penn, whose wisdom
was "derived from that book of gospel statutes,"
recognized Christian character as the basis of good
government. He states in Frame of Government of
Pennsylvania:

Governments like clocks, go from the motion men
give them; and as governments are made and moved
by men, so by them they are ruined too. Wherefore governments rather depend upon men, than men upon governments.... Let men be good, and the
government cannot be bad; if it be ill, they will cure it.[241]

At a later time William Penn told the Russian Czar, Peter the Great, that "if
thou wouldst rule well, thou must rule for God, and to do that, thou must be ruled

by Him.["]242

Section one of the Pennsylvania Charter of Privileges (1701) contains qualifications of officers where "all Persons who also profess to believe in Jesus Christ, the Saviour of the World, shall be capable (notwithstanding their other Persuasions and Practices in Point of Conscience and Religion) to serve this Government in any Capacity, both legislatively and executively."[243]

Georgia Colonists

Some of the earliest settlers to Georgia were German Lutherans who were driven out of their country when they refused to renounce their Protestant faith, and were invited by the Society in England for Propagating the Gospel to emigrate to Savannah. George Bancroft writes: "On the last day of October 1733, 'the evangelical community,' well supplied with Bibles and hymn-books, catechisms and books of devotion. . . — after a discourse and prayer and benedictions, cheerfully, and in the name of God, began their pilgrimage." They arrived at Charleston on March 18, 1734 and were welcomed by James Oglethorpe, the founder of Georgia.[244]

The Aitken Bible

Prior to America's independence almost every house in the colonies possessed and cherished the English Bible, yet, no English Bibles had ever been printed in the colonies (some had been printed in German and native Indian languages). It would have been piracy to do so. Only after independence were English Bibles printed. When the war cut off the supply of English Bibles, the Congress, in September 1777, resolved to import 20,000 Bibles

Front of Aitken Bible: "Whereupon, Resolved, That the United States in Congress assembled . . . recommend this edition of the Bible to the inhabitants of the United States."

from Scotland, Holland or elsewhere because "the use of the Bible is so universal and its importance so great."[245]

In 1782, Congress acted the role of a Bible society by officially approving the printing and distribution of the "Bible of the Revolution," an American translation prepared by Robert Aitken. The endorsement of Congress in the front of the Aitken

 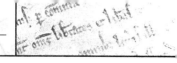

Bible read: "Whereupon, Resolved, That the United States in Congress assembled . . . recommend this edition of the Bible to the inhabitants of the United States."[246]

Oath of Office Taken on the Bible

At the first presidential inauguration George Washington laid his hand on the Bible and took the oath of office as prescribed by the Constitution, adding the words "so help me God," after which he leaned over and reverently kissed the Bible. Washington then went to the Senate and read his inaugural address. After this they all walked to St. Paul's Chapel for prayers and a service.[247] All the presidents have taken the oath of office on the Bible.

Washington taking the Presidential oath of office on the Bible.

2) The Bible formed the basis of America's civil laws.

Jamestown

Between 1609 and 1612 a set of laws was drawn up for the colony of Virginia. In these *Lawes Divine, Morall and Martiall, etc.* the colonists were required to serve God, to attend divine services, to not speak against God or blaspheme God's holy name, and to not speak or act in any way that would "tend to the derision, or despight [open defiance] of Gods holy word upon paine of death."[248] While this may seem extreme to us today, it nonetheless reveals their desire to live according to God's commands.

In 1619 the first representative assembly of the New World met in the church in Jamestown. It was begun by prayer. One of the resolves of this body was to encourage the farmers and plantation owners to open their homes to Indian youth with the purpose of converting them to Christianity and teaching them the precepts of God's Word.

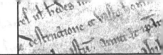

The Laws of the Pilgrims

The Pilgrims believed that God and His word were the supreme source of all authority. Their compilation of laws during the 1600s clearly revealed this. Their *Book of General Laws* (1671) begins by stating that "Laws. . . are so far good and wholesome, as by how much they are derived from, and agreeable to the ancient Platform of Gods Law."[249] As one reads through these laws it is obvious they looked to the Bible to assist them in formulating good and wholesome laws. They even gave Scriptural references to support their capital laws.

Fundamental Orders of Connecticut

This first American constitution was written by Rev. Thomas Hooker in 1638. The oath imposed on the magistrates bound them "to administer justice according to the laws here established, and for want thereof according to the rule of the word of God."[250] The oath of the governor (and similarly the Magistrate) ended with these words: "I . . . will further the execution of Justice according to the rule of Gods word; so helpe me God, in the name of the Lo: Jesus Christ."[251]

New Haven Colony

Established in 1638 under the guidance of Rev. John Davenport, this colony rested its frame of government upon the idea that "the Scriptures doe holde forth a perfect rule for the direction and government of all men in all duet[ies] . . . in the government of famyles and commonwealths."[252] God's Word was established as the only rule in public affairs. Bancroft wrote that "New Haven made the Bible its statute-book."[253]

Rev. Thomas Hooker

Massachusetts Body of Liberties

The Pentateuch (the first five books of the Bible) was the basis for the criminal code of the Massachusetts Body of Liberties. It was written in 1641 by a minister, Rev. Nathaniel Ward. If situations arose not addressed by the Body of Liberties, it states: "in case of the defect of a law in any case" the standard was "the word of God."[254] Article 65 states: "No custome or prescription shall ever prevaile amongst us in any morall cause, our meaneing is maintaine anythinge that can be proved to bee morrallie sinfull by the word of god."[255] The capital laws in the Body of Liberties give numerous scriptures as justification for carrying out the death penalty.[256]

Arbitrary Government Described (1644)

In explaining how the government of Massachusetts was to work, Governor John Winthrop wrote: "By these it appears, that the officers of this body politic have a rule to walk by in all their administrations, which rule is the Word of God, and such conclusions and deductions as are, or shall be, regularly drawn from thence."[257]

Code of the Connecticut General Court, 1650

No man's life, liberty, or property was to be taken except by specific law established and sufficiently published by the General Court (the legislature), "or in case of the defect of a law, in any particular case, by the Word of God."[258] The Connecticut Code of Law lists several crimes receiving the death penalty. Specific Scriptures are listed as justification for these capital laws. For example:

> If any person shall commit any willful murder, which is manslaughter, committed upon malice, hatred, or cruelty, not in a man's necessary and just defense, nor by mere casualty against his will, he shall be put to death. Ex. 21:12-14; Num. 35:30,31.

The Wren Building at the College of William and Mary. America's second college was started mainly due to the efforts of Rev. James Blair in order, according to its charter of 1691, "that the Church of Virginia may be furnished with a seminary of ministers of the Gospel, and that the youth may be piously educated in good letters and manners, and that the Christian religion may be propagated among the Western Indians to the glory of Almighty God."

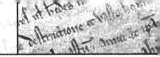

If any man steals a man or mankind, he shall be put to death. Ex. 21:16[259]

The Code also states that "the open contempt of God's Word, and messengers thereof, is the desolating sin of civil states and churches."[260]

Many other early constitutions, compacts, charters, and laws could be examined that reveal the central role of the Bible in shaping America's civil documents, such as the Charter of Rhode Island, the Frame of Government of Pennsylvania, the Declaration of Independence, various state constitutions, and the U.S. Constitution and Bill of Rights.

3) Education was rooted in the Bible.

The first schools in America were Christian. They were started by the church to teach people to be able to read the Bible (for example, the Boston Latin School in 1636). Early school laws reveal the biblical foundation of education.

Massachusetts School Laws of 1642 and 1647

In 1642 the General Court enacted legislation requiring each town to see that children were taught, especially "to read and understand the principles of religion and the capital laws of this country."[261] The laws of 1647 begin: "It being one chief project of that old deluder, Satan, to keep men from the knowledge of the Scriptures."[262] The General Court went on to order any town with 50 families to hire a teacher, and those that increased to 100 families to set up a school to prepare youth for the university.

Grammar School at Dorchester, Massachusetts

Rules adopted by town meeting in 1645 required the schoolmaster "to commend his scholars and his labors amongst them unto God by prayer morning and evening, taking care that his scholars do reverently attend during the same." The schoolmaster examined each student at noon on Monday to see what he had learned from the Sabbath sermon. On Friday afternoon at 2:00, he was to catechize them "in the principles of Christian religion."[263]

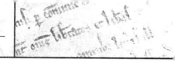

Connecticut School Laws, 1650

The laws of 1650 required localities to provide for the education of the youth. They began like that of Massachusetts: "It being one chief project of that old deluder, Satan, to keep men from the knowledge of the Scriptures."[264] A 1690 law declared: "This [legislature] observing that. . . there are many persons unable to read the English tongue and thereby incapable to read the holy Word of God or the good laws of this colony. . . it is ordered that all parents and masters shall cause their respective children and servants, as they are capable, to be taught to read distinctly the English tongue."[265]

Colleges

Colleges and universities were started to train ministers in the knowledge of the Scriptures. Two examples:

Harvard College (1636)

Started in 1636 by the New England Puritans to train godly ministers, they thought the greatest curse that could come upon the land would be an impotent, ignorant clergy. Even while strug-

Nassau Hall, College of Princeton, New Jersey. Like most early universities, Princeton was started by Christians for a Christian purpose. The trustees wanted "to cultivate the minds of the pupils ... and ... to rectify the Heart, by inculcating the great precepts of Christianity, in order to make them good Men."

gling to survive as a colony they undertook this task. Rules and precepts that were observed in the college include:

> Let every student be plainly instructed, and earnestly pressed to consider well, the main end of his life and studies is, to know God and Jesus Christ which is eternal life, John 17:3, and therefore to lay Christ in the bottom, as the only foundation of all sound knowledge and learning.

And seeing the Lord only giveth wisdom, let every one seriously set himself by prayer in secret to seek it of him Prov. 2:3.

Every one shall so exercise himself in reading the Scriptures twice a day, that he shall be ready to give such an account of his proficiency therein, both in theoretical observations of the language, and logic, and in practical and spiritual truths, as his tutor shall require, according to his ability; seeing the entrance of the word giveth light, it giveth understanding to the simple, Psalm 119:130.[266]

Regulations at Yale College, 1745

One of the original rules at Yale College shows the central place the Bible had:

1. All scholars shall live religious, godly, and blameless lives according to the rules of God's Word, diligently reading the Holy Scriptures, the fountain of light and truth; and constantly attend upon all the duties of religion, both in public and secret.[267]

We could examine scores of others colleges and see the biblical foundations. In fact 106 of the first 108 colleges were founded on the Christian faith.

Bookstores in early America had many Bibles and religious works.

The French political philosopher Alexis De Tocqueville observed that bookseller shops in the United States contained "an enormous quantity of religious works, Bibles, sermons, edifying anecdotes, controversial divinity, and reports of charitable societies."[268] They were providing what the American people wanted to read.

4) Textbooks were Christian

The Bible was the central text.

We saw in Chapter 5 on "Education" that early American textbooks were Christian. The Bible was the central text. Theological catechisms were very popular, with over 500 different ones used in colonial times. (Catechisms taught by using a series of questions and answers that were often memorized by the students.) The most

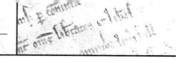

commonly used one was *The Foundation of Christian Religion gathered into six Principles*. Later, the *Westminster Catechism* became the most prominent one.

Use of biblical textbooks would be expected since the primary goal of education, as reflected by the New Haven Code of 1655, was to equip children to be "able duly to read the Scriptures ... and in some competent measure to understand the main grounds and principles of Christian Religion necessary to salvation."[269] This goal was promoted by the most prominent texts of the seventeenth through the nineteenth centuries, which included colonial hornbooks, the *New England Primer*, Webster's Blue Backed Speller, McGuffey's *Readers*, Murray's *Reader*, Young's *Civil Government*, and Butler's history.

A page from Webster's Blue Backed Speller.

The contrast of biblical education in early America with secular education of today can be seen by comparing the definition of words from Webster's original dictionary published in 1828 with dictionaries of today. Webster used thousands of Scriptural references and defined words biblically. Modern dictionaries give man-centered humanistic definitions. Citizens are ingrained with this non-Christian worldview not only in schools and from major arts and media outlets, but also when they define words.

We compared the definition of *immoral* in Chapter 5. Consider these definitions from Webster's 1828 Dictionary:

"RIGHT – 1. Conformity to the will of God, or to his law, the perfect standard of truth and justice. In the literal sense, *right* is a straight line of conduct, and *wrong* a crooked one. *Right* therefore is rectitude or straightness, and perfect rectitude is found only in an infinite Being and his will."

"GOVERNOR – 1. He that governs, rules or directs; one invested with supreme authority. The Creator is the rightful governor of all his creatures."

"PROPERTY – 4. The exclusive right of possessing, enjoying and disposing of a thing; ownership. In the beginning of the world, the Creator gave to man dominion over the earth, over the fish of the sea and the fowls of the air, and over every living thing. This is the foundation of man's property in the earth and in all its productions."[270]

When these words are defined using modern dictionaries, a completely dif-

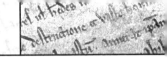

ferent worldview is presented. (See Review Question 6 at the end of this chapter which asks you to look up these words in a modern dictionary and compare the two definitions.)

5) The Founders acknowledged the centrality of the Bible.

Following are quotes from a few of America's Founding Fathers that show the importance of the Bible in their lives and thinking.

John Adams, President and Signer of the Declaration

"Suppose a nation in some distant Region, should take the Bible for their only law Book, and every member should regulate his conduct by the precepts there exhibited. . . . What a Eutopia what a Paradise would this region be."[271]

John Adams

Benjamin Rush, Signer of the Declaration

Benjamin Rush

"The great enemy of the salvation of man, in my opinion, never invented a more effectual means of extirpating Christianity from the world than by persuading mankind that it was improper to read the Bible at schools."[272]

"In contemplating the political institutions of the United States, I lament that we waste so much time and money in punishing crimes and take so little pains to prevent them. We profess to be republicans, and yet we neglect the only means of establishing and perpetuating our republican forms of government, that is, the universal education of our youth in the principles of christianity by the means of the bible. For this Divine book, above all others, favors that equality among mankind, that respect for just laws, and those sober

and frugal virtues, which constitute the soul of republicanism."[273]

Fisher Ames, Congressman and Author of House Version of First Amendment

"[T]he Bible [should] regain the place it once held as a school book[.] Its morals are pure, its examples captivating and noble. The reverence for the sacred book that is thus early impressed lasts long; and probably, if not impressed in infancy, never takes firm hold of the mind. One consideration more is important. In no book is there so good English, so pure and so elegant; and by teaching all the same book, they will speak alike, and the Bible will justly remain the standard of language as well as of faith."[274]

Samuel Adams

Samuel Adams, Signer of the Declaration and "Father of American Revolution"

To our founders, the Bible was more than a good book with good principles. It contains the message and words of life. Samuel Adams wrote to his daughter Hannah on Aug. 17, 1780:

"[Y] cannot gratify me so much, as by seeking most earnestly, the Favor of Him who made & supports you – who will supply you with whatever his infinite Wisdom sees best for you in this World, and above all, who has given us his Son to purchase for us the Reward of Eternal Life – Adieu, and believe that I have."[275]

Patrick Henry, "Orator of the American Revolution"

"The Bible is worth all the books that ever were printed, and it has been my misfortune that I have never found time to read it with the proper attention and feeling till lately. I trust in the mercy of heaven that it is not yet too late."[276]

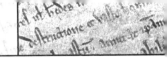

John Jay, First Chief Justice of the U.S. Supreme Court

"The Bible is the best of all books, for it is the word of God and teaches us the way to be happy in this world and in the next. Continue therefore to read it and to regulate your life by its precepts."[277]

John Quincy Adams, President

"[S]o great is my veneration for the Bible, and so strong my belief, that when duly read and meditated on, it is of all books in the world, that which contributes most to make men good, wise, and happy....

John Jay

"I advise you, my son, in whatever you read, and most of all in reading the Bible, to remember that it is for the purpose of making you wiser and more virtuous. I have myself, for many years, made it a practice to read through the Bible once every year....

"My custom is, to read four or five chapters every morning, immediately after rising from my bed. It employs about an hour of my time, and seems to me the most suitable manner of beginning the day...

"It is essential, my son, in order that you may go through life with comfort to yourself, and usefulness to your fellow-creatures, that you should form and adopt certain rules or principles, for the government of your own conduct and temper....

"It is in the Bible, you must learn them, and from the Bible how to practice them. Those duties are to God, to your fellow-creatures, and to yourself. 'Thou shalt love the Lord thy God, with all thy heart, and with all thy soul, and with all thy mind, and all thy strength, and thy neighbor as thyself'. ...They [our duties] are all to be learned in equal perfection by our searching the Scriptures.

John Quincy Adams

"Let us, then, search the Scriptures;... The Bible contains the revelation of the will of God. It contains the history of the creation of the world, and of mankind."[278]

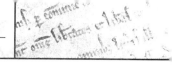

Thomas Jefferson, Author of Declaration

"The Bible is the cornerstone of liberty. A student's perusal of the sacred volume will make him a better citizen, a better father, a better husband."[279]

Thomas Jefferson

Benjamin Franklin, Signer of Declaration and Constitution

When members of the Constitutional Convention were discussing property qualifications for federal officials, Franklin used the Scriptures to speak against any such qualification. Madison records how Franklin said: "We should remember the character which the Scripture requires in Rulers, that they should be men hating covetousness."[280] When Franklin was presented at the Court of Versailles he tells us that a scripture verse, that his father used to quote to him when he was a boy, passed through his mind. That verse was: "Seest thou a man diligent in his business? He shall stand before kings."[281]

Benjamin Franklin

William Samuel Johnson, Signer of the Constitution

As President of Columbia College in New York, William Johnson gave a commencement speech where he reminded the graduates that the purpose of their education was "to qualify you the better to serve your Creator and your country. . . . Your first great duties, you are sensible, are those you owe to Heaven, to your Creator and Redeemer. . . . Remember, too, that you are the redeemed of the Lord, that you are bought with a price, even the inestimable price of the precious blood of the Son of God. . . . Love, fear, and serve Him as your Creator, Redeemer, and Sanctifier. Acquaint yourselves with Him in His Word and holy ordinances. Make Him your friend and protector and your felicity is secured both here and hereafter."[282]

William Samuel Johnson

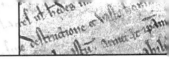

The Founders started numerous Bible societies.

Following our independence scores of local societies were started to circulate the Bible. Many of our Founding Fathers were greatly involved in these Bible societies, including:

- John Marshall (Supreme Court Chief Justice), Vice-president of American Bible Society
- James McHenry (Signer of Constitution), President of the Baltimore Bible Society
- John Langdon (Signer of Constitution), VP of the American Bible Society
- Rufus King (Signer of Constitution), Member of NY Bible Society
- John Quincy Adams, VP of the American Bible Society
- Elias Boudinot (President of the Continental Congress), Founder and first President of the American Bible Society, President of the NJ Bible Society
- Caleb Strong (Constitutional Convention), VP of the American Bible Society
- John Jay (Original Chief Justice of the US Supreme Court), President of the American Bible Society
- Charles Cotesworth Pinckney (Signer of Constitution), President of the Charleston Bible Society, VP of American Bible Society
- Rufus Putnam (General in American Revolution, Federal Judge), President of the Ohio Bible Society
- Benjamin Rush (Signer of Declaration), Founder and manager of the Philadelphia Bible Society
- Bushrod Washington (US Supreme Court Justice), VP of the American Bible Society

In 1816 sixty delegates representing 35 of these local societies gathered in New York City and formed the American Bible Society. During the first year 85 local societies joined with it. Elias Boudinot became the first President. Boudinot had been a member of the Continental Congress, chosen as President in 1782 and in that capacity a signer of the Treaty of Peace officially ending the war, a member of the first House of Representatives (1789-1796), and the Director of the National Mint (1796-1805). In accepting the office of President of the American Bible Society, Boudinot wrote: "I am not ashamed to confess that I accept the appointment of President of the American Bible Society as the greatest honor that could have been conferred on me this side of the grave."[283] He continued as president of the society until his death in 1821.

The first Supreme Court Chief Justice, John

Bible on which George Washington took the presidential oath, 1789.

Jay, served as President of American Bible Society as well. General Rufus Putnam founded the first Bible society west of the Alleghenies.

6) The Bible was the primary source of the Founders' worldview.

Noah Webster reflected the central role of the Bible in the personal and public life of the Founders, writing: "The Bible must be considered as the great source of all the truths by which men are to be guided in government, as well as in all social transactions.... The Bible [is] the instrument of all reformation in morals and religion."[284]

As mentioned in Chapter 4, the source of the political ideas of the American founding era were primarily drawn from the Bible, directly referenced in 34% of all citations with about 50% of the other citations from biblically thinking men.[285] The Bible had such an important role because almost all the Founders were Christians who were greatly shaped by the church and the teachings of the ministers. One historian summarized early American history, writing, "The people made the laws and the churches made the people."[286] The fact that the people made the laws was unique in history, because rulers' law was typical – the rulers made the laws and imposed them upon the people. In America the people could make the laws because they had been prepared by the church with a biblical understanding of how to make good and godly laws and had Christian character implanted within them so they would voluntarily choose to live in accordance with those laws.

First Great Awakening

While the early settlers of America were primarily Christians, many with a great zeal for God, each generation must obey God's Word and keep the internal flame of truth lit. By the time of the founding of the thirteenth original colony (Georgia, 1733), America at large, according to one writer, experienced a lull in religion. Jonathan Edwards described his town as experiencing

George Whitefield preached to large crowds throughout the colonies.

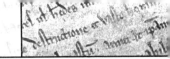

a "degenerate time" with "dullness of religion."[287] Future chaplain of the Congress Rev. Samuel Blair of Pennsylvania stated, "Religion lay as it were dying, and ready to expire its last breath of life in this part of the visible church."[288] The life of God had departed from many people and churches. God in His mercy, and in accordance with His plans in history, would bring a revival – a great awakening that not only impacted America, but many other nations.

A great outpouring of God's Spirit occurred through Jonathan Edwards, George Whitefield, Samuel Davies, and others, that united and set the colonies aflame. Benjamin Franklin, who became friends with Whitefield and often heard him preach, records in his autobiography in 1739 the great impact the revival had:

> It was wonderful to see the change soon made in the manners of our in-habitants. From being thoughtless or indifferent about religion, it seem'd as if all the world were growing religious, so one could not walk thro' the town in an evening without hearing psalms sung in different families of every street.[289]

Whitefield traveled up and down the colonies drawing huge crowds wherever he preached, whether in churches, streets, or fields. It is estimated that eighty per-cent of all Americans heard him speak.[290] Many thousands of people were converted and churches were filled. Godliness swept through colonies. Theological truths, in-cluding much new light, were transmitted to the families through the churches.

The ideas that came forth during the First Great Awakening not only addressed personal matters, but all areas of life. America's unique understanding of religious and civil liberty for all men blossomed during this awakening. The titles of sermons preached and printed during this time reveal that the biblical truth being recovered provided a blueprint for building a nation. A few of those sermons were:

- The Essential Rights and Liberties of Protestants (1744), Elisha Williams
- Civil Magistrates Must Be Just, Ruling in the Fear of God (1747), Charles Chauncey
- Unlimited Submission and Non-Resistance to the Higher Powers (1750), Jonathan Mayhew
- Religion and Patriotism, the Constituents of a Good Soldier (1755)
- The Advice of Joab to the Host of Israel Going Forth to War (1759), Thad-deus Maccarty
- Thanksgiving Sermon on the Repeal of the Stamp Act (1766), Charles Chauncey
- Election Sermon: Civil Government is for the Good of the People – the Character of Good Rulers, and the Duties of Citizens (1770), Samuel Cooke
- An Oration upon the Beauties of Liberty (1773), John Allen
- Scriptural Instructions to Civil Rulers (1774), Samuel Sherwood

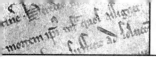

- Thanksgiving Sermon: The Christian Duty of Resistance to Tyrants – Prepare for War – Appeal to Heaven (1774), William Gordon
- Election Sermon: The Right of Self-Government is from God – the Divine Right of Kings Exploded (1775), Samuel Langdon
- The Bible and the Sword (1776), John Fletcher[291]

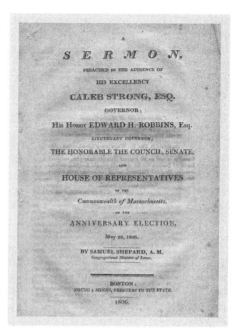

An Election Sermon preached in 1806 before the government leaders in Massachusetts. John Wingate Thornton wrote in *The Pulpit of the American Revolution*: "The clergy were generally consulted by the civil authorities; and not infrequently the suggestions from the pulpit, on election days and other special occasions, were enacted into laws. The statute-book, the reflex of the age, shows this influence. The State was developed out of the Church.

"The annual 'Election Sermon' — a perpetual memorial, continued down through the generations from century to century — still bears witness that our fathers ever began their civil year and its responsibilities with an appeal to Heaven, and recognized Christian morality as the only basis of good laws."

To transmit the theological, governmental, legal, economic, and general worldview coming forth from the Awakening, a number of new colleges and universities were established, mostly by various churches, including the College of New Jersey (Princeton, 1746), King's College (Columbia, 1754), Brown (1764), Rutgers (1764), Dartmouth (1770), and Hampden-Sidney (1776). The colonists understood a knowledgeable clergy and citizenry are essential to liberty.

In short, there would have been no American Revolution (1760-90) without the First Great Awakening (1735-70). The Founding Fathers, who gave us the Declaration of Independence and Constitution, were young men during the Awakening. This revival shaped their faith, character, and worldview, preparing them to give birth to an exceptional nation, the first Christian constitutional republic in history. It also gave the American people at large the qualities necessary to live in liberty – includ-

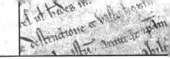

ing self-government, morality, biblical worldview, regard for life, and a fear of God.

The Bible, the Source of Ideas for American Independence

James McHenry

Churches and ministers were a great support in the cause of American liberty. The Bible provided the major source of ammunition for the clergy. Ministers had for years preached political sermons. Many of these were printed and read by the people. George Bancroft writes how the pastors were heard "with reverence by their congregations in their meeting-houses on every Lord's day, and on special occasions of fasts, thanksgivings, lectures, and military musters. Elijah's mantle being caught up was a happy token that the Lord would be with this generation, as he had been with their fathers. Their exhaustless armory was the Bible, whose scriptures furnished sharp words to point their appeals, apt examples of resistance, prophetic denunciations of the enemies of God's people, and promises of the divine blessing on the defenders of his law."[292]

The Bible Shaped Their Social Ideas

The Founders understood free and just societies can only be built upon biblical truth. Signer of the Constitution James McHenry said:

"The Holy Scriptures . . . can alone secure to society, order and peace, and to our courts of justice and constitutions of government, purity, stability, and usefulness. In vain, without the Bible, we increase penal laws and draw entrenchments around our institutions."[293]

One social evil that confronted America's Founders was slavery. Most of the Founders opposed slavery because it was inconsistent with the Bible. They saw it as a social evil that needed to be eradicated.[294] Benjamin Rush said:

Domestic slavery is repugnant to the principles of Christianity. . . . It is rebellion against the authority of a common Father. It is a practical denial of the extent and efficacy of the death of a common Savior. It is an usurpation of the prerogative of the great Sovereign of the universe who has solemnly claimed an exclusive property in the souls of men.[295]

In 1773, Patrick Henry wrote:

> Is it not amazing that, at a time when the rights of humanity are defined and understood with precision, in a country above all others fond of liberty, in such an age, we find men professing a religion the most humane, mild, meek, gentle, and generous, adopting a principle as repugnant to humanity as it is inconsistent with the Bible and destructive to liberty?. . . . I believe a time will come when an opportunity will be offered to abolish this lamentable evil; everything we can do is to improve it, if it happens in our day; if not, let us transmit to our descendants, together with our slaves, a pity for their unhappy lot and an abhorrence of slavery. We owe to the purity of our religion to show that it is at variance with that law which warrants slavery.[296]

Patrick Henry

In the mid-1800s the leader of the Underground Railroad, Levi Coffin, was motivated by the precepts of the Bible to aid fugitive slaves to escape to Canada. After listening to friends warn him of dangers to his life and property, Coffin responded: "I told them that I felt no condemnation for anything that I had ever done for the fugitive slaves. If by doing my duty and endeavoring to fulfill the injunctions of the Bible, I injured my business, then let my business go. As to my safety, my life was in the hands of my Divine Master, and I felt that I had his approval."[297]

The biblical faith of many slaves in America caused them to look to God for their deliverance: "[T]he slaves of the South . . . longed for liberty, but they looked for it through the intervention of others [rather than through violent insurrections]; they drew their hopes from the case of the Israelites led from Egypt by the hand of Moses; they trusted God would come to their aid in a similar way — raise up for them a Moses; and in this trust in Providence their faith was marvelous. The gospel of forgiveness had been preached to them by preachers both of the white race and their own, and the truths of the Bible, thus orally presented, had a wonderful influence in preparing them for the events about to follow."[298]

Christians in the North and the South led the anti-slavery movement of the mid-nineteenth century. (See Chapter 10 for more on the issue of slavery.)

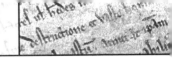

Numerous Bibles Were Available in Early America

The first book printed in America was the Bible. As mentioned earlier this was in the Algonquin language and was the work of John Eliot (1604-1690) who began evangelizing the Massachusetts Indians in the 1640s. Eliot organized the Indians who became Christians into communities. He wrote: "The Bible, and the Catechism drawn out of the Bible . . . are the ground-work of Community amongst all our Indian-Churches and Christians."[299]

Hundreds of different Bibles in numerous languages were in use in Colonial America. The Evans Early American micro-print collection (which contains the full text of all known existing books, pamphlets, and broadsides printed in the United States, or American colonies prior to Independence, from 1639 through 1800) has over 500 different Bibles listed.

THE

HOLY BIBLE,

CONTAINING THE

OLD AND NEW TESTAMENTS,

IN THE

COMMON VERSION.

WITH

AMENDMENTS OF THE LANGUAGE,

BY NOAH WEBSTER, LL. D.

NEW HAVEN:

PUBLISHED BY DURRIE & PECK.

Sold by Hezekiah Howe & Co., and A. H. Maltby, New Haven;
and by N. & J. White, New York.

1833.

Noah Webster's Bible, 1833.

Sabbath Observance

The Christian Sabbath has been observed and recognized by law from the beginning of America. Sabbath laws could be found in all the early colonies and states. Alexis de Tocqueville described the Sabbath observance of the 1830s in *Democracy in America*:

> In the United States, on the seventh day of every week, the trading and working life of the nation seems suspended; all noises cease; a deep tranquillity, say rather the solemn calm of meditation, succeeds the turmoil of the week, and the soul resumes possession and contemplation of itself. Upon this day the marts of traffic are deserted; every member of the community, accompanied by his children, goes to church, where he listens to strange language which would seem unsuited to his ear. He is told of the countless evils caused by pride and covetousness: he is reminded of the necessity of checking his desires, of the finer pleasures which belong to virtue alone, and of the true happiness which attends it. On his return home, he does not turn to the ledgers of his calling, but he opens the book of Holy Scripture; there he meets with sublime or affecting descriptions of the greatness and goodness of the Creator, of the infinite magnificence of the handiwork of God, of the lofty destinies of

man, of his duties, and of his immortal privileges. Thus it is that the American at times steals an hour from himself; and laying aside for a while the petty passions which agitate his life, and the ephemeral interests which engross it, he strays at once into an ideal world, where all is great, eternal, and pure.[300]

Pioneers and the Bible

As early Americans went west to settle new lands they carried the Bible and its truths with them. De Tocqueville wrote of the contrast of the physical homes of western pioneers and their personal characteristics: "Everything about him is primitive and unformed, but he is himself the result of the labor and the experience of eighteen centuries. He wears the dress, and he speaks the language of cities; he is acquainted with the past, curious of the future, and ready for argument upon the present; he is, in short, a highly civilized being, who consents, for a time, to inhabit the backwoods, and who penetrates into the wilds of the New World with the Bible, an axe, and a file of newspapers."[301] The Bible was the great civilizing and educational influence for these pioneers. De Tocqueville wrote of visiting log cabins in the wilderness that had a Bible if no other book.[302]

Revivals Impact the Nation

The Bible spurred numerous awakenings and revivals which had great effect in America's history. It also inspired much missionary work to the American Indians in the west. The states of Washington and Oregon were founded by missionaries, Marcus and Narcissa Whitman and Jason Lee. Johnny Appleseed not only planted orchards throughout the frontier, but he also planted the Word of God, carrying a Bible and sowing its truth wherever he went. One of the first explorers

An engraving from 1819 of a camp meeting revival.

of the west, Jedidiah Smith, always packed his Bible.

We have just touched on the great impact that the Bible has had on America. We could examine much more, including the records of the U.S. Congress, the words and laws of the state legislatures, and federal and state court rulings. The more you look, the more convinced you will become that there would be no America, the land of liberty, without God and the Bible. America became an exceptional nation because of her firm foundation in Christian principles as revealed in the Bible.

Supreme Court Chief Justice John Marshall said: "The American population is entirely Christian, & with us, Christianity & Religion are identified. It would be strange, indeed, if with such a people, our institutions did not presuppose Christianity, & did not often refer to it, & exhibit relations with it."[303]

As the Bible and its principles have been removed from our schools, missing from our leaders' ideas and actions, extirpated from the marketplace of ideas, and not adhered to by enough of our citizens, America has declined and will continue to decline.

America must once again restore the Bible to its place of influence. We must consider the Bible, in the words of Noah Webster, "as the great source of all the truths by which men are to be guided in government, as well as in all social transactions. . . . The Bible [is] the instrument of all reformation in morals and religion."[304]

Review Questions

- What six points of evidence are presented in this chapter to show that the Bible was of central influence in the colonization of America?

- What was the original seal of the Massachusetts Bay Colony? What did this mean and why did they choose this seal?

- Give one example of how the Bible formed the basis of America's civil laws.

- The first school laws began by saying, "It being one chief project of the old deluder, Satan, to keep men from the knowledge of the Scriptures." What does this mean?

- Why did the early settlers start colleges?

- Look up the definitions of *right, governor,* and *property* in a modern dictionary and compare them to the definitions from Webster's original 1828 dictionary (given in this chapter). How has the meaning of these words changed? Can you notice a difference in the worldviews of those who defined these words?

- If you have access to a Webster's 1828 Dictionary, compare definitions of other words (consider: marriage, sin, law, potato, just). (A hard copy 1828 can be ordered from face.net)

- Explain, with your observations, one of the Founder's quotes on the Bible.

- Many Americans today have been taught that our Founders were mostly atheists. How would you respond to this allegation?

- Why was the First Great Awakening important?

- How did the Bible shape the social ideas of early Americans?

CHAPTER 10

Advance of Liberty in Early America: Fruit of the Seed of the American Republic

The Declaration of Independence and U.S. Constitution

For over 150 years people who were primarily the product of the Protestant Reformation came to America and planted seeds that were to become a new nation, an exceptional nation, though not without faults. Christianity was the unifying factor of the Christian union that resulted from the American Revolution. The American Revolution was a Christian revolution. It was based upon biblical ideas,[305] and God's hand was evident throughout the events leading up to the war, during the eight years of fighting, and through the establishment of the United States Constitution in 1789.[306]

The Americans certainly saw God's hand in these events. George Washington summarized the colonists' view of God's involvement in the war when he wrote in 1778, referring to the first three years of the conflict: "The hand of Providence has been so conspicuous in all of this, that he must be worse than an infidel that lacks faith, and more than wicked, that has not gratitude enough to acknowledge his obligations."[307]

John Quincy Adams linked the founding of America to Christ's incarnation and God's plan to liberate mankind. He wrote in an 1837 oration:

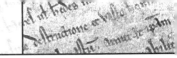

Is it not that, in the chain of human events, the birthday of the nation is indissolubly linked with the birthday of the Saviour? That it forms a leading event in the progress of the gospel dispensation? Is it not that the Declaration of Independence first organized the social compact on the foundation of the Redeemer's mission upon earth? That it laid the cornerstone of human government upon the first precepts of Christianity and gave to the world the first irrevocable pledge of the fulfillment of the prophecies announced directly from Heaven at the birth of the Saviour and predicted by the greatest of the Hebrew prophets 600 years before?[308]

Adams believed the principles of civil government and the principles of Christianity were linked together in the birth of America. The Declaration of Independence was our founding covenant, and its power and form were Christian. The same was true for the United States Constitution. It was formed with the view that men are sinful and cannot be entrusted with too much power. A constitution is needed to "chain down" rulers, by specifying the limited role of government, separating powers, and setting up checks and balances among the branches of government. In addition, frequent and fair elections were needed to hold officials accountable.[309]

Signing of the Constitution

The Famers of the Constitution declared that the forming of that document was a miracle of God. James Madison, the Father of the Constitution, wrote to Thomas Jefferson in France just a few weeks after the Convention: "It is impossible to conceive the degree of concord which ultimately prevailed, as less than a miracle."[310] Madison later wrote, "It is impossible for the man of pious reflection not to perceive in it [the Constitutional Convention] a finger of that Almighty hand."[311]

The President of the Constitutional Convention and the most influential of all the framers of the Constitution, George Washington, concurred, writing: "we may … trace the finger of Providence through those dark and mysterious events, which first induced the States to appoint a general Convention and then led them one after another … into an adoption of the system recommended by that general Convention." He thought the Constitution would most likely lay "a lasting foundation for tranquility and happiness," but knowing the source of blessing, his "earnest prayer" was "that the same good Providence may still continue to protect us and prevent us from dashing the cup of national felicity just as it has been lifted to our lips."[312]

Even the non-Christian Benjamin Franklin saw God's hand, writing: "Our General Convention ... when it formed the new Federal Constitution, [was] ... influenced, guided, and governed by that omnipotent and beneficent Ruler in whom all ... live, and move, and have their being."[313]

The prestigious literary journal, *The North American Review*, summarized the important nature of the Constitution, writing in 1867: "The American government and Constitution is the most precious possession which the world holds, or which the future can inherit. This is true — true because the American system is the political expression of Christian ideas."[314]

The Declaration and Constitution, arguably the most valuable civil documents for the advancement of liberty in history, were the fruit of the Christian seeds planted in the prior generations. There was much more good fruit. Great advancement and blessings came from the biblical foundation of America. After all, God promises that great blessing comes to those who obey His Word.

Advancement in Inventions, Technology, Scientific Discovery, Transportation, and Communication

The new nation of the United States, with its great liberty, provided the perfect environment for growth and advancement in every sphere of life. Beginning with the birth of America, there was an outburst of human energy, an exponential increase of inventions, and a great growth of wealth never seen before in history. Why? Was it because of great natural resources? No, for many nations have as many or more. Was it due to the special qualities of the European settlers? No, for some of these same people were starving in Europe. Was it because Americans worked harder than others in the world? Not really (though diligent labor was important in America's prosperity — the Puritan work ethic is foundational for America's success). What then? The primary reason was due to people living in Christian liberty. This liberty was a result of people having a biblical idea of man, family, education, government, law, and economics. A biblical worldview released character and ideas in men that propelled them forward in taking dominion over God's creation.

A nation is cultivated in direct relation to the amount of liberty it embodies — more liberty, greater productivity. Liberty is more important than type of soil, climate, natural resources, or other factors (though these, of course, have an effect). Free Americans turned the desolate plains into a garden; they turned the desert of Arizona into a fruit field; inhospitable Idaho into a potato mine, and so on.

Christianity produced personal liberty in the hearts and minds of men, which in turn produced religious, political, civil, and economic liberty. The ability to live free, direct their future, and benefit from their physical and mental labor brought

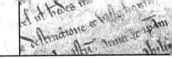

many new ideas and inventions to Americans, which produced great transformation in society.

Patent and copyright laws helped propel the many new inventions. These laws were based on the principle of property because the product of man's brain is property as well as the product of his hands. (Property is both external and internal.) Some of those inventions, discoveries, and advances include: Cotton gin, 1793; Bowditch publishes *The … Navigator* in 1802; Steamboat, 1807; Erie Canal, 1825; Railroad, 1826; Steam locomotive, 1830; McCormick reaper, 1831; Telegraph, 1832 (first line in 1844); Deere plow, 1833; Goodyear vulcanized rubber, 1839; Matthew Maury charts ocean currents, 1842; Safety pin, 1849; Sewing machine, 1846; Transatlantic cable, 1858; Transcontinental telegraph line, 1861; Transcontinental railroad line, 1869. Other inventions include the: electric light, telephone, phonograph, radio, mass produced automobile, airplane, television, computer. Advances occurred in many other fields as well, including medicine, business, and the social arena (e.g., the end of slavery, women's rights). Freedom and the ability to benefit from one's labor caused the United States of America to be the most inventive, progressive, and prosperous nation in history.

The McCormick Reaper (1831)

Cyrus Hall McCormick, the inventor of the reaper (a machine which cut grain), was a great example of a Christian inventor and businessman. He was a "reaper" in the Kingdom of God who instituted many new principles of business which reflected his biblical view of life. He advanced civilization and destroyed famine by using his God-given talents to fulfill his calling.

His invention of the reaper, and the ensuing business of making and selling reapers, lay the foundation for the advancement and prosperity of America, for it enabled one man to do the work of many, increasing his productivity many-fold. One biographer wrote:

Cyrus Hall McCormick

> He instructed the wheat-eating races how to increase the "seven small loaves" so that the multitudes should be fed. He picked up the task of feeding the hungry masses – the Christly task that had lain unfulfilled for eighteen centuries, and led the way in organizing it into a system of international reciprocity.[315]

Cyrus, born in 1809, grew up on a farm in the Shenandoah Valley of Virginia. His father had worked to invent a reaper from the time Cyrus was a child, but was unsuccessful. Seeing his father's attempts was part of his inspiration to invent. Another motive came from experiencing the back-breaking work of harvesting grain by hand. For thousands of years mankind had harvested grain by hand using simple tools, sickles or scythes. When the crops ripened, men labored day and night to gather the grain before it rotted in the field. The size of their planted fields depended upon the amount of manual labor available for the harvest. McCormick's reaper multiplied the potential productivity of men and transformed farming.

Cyrus' first successful reaper was tested in July 1831 on a small patch of wheat on his father's farm. Cyrus gave a public exhibition a few days later at the nearby town of Steele's Tavern. With his reaper drawn by two horses he cut six acres of oats in an afternoon. This was an amazing feat equal to the work of six laborers with scythes or 24 peasants with sickles.

In 1832, he gave a large-scale public exhibition to one hundred people in the town of Lexington. This brought a wider recognition of his invention and praise from many sources. A noted professor declared that "this machine is worth a hundred thousand dollars." No praise was more encouraging than the words of his father who said, "It makes me feel proud to have a son do what I could not do."[316]

Many other people had attempted to invent a reaper—Cyrus was the 47th person to secure a patent for a reaper — but none of them worked properly or could have developed into a successful machine for they lacked the proper operational design. His invention combined for the first time the seven mechanical elements necessary for a working reaper. Those who built their own reapers after this time copied McCormick's basic design.

Cyrus Hall McCormick is remembered as the inventor of the reaper, but he did much more than that. He also invented the business of making and selling reapers, and he did it in a biblical manner, with Kingdom fruit. His work impacted the world. "He did more than any other member of the human race to abolish the famine of the cities and the drudgery of the farm — to feed the hungry and straighten the bent backs of the world."[317]

McCormick had built a successful reaper, but no one knew about it. Promoting the value and importance of the reaper was just as important as building it. He built the machine, so now he had to build the business. Cyrus worked harder and longer to build his business than he did to build his reaper. "His whole soul was wrapped up in his Reaper," said one of his neighbors.[318]

In the summer of 1832 while looking out over rolling fields of wheat the thought came to him, "'Perhaps I may make a million dollars from this Reaper.' This thought was so enormous that it seemed like a dream—like dwelling in the clouds—so remote, so unattainable, so exalted, so visionary."[319] For years it appeared only that, a vision. In fact, it took **nine years** before McCormick found anyone with enough money and courage to buy a reaper from him. He had invented a machine

that would transform every farmer that obtained one (and, in time, agriculture the world over) yet no one bought one for nine years. During that time he struggled greatly and instead of making any money toward his vision of a million dollars, he actually lost money. He even had to give up his farm to creditors, but he held on to his reaper. His indomitable spirit would not give up on his vision.

McCormick Reaper

In 1839 he opened the first of the world's reaper factories in the little log workshop near his father's house and began to make reapers. But even so it was not until over a year later that he sold his first reaper to Abraham Smith. During those first years of failure "Cyrus McCormick hung to his Reaper as John Knox had to his Bible."[320] In the next decade as he traveled around the country and promoted his reaper, he became so identified with his invention that he was often called "the Reaper Man."

During the 1840s, he gradually began to sell more and more reapers, but as he looked to expand his business he recognized Virginia was not the place to do it, so he traveled to the Midwest and opened up a factory in a little mud-town called Chicago. As he looked for ways to sell his reapers throughout the states he created "a new species of commercial organization which is by many thought to be fully as remarkable as his invention of the Reaper."[321]

Workshop where McCormick invented his reaper.

Cyrus McCormick probably did more than any man in history to elevate men out of poverty, and he did so in a biblical way. He did not seek to use governmental force to take from the productive and give to the nonproductive (as modern socialist states do), but he gave the common farmer a tool that made him twenty or thirty times more productive, hence increasing greatly his wealth creation potential.

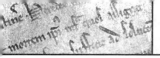

The Morse Telegraph (1832)

Samuel F. B. Morse invented the telegraph in 1832 and worked during the next decade to improve it. The first inter-city line was tested in 1844, when a message was sent from the Capitol Building in Washington to Baltimore.

The invention of the telegraph was one of the most significant technological discoveries in history. It ranks with the printing press in its impact in the area of communication. The message from Washington to Baltimore took a few minutes, which before would have taken about a day. When cables were laid across the Atlantic and across the continent, messages that would have taken days and weeks, now took just a moment.

Samuel F.B. Morse said of his telegraph, "Not what hath man, but 'What hath God wrought!'"

The *New York Herald* declared Morse's telegraph "is not only an era in the transmission of intelligence, but it has originated in the mind . . . a new species of consciousness." Another paper concluded that the telegraph is "unquestionably the greatest invention of the age."[322]

Morse was a Christian who believed he had been chosen by God to invent the telegraph and, for the first time, harness the use of electricity. This discovery would contribute greatly to the advancement of man and the fulfilling of God's purpose for mankind. Annie Ellsworth, a friend of Morse's, composed the first message sent over the Washington-Baltimore line on May 24, 1844. She "selected a sentence from a prophecy of the ancient soothsayer Balaam" — "What hath God wrought!"[323] Of this message Morse wrote:

> Nothing could have been more appropriate than this devout exclamation, at such an event, when an invention which creates such wonder, and about which there has been so much scepticism, is taken from the land of visions, and becomes a reality.[324]

Morse considered it remarkable that he, an artist, "should have been chosen to be one of those

Plaque in the Capitol commemorating Morse's invention with the first words transmitted: "What Hath God Wrought."

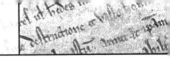

to reveal the meaning of electricity to man! How wonderful that he should have been selected to become a teacher in the art of controlling the intriguing 'fluid' which had been known from the days when the Greeks magnetized amber, but which had never before been turned to the ends of common man! 'What hath God wrought!' As Jehovah had wrought through Israel, God now wrought through him."[325] Morse wrote to his brother:

> That sentence of Annie Ellsworth's was divinely indited, for it is in my thoughts day and night. "What hath God wrought!" It is His work, and He alone could have carried me thus far through all my trials and enabled me to triumph over the obstacles, physical and moral, which opposed me.
>
> "Not unto us, not unto us, but to Thy name, O Lord, be all the praise."
>
> I begin to fear now the effects of public favor, lest it should kindle that pride of heart and self-sufficiency which dwells in my own as well as in others' breasts, and which, alas! is so ready to be inflamed by the slightest spark of praise. I do indeed feel gratified, and it is right I should rejoice with fear, and I desire that a sense of dependence upon and increased obligation to the Giver of every good and perfect gift may keep me humble and circumspect.[326]

Morse would remark in a speech many years later:

> If not a sparrow falls to the ground without a definite purpose in the plans of infinite wisdom, can the creation of an instrumentality, so vitally affecting the interests of the whole human race, have an origin less humble than the Father of every good and perfect gift? I am sure I have the sympathy of such an assembly as is here gathered, if in all humility and in the sincerity of a grateful heart, I use the words of inspiration in ascribing honor and praise to him to whom first of all and most of all it is pre-eminently due. "Not unto us, not unto us, but to God be all the glory." Not what hath man, but "What hath God wrought!"[327]

Morse Telegraph 1837

Matthew Maury Charts Ocean Currents (1842)

Inspired in his life work by Scripture, Matthew Fontaine Maury was sustained by industry derived from his Christian faith. As an enlightened seer in new fields of science and guided by his biblical worldview, he played a significant role in advancing civilization. He was one of the greatest men America has ever produced.

Maury's accomplishments include: 1) He was the father of oceanography, 2) He charted the ocean and wind currents, 3) He mapped out and proposed sea routes, including laying down lanes for steamers in the North Atlantic, 4) He developed the National Observatory, 5) He was instrumental in founding of U.S. Naval Academy, 6) He proposed the idea for a U.S. Meteorological Society or National Weather Bureau, 7) He was a key consultant for the laying of the transatlantic telegraph cable, 8) He invented the first floating mines and the first electric torpedoes, 9) He wrote many influential science books. Matthew Maury literally fulfilled the ancient mandate of God to take dominion over the earth (Gen. 1:26-28).

Scriptural Inspiration

Matthew Maury's faith was evident in his work and in his writings, where he often quoted the Bible. He said the same God who was the author of the Bible was also the author of nature. In both God gave a divine revelation of Himself to mankind, and that the message of the two were never contradictory. He also said "to remember that the earth was made for man."[328]

Maury was originally inspired to find the ocean currents as Scripture was read to him. A monument honoring Maury was dedicated in Richmond, Virginia, in 1929. A writer for the Richmond Times, Virginia Lee Cox, spoke of this biblical inspiration in describing the monument in a newspaper article of the day. Cox wrote:

Matthew Maury

On the plinth of the monument in the flattest relief are figures of fish, representing Maury's interest in the paths of the sea. The story goes that once when Maury was ill he had his son[329] read the Bible to him each night. One night he read the eighth Psalm, and when he came to the passage—"The fishes of the sea and whatsoever walketh through the paths of the sea" — Maury had him read it over several times. Finally he said, "If God says there are paths in the sea I am going to find them if I get out of this bed." Thus the Psalm was the direct inspiration for his discoveries....

In his right hand are the pencil and the compass, and in his left hand a chart. Against his chair is the Bible, from which he drew inspiration for his explorations. The sculptor has caught amazingly the spirit of the man.[330]

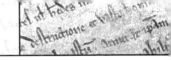

Another Maury Monument—in the Goshen Pass on the bank of the North Anna River, erected by the state of Virginia in 1923—also reveals his biblical inspiration. The bronze tablet on the monument contains these words:[331]

MATTHEW FONTAINE MAURY, Pathfinder of the Seas, The Genius who first snatched from ocean & atmosphere the secret of their laws. Born January 14th, 1806. Died at Lexington, Va., February 1st, 1873.... Every mariner for countless ages as he takes his chart to shape his course across the seas, will think of thee. His Inspiration Holy Writ: Psalms 8 & 107, Verses 8, 23, & 24; Ecclesiastes Chap. 1, Verse 8; A Tribute of his Native State Virginia, 1923

The Scriptures that inspired Maury were: Psalm 8:8 — "The fowl of the air, and the fish of the sea, and whatsoever passeth through the paths of the seas." Psalm 107: 23-24 — "They that go down to the sea in ships, that do business in great waters; these see the works of the Lord, and his wonders in the deep." Eccl. 1:8—"All things are full of labor; man cannot utter it: the eye is not satisfied with seeing, nor the ear filled with hearing."

Maury looked to the Bible when it gave insight into scientific knowledge. For example, he writes in *The Physical Geography of the Sea*:

Maury Monument in Richmond. "Against his chair is the Bible, from which he drew inspiration for his explorations."

> And as for the general system of atmospherical circulation..., the Bible tells it all in a single sentence: "The wind goeth toward the south, and turneth about unto the north; it whirleth about continually, and the wind returneth again according to his circuits." – Eccl., i., 6.[332]

Maury frequently mentioned the work of God in his scientific writings. "The ocean of air like the ocean of water, is never at rest. It has its waves and its currents." After giving three offices of winds that make life on earth possible, Maury wrote: "Discharging these various offices, they verify the Psalmist's words, 'God maketh the winds his messengers.'"[333]

Maury believed giving yourself to a useful and God-ordained occupation was the secret of happiness. He "found that occupation, for some useful end or other, was the true secret of happiness."[334] Once a man found this occupation, Maury be-

lieved industry was essential for success. He wrote: "It's the talent of industry that makes a man. I don't think that so much depends upon intellect as is generally supposed; but industry and steadiness of purpose, they are the things."[335]

A Biblical Seer

Maury was able to accomplish so many significant things because he attempted to look at creation from a lofty position, from the view of the Creator. One of his biographers wrote:

> The thing above all others that made Maury a great man was his ability to see the invisible. He was a seer. He saw the cable before it was laid. He saw a railroad across the continent before it was built. He saw a ship canal from the Mississippi to the Great Lakes before it was dug. . . . He was a seer and a pathfinder not only on the seas, but under the seas, across the lands, and among the stars.[336]

He saw so much because he knew the Bible, believed it, and saw the harmony between what it taught and the natural sciences. He wrote that, "Physical geography confesses the existence, and is based on the biblical doctrine that the earth was made for man. Upon no other theory can it be studied; upon no other theory can its phenomena be reconciled."[337] In the same speech, he also declared:

> I have been blamed by men of science, both in this country and in England, for quoting the Bible in confirmation of the doctrines of physical geography. The Bible, they say, was not written for scientific purposes, and is therefore of no authority in matters of science. I beg pardon! The Bible is authority for everything it touches. . . . The Bible is true and science is true. The agents concerned in the physical economy of our planet are ministers of His who made both it and the Bible. The records which He has chosen to make through the agency of these ministers of His upon the crust of the earth are as true as the records which, by the hands of His prophets and servants, He has been pleased to make in the Book of Life. They are both true; and when your men of science, with vain and hasty conceit, announce the discovery of disagreement between them, rely upon it the fault is not with the Witness or His records,

Matthew Maury said concerning Psalm 8:8, "If God says there are paths in the sea I am going to find them."

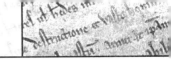

but with the "worm" who essays to interpret evidence which he does not understand.[338]

Maury, as has been true of most of the significant scientists in history, accomplished his great work because he had a biblical view of life and science. He realized the Creator of the Universe is orderly and caused His creation to operate according to set laws. Maury believed God wants man to discover and apply those laws as part of his mission to take dominion over the earth. Maury wrote:

> As a student of physical geography I regard the earth, sea, air and water as parts of a machine, pieces of mechanism not made by hands, but to which, nevertheless, certain offices have been assigned in the terrestrial economy. It is good and profitable to seek to find out these offices, and point them out to our fellows; and when, after patient research, I am led to the discovery of any one of them, I feel with the astronomer of old as though I had 'thought one of God's thoughts!' — and tremble.[339]

There are many other technological and scientific advances that were part of the good fruit of the American republic. Christians were ubiquitous in this and all spheres of advancement. An engraving on the base of a statue in United States Capitol of Dr. Crawford W. Long says:

> Discoverer of the use of sulphuric ether as an anaesthetic in surgery on March 30, 1842 at Jefferson, Jackson County, Georgia U.S.A. "My profession is to me a ministry from God."

Statue of Dr. Crawford W. Long in the U.S. Capitol

Growth of Education

Education for all people is a Christian idea. It motivated the early colonists to start schools and colleges, and is why the Bible was their central textbook. Americans' biblical faith continued to be manifested through education in the nineteenth century.

Noah Webster

The most important educator of the nineteenth century was Noah Webster, the father of American scholarship and education. He was a devout Christian whose biblical philosophy of education is clearly reflected in his enormous work. He produced a series of self-teaching textbooks out of his desire to teach truth to the American people and make the nation intellectually independent of England and Europe.

Webster's *Blue Backed Speller* (mentioned in Chapter 5) was first published in 1783 and did more for American education than any other single book except the Bible. Selling over 100 million copies in a century, its premise was that "God's word, contained in the Bible, has furnished all necessary rules to direct our conduct." As Americans settled the west, they carried their Bible and Webster's speller.

After America won her independence from Great Britain and established herself as a constitutional republic, Webster worked to see that our liberty and growth continued by providing edu-

Noah Webster

cational tools that imparted the principles that originally gave birth to our nation. He recognized that the success of our system of government depended upon the quality of education. He saw this education as the responsibility of the parents and the individual. He stressed that its basis must be upon Christianity. Webster stated:

> In my view, the Christian religion is the most important and one of the first things in which all children, under a free government, ought to be instructed…. No truth is more evident to my mind than that the Christian religion must be the basis of any government intended to secure the rights and privileges of a free people.[340]

Noah Webster worked about twenty-six years on *An American Dictionary of*

IM-MOR'AL, a. [*in* and *moral.*] Inconsistent with moral rectitude ; contrary to the moral or divine law ; wicked ; unjust ; dishonest ; vicious. Every action is *immoral* which contravenes any divine precept, or which is contrary to the duties which men owe to

Webster's definition of immoral reflects the
Biblical worldview of early America.

the English Language. By the time of its completion and publication in 1828, Webster had mastered 28 languages. This colossal work reflects the industry, scholarship, and Christian character of this great yet humble man. His dictionary, which was the first American dictionary and the grandfather of all others, defines words biblically and generously uses scriptural references, in great contrast to modern dictionaries.

Noah Webster's life can be characterized as prolific. In addition to his dictionary and textbooks — the *Blue Backed Speller,* a *Grammar,* a *Reader,* a *United States History* — he wrote much more on religious, political, educational, musical, economic, commercial, medical, social, and scientific topics. He was also the first person to publicly promote the idea of a constitutional convention. His efforts brought about copyright legislation at state and national levels. He served in state government, published a magazine and newspaper, founded a college, and translated the first American revised version of the Bible. While doing all these things, his family was not neglected as he lovingly raised seven children.

In light of such an astoundingly productive life, Noah Webster's statement in the preface to his 1828 American Dictionary particularly reveals his Christian character. He said:

> And if the talent which he [God] entrusted to my care, has not been put to the most profitable use in His service, I hope it has not been "kept laid up in a napkin," and that any misapplication of it may be graciously forgiven.[341]

Men with the character and worldview of Noah Webster educated the generations of Americans that secured this country as the most free and prosperous nation the world has seen. The continuance of a positive course for our nation will only occur as men like Webster reestablish our educational system upon the Bible, removing any dependence upon man's own intellect.

William McGuffey

William Holmes McGuffey (1800-1873) was a Presbyterian minister, university professor, and an author. He taught at a number of different colleges, ending his career as the professor of moral philosophy at the University of Virginia (the last 28 years of his life). He authored the profoundly influential *McGuffey Readers,* which earned him the right to be called "The Schoolmaster of the Nation." His textbooks (the first two volumes published in 1836, with six volumes by 1857) were de-

William McGuffey

signed to "fit the child's education to the child's world" and to build character as well as vocabulary. One hundred and twenty-two million copies were sold in 75 years. They were the standard text for nearly one century in many parts of the country. They were still selling well in the 1960s (30,000 a year) and continued to be used in some public schools. They are popular with many homeschoolers today.

His *Readers* promote the theistic, Calvinist worldview and ideas of salvation, righteousness and piety that were found in the *New England Primer* the century before. They "represent the most significant force in the framing of our national morals and tastes" other than the Bible. In the Preface to the *Fourth Reader*, he wrote:

> From no source has the author drawn more copiously, in his selections, than from the sacred Scriptures. For this, he certainly apprehends no censure. In a Christian country, that man is to be pitied, who at this day, can honestly object to imbuing the minds of youth with the language and spirit of the Word of God.[342]

John Westerhoff writes:

> From the First to the Fourth Reader, belief in the God of the Old and New Testaments is assumed. When not mentioned directly, God is implied: "You cannot steal the smallest pin ... without being seen by the eye that never sleeps." More typically, however, lessons make direct references to the Almighty: "God makes the little lambs bring forth wool, that we may have clothes to keep us warm.... All that live get life from God.... The humble child went to God in penitence and prayer.... All who take care of you and help you were sent by God. He sent his Son to show you his will, and to die for your sake."
>
> When we investigate the content of McGuffey's Readers, three dominant images of God emerge. God is creator, preserver, and governor.[343]

Colleges

Previously we mentioned the Christian foundation of most of the early colleges and universities, from the first college, Harvard, to those that sprang up during the First Great Awakening. This continued into the 1800s. In 1860 there were 246 colleges in the United States. Over 90 percent of these were Christian or were started for a Christian purpose.[344] Ministers remained as presidents of most colleges up to the end of the nineteenth century.

Even though the Christian faith was central at most schools, seeds of secularism began to be planted. In the early 1800s Unitarians took control of Harvard University. Though originally rooted in the Bible, Unitarianism gradually drifted farther and farther away from biblical ideology, with a corresponding shift occurring in Unitarian churches and in colleges controlled by that belief system.

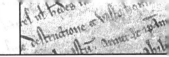

The rise of modern state education began in Massachusetts due to the efforts of Horace Mann. In 1838 he became the first secretary of education of Massachusetts public schools. Many today see this as a great step forward, but his action paved the way for a state financed, state directed, and ultimately state controlled education system that has usurped not only the authority of localities, but more importantly that of parents to direct the education of children. The Bible remained in the schools for generations (though it was no longer THE text, but one of many texts), but over time it has not only ceased to be used as a text, but the liberating philosophy of a biblical worldview has been replaced by a secular, immoral, man-centered view of life.

The first compulsory school laws were enacted in Massachusetts in 1852 and over time every state has followed suit. As a consequence, the government now compels youth to learn certain ideas, including moral and religious ideas since all education is ultimately religious (see Chapter 2).

Political and Geographical Advancement

After independence, western exploration and settlement occurred rapidly, adding many new states to the original thirteen. In 1775 Daniel Boone blazed the Wilderness Road through the Cumberland Gap to explore and settle Kentucky. He would later explore and move farther west. John Chapman was a missionary explorer who sowed the Word of God to any pioneers he encountered. As he traveled west he also planted many apple trees to provide food for future settlers. Chapman, who became known as Johnny Appleseed, sought to provide spiritual and physical sustenance.

The purchase from France of the Louisiana Territory under President Thomas Jefferson in 1803 nearly doubled the size of the United States. Lewis and Clark first explored this territory, but many other explorers followed them, including Jedidiah Smith who always packed his Bible.

One of the leaders in Texas' independence from Mexico in 1836 was Gail Borden. He ran the only newspaper in the area and printed important government papers and news of the war. Though professing the Christian faith years before, it was not until 1840 that Borden was baptized. That year was the first time an ordained Baptist minister came to Galveston, where Borden lived, to organize a church. Gail

Gail Borden was the first person baptized in the Gulf of Mexico west of the Mississippi River.

and his wife Penelope were the first to ask for this ordinance. "It was reputedly the first baptismal service in the Gulf west of the Mississippi River."[345] Borden later invented condensed milk, the reason most people know his name today.

Missionaries Marcus and Narcissa Whitman blazed the Oregon Trail, in 1836. The first great emigration was led by Marcus in 1843. He was also instrumental in the United States acquiring the Oregon Territory in 1846.[346]

Barbary Powers War (1801-05, 1815), America's First War against Muslim Terrorists

America's war with Muslim terrorists did not begin after the bombing of the Twin Towers in New York City on September 11, 2001. Nor did it begin with the bombing of the Beirut Barracks in Lebanon in 1983. In fact, the first war we fought as a new nation was against Islamic terrorists.

Muslims have long been at war with Christendom, on and off for fourteen centuries. By the late eighteenth century a "peaceful warfare" had developed. To carry on commerce within the Mediterranean Sea without fear of molestation from the Muslims, it was the custom for European powers to pay tribute to the pirates of the Barbary States (Algiers, Morocco, Tripoli, and Tunis). These states were located in North Africa, which the Muslims had controlled for centuries. European nations found it easier to pay the bribes than fight. Thus the unholy alliance of the Muslim states with nations like England, France, and Spain only served to build up the terrorists. The economic system of tribute, ransom, and bribery was well established when America entered onto the scene.

After American independence, American crews and ships came under the direct threat of the pirates as they began to sail under a new flag. The pirates saw the opportunity for fresh booty in ships and slaves. The U.S. Ambassadors to France, Thomas Jefferson, and Britain, John Adams, were ordered to do what they could to make peace. Jefferson argued the best long-term solution was to establish a navy, writing, "I very early thought it would be best to effect a peace through the medium of war."[347] He pointed out that the cost of establishing and maintaining a navy "would amount to little more than we must pay, if we buy peace,"[348] that is, pay the tribute demanded by the pirates.

In May 1786, Jefferson and Adams met in London with the resident Tripolitan ambassador,

President Thomas Jefferson directed America's first war against Muslim terrorists.

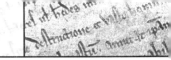

Sidi Haji Abdul Rahman Adja, to try and negotiate a treaty to end the threat from the Barbary pirates. They asked the ambassador why the Muslim states were so hostile to the new American republic that had done nothing to provoke such animosity. Ambassador Adja answered, "that it was founded on the Laws of their Prophet, that it was written in their Koran, that all nations who should not have acknowledged their authority were sinners, that it was their right and duty to make war upon them wherever they could be found, and to make slaves of all they could take as Prisoners, and that every Musselman who should be slain in Battle was sure to go to Paradise."[349] (Jefferson would later buy a Koran to learn for himself if it really taught this strange doctrine.)

With no means of resistance, the United States concluded a treaty in 1786 with the ruler of Morocco where the U.S. would pay money and give presents in exchange for captive Americans and future immunity. This treaty still applied in 1789 when the new U.S. Constitution went into effect. Paying tribute had been going on for centuries. Great Britain made a treaty with the Barbary States in 1662 to purchase immunity for its merchant shipping.[350] Having no other option, since the newly founded United States had no navy, President Washington continued the custom of paying tribute. This irked him greatly, but this was the only way to protect American commerce and American citizens from capture and imprisonment. Without the tribute payment, and at times with it, the pirates would capture ships and hold the captains and crew for ransom. They were held in horrid conditions, and many died from hardships of captivity.

Under Washington, funds had been appropriated to build a navy. Adams had access to these ships but did not think the American people were prepared for a protracted war in far off northern Africa, so he continued paying tribute. When Jefferson became President, he had had enough. He decided to use our treasury, not, in the words of the U.S. Consul to Tunis William Eaton, "to buy oil of roses to perfume that pirate's beard," but rather to send "gun batteries to chastise his temerity."[351] When Jefferson refused to pay tribute to the Barbary pirates, they declared war of sorts upon the United States and began to attack American ships in the area, stealing property and imprisoning citizens. Jefferson sent troops to protect American

Stephen Decatur boarding a Muslim pirate gunboat during the bombardment of Tripoli, August 3, 1804.

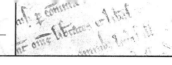

interests. War continued until 1805 when a treaty of peace was signed on June 10 where the Barbary pirates agreed to end hostilities.

In 1815, while America was fighting the War of 1812, the leader of the Muslim terrorists in Algiers (having the title, the Dey) renewed his plunder of American commerce thinking the war would keep the U.S. from being able to respond. After pirates seized American vessels and citizens, Congress approved action against the Barbary powers. Capt. Stephen Decatur sailed from New York with 10 ships and captured enemy ships and sailed into the harbor of Algiers. He forced the Dey to release all prisoners without ransom and to agree to a peace treaty where no tribute would be paid again, nor American commerce molested. Decatur obtained similar guarantees from Tunis (July 26) and Tripoli (August 5).

America set an example for Europe of chastising and humbling a lawless band of pirates and ended the practice of paying tribute to Muslim terrorists. Expressions of submission were obtained from these powers by the United States such as had not been obtained by any other nation. Pope Pius VII said: "The Americans have done more for Christendom against the pirates of Africa than all the powers of Europe united."

Political Figures

Just as during the founding era, the majority of the governmental leaders of the nineteenth century were Christians, including such men as Chief Justices John Jay and John Marshall, Presidents John Quincy Adams and James Garfield, and Senator Daniel Webster. President Andrew Jackson was converted later in life, and President Abraham Lincoln likely embraced the Christian faith as well.[352]

Daniel Webster

Daniel Webster was a great Christian states-man and orator, and served almost a decade in the U.S. House, nearly two decades in the U.S. Senate, and as the Secretary of State for three different Presidents. He believed that to become a great orator one must study the Word of God. He practiced his own oratory by reciting the Bible aloud.

Webster's old Senate desk is still in the Capitol, in the current Senate Chamber. It is used by the senior Senator from New Hampshire, the state of Webster's birth. As a Senator he used a penknife

Daniel Webster

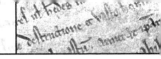

to inscribe his name in the bottom of his desk. (Others have followed his example.) He developed a love for penknives at an early age. One of Daniel's first school teachers, Master James Tappan, told the story of how he got his first penknife (at around age 6-8):

> Daniel was always the brightest boy in the school. . . . He would learn more in five minutes than any boy in five hours. . . . One Saturday, I remember, I held up a handsome new jack-knife to the scholars and said the boy who would commit to memory the greatest number of verses in the Bible by Monday morning should have it. Many of the boys did well; but when it came to Daniel's turn to recite, I found that he had committed so much [to memory] that after hearing him repeat some sixty or seventy verses, I was obliged to give up, he telling me that there were several chapters yet that he had learned. Daniel got that jack-knife.[353]

Webster's love for the Bible remained throughout his life. He understood obedience to God's truth produces great blessings for a nation. He said, "Whatever makes men good Christians, makes them good citizens."[354] He gave this warning that is very pertinent for today:

> If we and our posterity shall be true to the Christian religion, if we and they shall live always in the fear of God and shall respect His Commandments, . . . we may have the highest hopes of the future fortunes of our country; . . . . But if we and our posterity neglect religious instruction and authority, violate the rules of eternal justice, trifle with the injunctions of morality, and recklessly destroy the political constitution which holds us together, no man can tell how sudden a catastrophe may overwhelm us that shall bury all our glory in profound obscurity.[355]

Senator Webster was known for his great oratorical skills – skills which he said were acquired through much labor. One day as the Senate was discussing the extent of the British Empire, Webster displayed his great eloquence when he remarked:

> She has dotted the surface of the whole globe with her possessions and military posts, whose morning drum-beat, following the sun and keeping company with the hours, circles the earth daily with one continuous and unbroken strain of the martial airs of England.

When they left the Senate one member complimented Mr. Webster on his brilliant language, and said that his remarks struck him greatly, especially considering they were impromptu. To this Webster replied:

> You are mistaken, the idea occurred to me when I was on the ramparts of Quebec some months ago. I wrote it down and rewrote it, and after several

trials got it to suit me, and laid it up for use. The time came today, and so I put it in.[356]

James Garfield

In 1881 James A. Garfield was inaugurated the twentieth President of the United States. About six months after taking office he was assassinated. Were it not for God's Providence, he would have died many years earlier in his youth.

As a boy, Garfield worked on a canal. He was unable to swim which almost proved fatal one day when he fell into the water. While gasping for breath and trying to keep above water, he grabbed hold of a tow rope that had accidentally fallen into the water. As he was sinking he somehow managed to throw the rope, which wrapped around a fixture on the barge, and he then pulled himself to safety. After recovering, Garfield attempted for three hours to throw the same rope around the same fixture and have it attach, but he was unable to duplicate the feat.

James Garfield

Garfield concluded that God had providentially saved his life. He went on to attend seminary and became a minister for the Disciples of Christ denomination. He led hundreds to Christ, publically debated evolutionists, and influenced the public sector in many different ways. He was elected to Congress and eventually became President.

In 1876, at the Centennial of our Declaration of Independence, Garfield wrote these words, which must be understood by Americans today:

> Now, more than ever before, the people are responsible for the character of their Congress. If that body be ignorant, reckless, and corrupt, it is because the people tolerate ignorance, recklessness, and corruption. If it be intelligent, brave, and pure, it is because the people demand these high qualities to represent them in national legislature…. Congress must always be the exponent of the political character and culture of the people; and if the next centennial does not find us a great nation, with a great and worthy Congress, it will be because those who represent the enterprise, the culture, and the morality of the nation do not aid in controlling the political forces which are employed to select the men who shall occupy the great places of trust and power.[357]

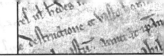

Arts and Literature

Like all other areas of life, arts and literature advanced after independence. Quaker Benjamin West was the first prominent American painter, beginning his career before the American Revolution and conducting most of his work in England. Many others followed him including Washington Allston, Charles Wilson Peale, Thomas Sully, Samuel F.B. Morse, John Trumbull, and Emanuel Leutze.

American Landscape Painters

American painting has suffered the same fate as American history – its Christian and moral foundations have been covered up, distorted, and lost. It is especially evident with the landscape painters of the nineteenth century. The prominent painters of the Hudson River School, covering the years 1825-1860, included Frederic Edwin Church, Thomas Cole, Jasper Francis Cropsey, and Asher Brown Durand.

"For these painters there was a moral purpose in being an artist; art was a sacred obligation…. The paintings of the Hudson River School … are filled with light, the most obvious manifestation of God's presence, expressing man's harmony with nature, seen as a second chance for mankind in the new Eden of the American wilderness."[358]

These were not "religious" paintings of obvious religious themes, like many from the Middle Ages, but Christian paintings, reflecting God's nature and light in His creation, through the excellence of the scenes, styles, and techniques.

In the modern relativistic world, "Beauty [has] suffered the same fate as morality."[359] Just as there is no standard for moral behavior, there is no standard for beauty when looking at art — beauty is only in the eye of the beholder. The random strokes of a monkey on a canvas can be just as beautiful as the masterful brush of Da Vinci on the Last Supper. It all depends on who is evaluating them. The recent tax-payer funded work that demeaned Christ can be art to some modern subjective viewers, for there is no objective standard by which to judge beauty or art.

But a secular humanistic worldview is not founded upon truth and cannot sustain itself. Thus, beauty and goodness continue to be acknowledged. "Beauty . . . has survived its harshest critics." "Goodness, beauty, and truth have thus outlasted the critique of those that constituted modernism."[360]

The Hudson River Painters are the fruit of the American Christian Republic. Art, like every other field, reflects the Christian foundation of America; but art also helps to preserve and propagate the Christian seed. The Hudson River School reflected the biblical morality and worldview of the founding generation of Americans. They "saw the American landscape as blessed by God." These artists believed that "the arts play a critical role in a civilization, not only in defining and dissemi-

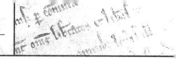

Thomas Cole, View on the Catskill Early Autumn 1837

nating core values, but also as a barometer of moral character." Jasper Cropsey wrote in 1846: "No moral and refined work of art could be produced by an immoral man." For Cropsey, "the artist was a knight who wields not a sword but a brush in his pursuit of spiritual and moral perfection." He saw himself on "a holy quest," involved in "spiritual warfare."[361]

Filmmakers today are like these artists of earlier centuries. In the 1800s people paid money to see paintings, which would at times be displayed in traveling exhibits. Before the invention of the camera there were few pictures, so they had a great effect on the viewers. "There was a moral purpose in being an artist." "One was called to art much as one was called to the ministry. It became a sacred obligation. And nowhere was the obligation more important than in the new republic."[362]

"Genesis instructed these nineteenth-century artists that, when God created the Earth, Seas, Heaven, Sun, Moon, Man, Woman, and all living and growing things, he saw that it was good: 'And God saw the light, that it was good: and God divided the light from the darkness.' This process of creating and seeing was repeated each time, until at the end of the sixth day, 'God saw everything that he had made, and behold, it was very good.... and he rested on the seventh day.' The human ability to see, to judge, to comprehend the universe, was understood to be part of the divine spirit. Seeing implies an aesthetic function, but it was far more than that for these artists. Ruskin wrote that 'the greatest thing a human soul ever does in this world is to see something.... to see clearly is poetry, prophesy, and religion, — all in one.' We are drawn to the artists of the Hudson River School because they enable us to see what they saw with fresh eyes: the beauty of nature, the glory of God, and the virtue of America."[363]

Jasper Francis Cropsey, Wyoming Valley

The Hudson River Painters had a vision to transmit God's paradise and preserve it through biblical renewal in all spheres of life. They were aware of the gradually encroaching secularism in Western Civilization, especially seen in European art and culture. They hoped to keep this destructive force from overtaking America, not by using all their energy to attack that which was pagan, but by presenting godly beauty and truth in their art. They understood that "cultural renewal is not about destroying a golden calf — an image of a bankrupt ideology — but about creating works of the highest standards that celebrate the beauty of holiness."[364]

Authors

While some of the early American authors were not Christians, like Edgar Allen Poe, Herman Melville, and Henry David Thoreau, they often reflected a Christian view of man and life in their writings. For example, Poe clearly reveals the negative consequences of man's sinfulness, though he fails to give a biblical solution to this problem. Others uphold higher biblical themes, like Henry Wadsworth Longfellow, James Fenimore Cooper, and Washington Irving.[365]

One of the bestselling novels of all time was written by a Christian, General Lew Wallace. He is honored by a statue in the U.S. Capitol Building. Wallace wrote *Ben Hur: A Tale of the Christ* after he was challenged by "the great agnostic," Robert Ingersoll, to try to prove that Jesus was the Son of God. Through his extensive research and travels to the Holy Land, he became a Christian and went on to write the great Christian classic and bestselling novel of the nineteenth century. *Ben Hur* undermined Ingersoll's message and advanced Christianity mightily. It influenced many, including President Ulysses S. Grant, who read it through in a day-and-a-half. President Garfield wrote a nationally published letter recommending *Ben Hur*.

Challenges to Liberty and the Need of Continual Energetic Faith

With increasing liberty comes the need for increasing godly character among the citizens to support the liberty. Without this internal support, a free society will quickly become depraved. The decay begins in man's heart, but will quickly express itself in society. A declining society, with increasing crime and corruption, leads to the need for greater external constraints to control the uncivil, which leads to loss

Lew Wallace, Statue in U.S. Capitol

 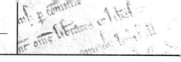

of liberty. Biblical revival and renewal, therefore, are needed for liberty to grow.

Continued Growth of Christianity and the Second Great Awakening

As a new nation, America had more liberty and prosperity than any people in history. Yet, in spite of this their internal divine fire began to go out. God in His mercy moved on the nation again in what is called the Second Great Awakening.

The Second Great Awakening occurred in different phases over many years. It began in the late 1700s in the wilderness of Kentucky in the days of Daniel Boone. Over time, it spread throughout the nation. Many prominent individuals were impacted. When this revival swept through Connecticut in 1808, the well known educator Noah Webster was dramatically converted, although he had attended church all his life and generally had a biblical worldview. He was just beginning his twenty-year labor on his *American Dictionary of the English Language*. His definitions and biblical references reflect the transformation he experienced. The awakening continued on and off in different parts of America up until and during the Civil War. Other nations saw revival as well.

Salvation came to many, in camp meetings in the western wilderness, in homes and businesses, and in churches in the North and South. Because of this revival and the biblical foundation of the nation, Christianity continued to be the predominate force in the first half of the 1800s. We have mentioned how the Founding Fathers started and served as officers in numerous Bible societies. The American Bible Society formed in 1816 when 35 Bible Societies joined together, and 85 other local societies joined with it the first year. Elias Boudinot, President of the Continental Congress in 1782, became its first president. Its officers included the first Chief Justice of the U.S. Supreme Court, John Jay, President John Quincy Adams, and Supreme Court Chief Justice John Marshall.

In addition to Bible Societies, Christianity gave impetus for the founding of abolition societies, philanthropic societies, the American Tract Society, the American Sunday School Union (1824), and America's first branches of the YMCA (in Boston, 1851) and YWCA (in Boston, 1866).

Missions Movements and Missionaries

Modern missions were birthed in the eighteenth century in Great Britain and the United States. We have seen that a central motive for the colonization of the original thirteen colonies was the propagation of the Gospel. This motive continued to influence the establishment of other states after we became a nation. Ministers led the settlement of the Oregon Territory, Rev. Jason Lee in the state of Oregon and Marcus and Narcissa Whitman in Washington.

Marcus Whitman, a medical missionary and Christian patriot, was the man who saved the Oregon Territory and assured it would be a part of the United States. Called to the Northwest by a desire to see the Indians taught the liberating principles of the Bible, the daring action of this "man of destiny" paved the way for the establishment of the states of Washington, Oregon, and Idaho. Biographer William Mowry writes:

Braving the cold and the snows of the Rocky Mountains, he crossed the continent on horseback to warn our government at Washington and to encourage the hardy pioneers of the frontier to emigrate to Oregon, assuring them that they could carry their wagons and their families through to the Columbia, for he had gone there himself with his wife and his wagon.[366]

Statue of Marcus Whitman in the U.S. Capitol with his Bible in one hand and his medical bag in the other

The tragic and sad end of the story of Marcus and Narcissa Whitman reminds us that "the blood of the martyrs is the seed of the church." Their story clearly reveals the providence of God in the march of history—that nations do not, in the words of historian George Bancroft, "float darkling down the stream of the ages without hope or consolation, swaying with every wind and ignorant whither they are drifting" but that "there is a superior intelligence and love, which is

In the winter of 1842-43, Whitman made a daring trip over the Rocky Mountains and traveled to Washington, DC, to meet with President John Tyler and Secretary of State Daniel Webster (left) and urge them to not give away the Oregon Territory.

moved by justice and shapes their courses." The Whitmans' story will also inspire us to practice "heroic, patriotic, and Christian virtues."[367]

When Marcus & Narcissa reached the Continental Divide, July 4, 1836, on their initial trip to the northwest, they claimed the Oregon Territory for God and the United States. Rev. Spalding wrote: "They alighted from their horses and kneeling on the other half of the continent, with the Bible in one hand and the American flag in the other, took possession of it as the home of American mothers and of the Church of Christ."[368]

Christian Philosophy of Government Seen in the United States

Americans had a biblical philosophy of government. What governments did in Europe the private sector did in the United States, and that much more effectively. DeTocqueville wrote how America assisted the poor and established voluntary associations for every imaginable purpose, meeting needs much better than in Europe. In Europe the state controlled the development of the telegraph, in America the private sector did so. Comparing the growth of the telegraph in the USA and Europe shows the superiority of the free market system. A New York newspaper wrote in 1846, two years after Samuel F. B. Morse's line from Washington to Baltimore was complete:

> While England by her government has got with great labor 175 miles of telegraph into operation … the United Sates, with her individual enterprise, has now in successful operation 1269 miles. This is American enterprise.[369]

This comparison reflects different governmental philosophies in the new Christian republic and the old European statist governments. This "American enterprise" is still reflected today in many ways. You can find a huge variety of almost any kind of product and service. The growth of homeschool materials

Samuel F.B. Morse exhibiting the telegraph. Alexander Hamilton wrote that the free enterprise system encourages industry and invention.

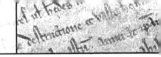

is one example. Americans are still a creative and productive people because they have the freedom to pursue their ideas and to benefit from the fruit of those ideas. However, more government control, regulation, and taxes are stifling creativity and productivity. Businesses are growing in states with less taxes and regulations (many states in the South) and leaving others with high taxes and more controls (like California and various New England states). Some businesses are going to other nations to escape big government.

The Diminishing Influence of Christianity

During the nineteenth century a number of factors contributed to a gradual diminishing influence of Christianity in America. One of those was the rise of Unitarianism. Today Unitarianism is often non- and sometimes anti-Christian, but in its beginning in America in the late 1700s into the early 1800s it held the Bible and the Words of Jesus as its standard for theological belief. This is why some of our Christian Founders, like John Quincy Adams and Joseph Story, could associate with early Unitarianism. However, over time it was slowly reshaped into an ethical theism which embraced humanism, pragmatism, evolutionism, and other anti-Christian beliefs. Many churches and colleges were influenced by Unitarianism.[370]

A second factor that caused biblical Christianity's influence to decline in America was the influx of immigrants from Europe who did not adhere to *sola scriptura*, that belief in the centrality of the Bible held by the first colonists. Liberty in America attracted many immigrants, most coming from Europe during the nineteenth century. Some were Protestants, and many were Catholics, who often held to a form of religion but were usually deficient in biblical knowledge and worldview. Some were non-Christians. To maintain liberty and prosperity, a Christian nation must impart to new citizens the biblical character and worldview that initially formed the foundation of the nation. If this is not done, the nation will gradually decline. While many of the new immigrants were infused with a vibrant Christian faith, large numbers were not, and their non-biblical ideology negatively affected the nation.

A third factor contributing to the diminishing influence of Christianity in the nineteenth century was the rise of materialism. Prosperity is the natural by-product of biblical faith. However, we must be careful not to let the love of money creep into our lives. A prominent puritan minister of the late seventeenth century Cotton Mather said: "Religion begot prosperity, but the daughter hath consumed the mother." Christianity laid the foundation for the great prosperity that arose in the United States, but for many people, seeking wealth became more important than seeking the source of wealth, God Himself. God told the children of Israel that when they entered the Promised Land they would prosper if they obeyed Him, but He warned them not to forget Him and worship other Gods, for if they did they would perish

(Deuteronomy 30:5, 8-10, 17-18; 8:11-14, 17-18). Many Americans have failed to heed this warning, beginning in the nineteenth century but even more so today.

The Church Must Continually Disciple the Nation.

Eternal vigilance is the price of liberty. Each generation must maintain and propagate the principles of liberty. The American Revolution was a product of the pulpit. The church imbued the citizens with the character and ideas necessary for freedom. Parents in turn transmitted these to their children. However, as the nation moved toward the mid-1800s the church failed to carry on the example of the Revolutionary era. Consequently, the negative factors mentioned above began to grow. In addition, the failure of the new American nation to deal with the institution of slavery was devastating.

The Issue of Slavery

Cotton Mather: "Religion begot prosperity, but the daughter hath consumed the mother."

England outlawed slavery in 1833 due to the influence of Christians, especially William Wilberforce. America's road to end slavery was much more difficult.

The majority of the Founding Fathers believed slavery was fundamentally wrong; it was an evil institution that needed to be abolished. Charles Carroll, signer of the Declaration from Maryland, expressed the majority view when he said, "slavery … is admitted by all to be a great evil."[371] Washington wrote, "that there is not a man living who wishes more sincerely than I do to see a plan adopted for the abolition of it [slavery]."[372]

However, slavery had been around since time began, present in almost every nation in history; thus they believed such an entrenched social problem must be overcome gradually. Some of them owned slaves and yet were leaders in anti-slavery organizations which were working to change the laws as well as educate and prepare slaves for independence.

During the drafting of the Declaration of Independence in 1776 Jefferson wanted to condemn slavery outright, but some thought it potentially too divisive to deal with while they were trying to present a united front. They also avoided it in their Articles of Confederation in 1777 since most considered it under the jurisdiction of the states.

Many states and individuals had already been acting upon their anti-slavery beliefs. Some of the first anti-slavery laws in history were enacted in colonial New England. There had always been free blacks in America who owned property, voted, and had the same rights as other citizens. Black slaves who fought during the Revolutionary War won their freedom in every state except South Carolina and Georgia. Many of the Founders started and served in anti-slavery societies. With independence came the freedom for the states to enact new laws—by 1804 eight northern states had abolished slavery. In the South, many individuals, including George Washington, who owned slaves set them free.

The issue of slavery was considered at the Constitutional Convention. Though most delegates were opposed to slavery, they compromised on the issue when the representatives from Georgia and South Carolina threatened to walk out. The delegates realized slavery would continue in these states with or without the union. They saw a strong union of all the colonies was the best means of securing their liberty (which was by no means guaranteed to survive). They did not agree to abolish slavery as some wanted to do, but they did take the forward step of giving the congress the power to end the slave trade after 20 years. No nation in Europe or elsewhere had agreed to such political action.

Even so, many warned of the dangers of allowing this evil to continue. George Mason of Virginia told the delegates:

> Every master of slaves is born a petty tyrant. They bring the judgement of heaven upon a country. As nations cannot be rewarded or punished in the next world, they must be in this. By an inevitable chain of causes and effects, Providence punishes national sins by national calamities.[373]

The constitutional provision of counting the slaves as three-fifths for purposes of representation was not pro-slavery or black dehumanization; it was a political compromise between the North and the South. The three-fifths provision applied only to slaves and not free blacks, who voted and had the same rights as whites (and in some Southern states this meant being able to own slaves). While the Southern states wanted to count the slaves in their population to determine the number of congressmen from their states, slavery opponents pushed to keep the Southern states from having more representatives, and hence more power in Congress.

George Mason

The former slave and famous abolitionist Frederick Douglass, who first thought the Constitution was pro-slavery, saw the liberating nature of the Constitution after he escaped slavery and studied the document, writing:

> [T]he Constitution is a glorious liberty document. Read its preamble; consider its purposes. Is slavery among them? Is it at the gateway? Or is it in the temple? It is neither.... [I]f the Constitution were intended to be, by its framers and adopters, a slaveholding instrument, why neither slavery, slaveholding, nor slave can anywhere be found in it?... Now, take the Constitution according to its plain reading and I defy the presentation of a single pro-slavery clause in it. On the other hand, it will be found to contain principles and purposes entirely hostile to the existence of slavery.[374]

Frederick Douglass

National Sins

Congress passed and President Washington signed the Northwest Ordinance in 1789, which prohibited slavery in the new states. They also banned the exportation of slaves from any state in 1794. All intentions of that generation were united in their goal to abolish slavery. God wanted to show the world how a Christian nation would deal with such a major social problem. However, America failed to deal with slavery as God had intended. It had begun to take steps to end slavery but failed to follow through to completion.

The view of the Founders that American slavery was an evil that should be abolished changed for many by the 1830s. Instead of speaking against slavery and working to abolish it, many people, and even many churches, began to attempt to justify it, both constitutionally and biblically. In that decade the three major Protestant church denominations split over the issue of slavery. Once the churches divided, it was almost certain that the nation would divide.

Since America did not deal with the evil institution of slavery, God did. And He used a devastating war to do so — a war that brought judgment upon both the North and South, with the loss of over half a million lives. The South, the place where slavery was entrenched, was especially hard hit, as one out of seven adult males of child-bearing age was killed during the war.

The Civil War had both positive and negative results. The positive: slavery was abolished and the union was preserved. The negative: power began to be centralized in the national government, and the idea of federalism incorporated into the nation by the Founders (with a balance of power between the state and national governments) began to be lost.

Through it all, the principles of the Declaration prevailed, in particular, the

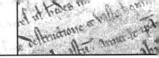

idea that all men are created free and have equal rights before the Creator, including a right to life, liberty, and property. This Christian idea continued to advance in history. The elimination of slavery in America was the catalyst that led to the overthrow of slavery throughout much of the world.

Advancements Continue

Though seeds contrary to biblical ideology began to be planted in the mid to late 1800s, the more powerful biblical ideas sown in the prior centuries continued to bear much fruit toward the end of the nineteenth century and the beginning of the twentieth. Unfortunately, over time the contrary seeds began to produce much bad fruit, as we will see in the next chapter.

 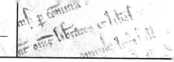

Review Questions

- What is the importance of the Declaration of Independence and the U.S. Constitution?
- Read the Declaration of Independence and identify biblical principles in this document.
- The Declaration states that all men are created equal. Are all men equal? What does it mean that all men are equal? How are all men equal?
- What causes advancement within a society?
- Describe the contribution to man's advancement of one of these Christian men: Cyrus McCormick, Samuel Morse, or Matthew Maury.
- Why was Noah Webster called the Father of American Scholarship and Education? What motivated him to seek to educate all Americans?
- The Marine Corps Hymn contains the words, "to the shores of Tripoli," which is in reference to the Barbary Pirates War. What was this war all about?
- Daniel Webster was known as one of America's great orators. What can we learn from him regarding how to prepare to be a great orator (or preparation for any great accomplishment)?
- What insights does James Garfield's quote from his 1876 centennial address give regarding the state of our nation today?
- Who were the Hudson River Painters? What lessons can we learn about art from them?
- What is necessary for liberty to be maintained and advance in a nation?
- How has America displayed a Christian philosophy of government?
- Explain what Cotton Mather meant when he said, "Religion begat prosperity, but the daughter hath consumed the mother."
- Give some examples of how the Founding Fathers viewed slavery. What action did they take regarding slavery? How did this view change over time? What was the consequence of this?

Chapter 11

Decline of the American Republic in the 20ᵗʰ Century: Growth of a Different Seed

Advancements Continue in Later 1800s and Early 1900s from Christian Seeds Planted in Prior Centuries

Biblical truth is powerful, so much so that its seed continues to bear fruit for many generations. For the past century and more, we have sown ungodly, humanistic ideas in all areas of life; yet even so, we still remain the most free and prosperous nation in the world (though in recent times we have been losing ground). We owe our freedom to the Christian foundations of the nation, coupled with the efforts of many people to continue to transmit biblical Christianity and truth.

Towards the end of the nineteenth and into the twentieth century, advancements continued from the Christian seeds while at the same time thorns began to grow from non-christian ideas. The biblical seeds of liberty also affected other nations, with liberty advancing in Europe with the end of serfdom in the nineteenth century. Technological advancements in the U.S. and Europe produced the radio, automobile, airplane, television, computer, and space flight. Economic and agricultural advances occurred due to the influence of such Christian men as George Washington Carver and John Wanamaker.

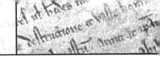

George Washington Carver Applied the Truth and Transformed the Economy of the South

George W. Carver was born into slavery just before the close of the Civil War. His mom was a slave, but after emancipation she stayed in Missouri with the family who had owned her. George and his mother were carried off from the Carver family by raiders when he was just a baby. Mose Carver offered 40 acres and a horse (since he had no cash) to a man to find the mother and child. He brought back George, but was unable to find the mother. George, therefore, grew up on the Carver farm, but in relative poverty.

George W. Carver

As a child he loved the woods and plants and things related to botany. He was very observant of nature and always asked questions. He also enjoyed using his hands. At about age ten he left the farm and worked his way through high school. As a young man he worked hard and saved money to go to a certain college, but was not allowed to attend. A couple helped him to go to an artist school, but he found there were no jobs for an artist. He eventually was able to study his first love, agriculture.

After obtaining his university degree, Carver was invited by Booker T. Washington to teach at his newly formed Tuskegee Institute in Alabama. His work while there transformed the economy of the South and affected many nations as well.

Carver would rise every morning at 4:00 AM, read the Bible, and seek God concerning what He wanted him to do. Toward the end of his life Carver remarked: "The secret of my success? It is simple. It is found in the Bible, 'In all thy ways acknowledge Him and He shall direct thy paths.'"[375]

One thing Carver sought God concerning was how to improve the economy of the southeastern part of the United States. Continual planting of cotton had depleted the soil and the invasion of the boll weevil was destroying much of the cotton crop.

Biographer Rackham Holt wrote that, "He devoutly believed that a personal relationship with the Creator of all things was the only foundation for the abundant life. He had a little story in which he related his experience:

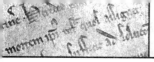

I asked the Great Creator what the universe was made for.

"Ask for something more in keeping with that little mind of yours," He replied.

"What was man made for?"

"Little man, you still want to know too much. Cut down the extent of your request and improve the intent."

Then I told the Creator I wanted to know all about the peanut. He replied that my mind was too small to know all about the peanut, but He said He would give me a handful of peanuts. And God said, "Behold, I have given you every herb bearing seed, which is upon the face of the earth … to you it shall be for meat…. I have given every green herb for meat: and it was so."

I carried the peanuts into my laboratory and the Creator told me to take them apart and resolve them into their elements. With such knowledge as I had of chemistry and physics I set to work to take them apart. I separated the water, the fats, the oils, the gums, the resins, sugars, starches, pectoses, pentosans, amino acids. There! I had the parts of the peanuts all spread out before me.[376]

Carver's story teaches us the importance of preparation in fulfilling God's plan for our lives. Carver had labored hard to develop his skills of chemistry. Consequently, God could answer the question Carver posed to Him. God could not reveal the answer to this question to me today; I would need much preparation before I would be in a position to understand and act upon the answer. Diligent preparation is vital to understand and fulfill our calling. God may not answer many of our inquiries or lead us deeper into our providential purpose because we have not learned enough or been properly prepared to hear and understand what He may say. It is important to learn this lesson. To continue with Carver's story, he relates:

I looked at Him and He looked at me. "Now, you know what the peanut is."

"Why did you make the peanut?"

The Creator said, "I have given you three laws; namely, compatibility, temperature, and pressure. All you have to do is take these constituents and put them together, observing these laws, and I will show you why I made the peanut."

I therefore went on to try different combinations of the parts under different conditions of temperature and pressure, and the result was what you see.[377]

The results: Carver discovered over 300 uses for the peanut. Food items included nuts, soup, a dozen beverages, mixed pickles, sauces, meal, instant and dry coffee. Other items included: salve, bleach, tan remover, wood filler, washing powder, metal polish, paper, ink, plastics, shaving cream, rubbing oil, linoleum, shampoo, axle grease, synthetic rubber.

He produced milk which would not curdle in cooking or when acids were added. Long-lasting cream and cheese could be made from this milk. "This milk proved to be truly a lifesaver in the Belgian Congo. Cows could not be kept there because of leopards and flies, so if a mother died her baby was buried with her; there was nothing to nourish it. Missionaries fed the infants peanut milk, and they flourished."[378]

George worked with many other plants and items — making 107 products from sweet potatoes; making synthetic marble from sawdust; and making wallboard from many different Southern plants.

For his work, Carver received many awards and became the advisor to many world leaders, including President Franklin Roosevelt, Mahatma Gandhi, and Thomas Edison. In all his work he never failed to acknowledge God. In 1921 when he testified before a committee of Congress, he was asked by the Chairman:

George Washington Carver said: "My purpose alone must be God's purpose — to increase the welfare and happiness of His people."

"Dr. Carver, how did you learn all of these things?"
Carver answered: "From an old book."
"What book?" asked the Senator.
Carver replied, "The Bible."
The Senator inquired, "Does the Bible tell about peanuts?"
"No Sir" Dr. Carver replied, "But it tells about the God who made the peanut. I asked Him to show me what to do with the peanut, and he did."[379]

Carver looked for divine direction and saw God as the revealer of truth. He said:

I discover nothing in my laboratory. If I come here of myself I am lost. But I can do all things through Christ. I am God's servant, His agent, for here God and I are alone. I am just the instrument through which He speaks, and I would be able to do more if I were to stay in closer touch with Him. With my prayers I mix my labors, and sometimes God is pleased to bless the results.[380]

He knew his purpose in life: "My purpose alone must be God's purpose — to increase the welfare and happiness of His people."[381] Godly service, not money or fame, was his primary motivation. In fact, Edison offered him a job with a six-figure income, a fortune in those times, but he turned it down so he could continue his agricultural work in his laboratory that he called "God's little workshop." "George Washington Carver worked for the riches of God rather than the wealth of this world."[382]

Carver helped transform the economy of the South, and affected agriculture all over the world. Carver had to overcome all kinds of obstacles to fulfill his destiny (only a few have been mentioned here). In all of these he persevered, labored hard, and pursued the desires in his heart. He had a great impact upon many people, upon agriculture, and the economy at large.

John Wanamaker

John Wanamaker was the founder of the modern department store and a business pioneer. In 1911 he opened a new store in Philadelphia that was so noteworthy that President Taft dedicated it. He said that the department store that Wanamaker pioneered was "one of the most important instrumentalities in modern life for the promotion of comfort among the people,"[383] and that it would be "a model for all other stores of the same kind throughout the country and throughout the world."[384] Thirty thousand people attended this event. Words on the dedication tablet reveal the success of the Wanamaker store was due to "freedom of competition and the blessing of God."[385]

John Wanamaker

When John Wanamaker was a boy, he went to a jewelry store in Philadelphia on a Christmas Eve to buy his mom a gift. He said,

> "I had only a few dollars saved up for the purpose. I wanted to buy the best thing these dollars would buy. I guess I took a long time to look at the things in the jewelry cases. The jeweler was growing impatient. Finally I said 'I'll take that,' indicating a piece — just what it was I do not recall.
>
> "The jeweler began wrapping it up. Suddenly I saw another piece that I thought would better please my mother. 'Excuse me, sir,' I said, 'but I have changed my mind, I'll take this piece instead of the one you are wrapping.'
>
> "You can imagine my surprise and chagrin when the jeweler answered;

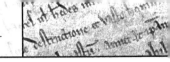

'It's too late now. You've bought the first piece and you must keep it.' I was too abashed to protest. I took what I had first bought, but as I went out of the store I said to myself:

"'When I have a store of my own the people shall have what they want … and what they ought to have.'"[386]

This incident helped create the foundation of his business.

John Wanamaker was much more than a successful merchant. He founded a new system and philosophy of business, based upon the biblical view of man. He was a merchant pioneer who believed that "the Golden Rule of the New Testament has become the Golden Rule of business."[387] Though at times he was cynically called "Pious John" by those who thought religion had no place in business, he showed that Christianity was essential for good business.

Christianity provided the character necessary to keep the many temptations of business from blowing the merchant "over the precipice and be ruined"[388] and also the principles necessary to build a successful business. He understood stores were much more than buildings with stocks and fixtures, saying the soul of the work-men must give life to the structure, not only providing needed goods for people but "meeting the greater future of the nation" and leading "the world in its nobler civilization by its advancing education and commerce."[389]

He revolutionized business by establishing the one-price system, the money-back guarantee, the marking of the quality of goods, and the service oriented store. He was the "father of modern advertising," in that the volume of advertizing became so great as other merchants followed his lead of having daily ads in newspapers, that this gave birth to the modern newspaper and magazine, making them affordable to all.

Money did not motivate John Wanamaker to build a successful business. His desire was to serve the people. Money came as a by-product of service.

He exemplified the historical truth that capitalism is a product of Calvinism. Calvinism taught that work is an important part of Godliness; that God requires uprightness in all one's dealing in business; that keeping account of one's dealings in business is like God keeping account of man's actions before God. Calvinism im-parts a zealousness to succeed and an understanding of the importance of savings and frugality.

He had poor health (he was rejected for service in the Civil War because of this), but labored six days a week in the business and community, as well as every Sabbath (in teaching in the church and Sunday school) for 70 years.

He had only about two years of formal schooling, yet became one of the world's leaders in business, served in the cabinet of President Benjamin Harrison as Post-master-General, and assisted in many voluntary associations. President Taft called him "the greatest merchant in America."[390]

He applied the Golden Rule to employees and customers. He promoted bet-

Wanamaker's Philadelphia store.

ter working conditions, including fewer work hours per week, retirement plans, medical plans, better work environment (with lockers, cafeterias, recreation clubs). He operated with the view that all his employees were part of the Wanamaker family. With both customers and employees in view, he pioneered store comforts: heat and ventilation, elevators, electric lights, and ease of access.

His Philadelphia store became the largest in the world. It was much more than just its physical size. It had a spirit, a personality. The employee sought to serve the customer and had his well-being in mind. The store entertained, educated, and performed special services. People enjoyed visiting, whether they bought items or not, and were refreshed from the visit. Universities studied his stores to learn successful economic principles. They could see them at work. His success came from his character.

Wanamaker said, "Commerce . . . is the very life blood that pulsates through every fibre of a healthy body politic."[391] What Wall Street or investment banks did was of no matter unless commerce was full of life and advancing.

He believed strongly in the free market and individual enterprise, with government involved only in keeping the market free and fair. The best means of advancing the economy and producing the growth of business in a nation was to keep taxes low, cut government regulations, and encourage competition. "Business thrives on competition," he wrote, "and that the people's interests in getting better merchandise and lower prices are always improved when competition is unstifled!"[392]

Unfortunately, as the twentieth century progressed, the rise of socialism and secularism in the nation began to stifle the free market and limit liberty in many ways.

Rise of Secularism/Statism

Secularism, or secular humanism, is the belief that there is no god, no ultimate authority outside of man, and that man is the center of the universe. As such he is the source of law, the sovereign one. He determines what is truth, or even if truth exists. Secular man sits upon the throne of the universe. Atheism, materialism,

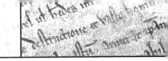

and evolution are at the heart of this worldview. Secularism is the mother of many worldviews, including communism, Marxism, socialism, statism, and in reality all man-made religions.

Statism, and its many forms (socialism, communism, Marxism, fascism, socialist democracy), goes hand-in-hand with secularism. As defined before, statism is the belief that the civil government (or man via civil government) is the ultimate authority in the earth and as such is the source of law, morality, and righteousness (that which is right and wrong). Statism is a religious belief.

Rise of Secularism in the Church

The rise of secularism in American society began in the church. Minister and "Father of American Geography," Dr. Jedidiah Morse, preached an insightful Election Sermon in 1799 from the biblical text, "If the foundations be destroyed, what can the righteous do?" (Psalm 11:3), stating:

Jedidiah Morse

> To the kindly influence of Christianity we owe that degree of civil freedom, and political and social happiness which mankind now enjoys. In proportion as the genuine effects of Christianity are diminished in any nation, either through unbelief or the corruption of its doctrine, or the neglect of its institutions; in the same proportion will the people of that nation recede from the blessings of genuine freedom, and approximate the miseries of complete despotism. I hold this to be a truth confirmed by experience. If so, it follows, that all efforts made to destroy the foundations of our holy religion, ultimately tend to the subversion also of our political freedom and happiness. Whenever the pillars of Christianity shall be overthrown, our present republican forms of government and all the blessings which flow from them, must fall with them.[393]

He identified three reasons why the "genuine effects of Christianity are diminished in any nation:" (1) unbelief, (2) corruption of its doctrine, and (3) neglect of its institutions. If fewer people believe the Christian faith, the nation will obviously slide farther and farther away from God. Thus, unbelief is one reason for America's secularization.

Another important reason for a declining America is corruption of doctrine

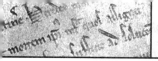

within the church (as both an institution and the entire body of individual believers). By corrupt doctrine Morse meant not merely theological doctrine (like the doctrine of the Word of God, the nature of God, the nature of man, redemption, etc.), which are very important and do affect society. He also meant the general doctrines that Paul refers to in Acts 17:24-28: (1) Creation – "God made the world;" (2) Lordship – "He is Lord of heaven and earth;" (3) Providence – "He Himself gives to all life and breath and all things; … For in Him we live and move and exist;" (4) Sovereignty – "He made … every nation … having determined their appointed times and the boundaries of their habitation." A corrupt view of these doctrines has had an immensely negative impact in the church's ability to disciple the nation. In fact, embracing such corrupt doctrine has caused the church to retreat from society, thinking God is only concerned about the hereafter and saving souls from the earth which is a sinking ship.[394]

A third reason for America's secularization is that Christians have neglected societal institutions – the family, schools, government, the economy, etc. Christians developed and governed these institutions for the first three centuries of America's history. Due to false thinking (corrupt doctrine) Christians retreated from government, media, education, and law because they saw these things as secular, dirty and non-spiritual. The vacuum they left was filled by secularists who controlled these spheres for most of the twentieth century and on to the present.

The implications of unbelief, corruption of doctrine, and neglect of institutions are great: the rise of the social gospel; Christians and churches neglecting their responsibilities to assist the poor, educate children, and prepare people to govern; the state doing much of what the church and private sector is supposed to do; and the rise of secularism in every sphere of life.

Rise of Secularism in Education

Horace Mann's work in Massachusetts in the years 1837-1848 paved the way for modern state financed, state directed, state controlled, and state mandated education, superseding parental and local control. It was also around this time that the Bible began to be removed as the central textbook. Once viewed as the source of salvation, morality, truth, and knowledge it gradually came to be seen as one of many textbooks. In recent years it has been removed from most public schools, even as use as a religious text. It certainly does not form the foundation for the philosophy of education in

Horace Mann

the nation as it did for centuries.

In the late 1800s and early 1900s, secularists Charles and Mary Beard began to popularize Marxist, socialist ideas in the many revisionist history books they wrote and introduced to schools. These were so radical that even modern academics reject much of what they taught, but their ideas were, nonetheless, sown throughout the nation. In the first half of the twentieth century the godfather of modern progressive education, John Dewey, had much success in introducing socialistic ideas in colleges, especially through training teachers. They in turn carried this philosophy to local secondary schools.

Colleges, which were originally started by churches or for Christian reasons, gradually became more and more secular. Ministers ceased to be hired as their presidents. Today 80-90% of the staff of most major universities is liberal. Christian professors are becoming a rare item, and many must keep their belief quiet if they want to keep their job.

Today, public schools, in essence, serve as the pulpits for the modern religion of secular humanism, spreading its tenets of relativism, positivism, and humanism.[395] All citizens are compelled via their tax dollars to support this religion, whose ideology is undermining liberty and destroying the unique nation our Founders gave us. All teachers and administers are certainly not ungodly, as there are many godly people involved in public education and many still communicate truth and biblical ideals, but the philosophy, content, and structure of the public educational system has long ago abandoned its biblical roots and is becoming more and more hostile to the Christian faith.

Rise of Secularism in Law

Roscoe Pound

In his Spirit of the Common Law, Roscoe Pound, who was president of Harvard Law School in the 1920s, revealed the nature of the rise of secularism in law in America. (The secularization of law had begun decades before at Harvard Law School under the direction of Christopher Columbus Langdell.[396]) Pound recognized the Christian foundation of law in the United States but did not directly attack it. In fact, he said that the old Christian legal foundation was good and produced many good results; but, he went on to say that this foundation was not good enough to bring us into the modern era. According to him, we needed a new law system, one founded on a different premise. Pound and others claimed that law was rooted in the best that society had to offer—in the consensus of the society and what they deemed best for mankind—and as society grew and became better, the law would change with it. Evolving law and the sovereignty of the state replaced the absolutes of God's law. Pound said "the state takes the place of Jehovah."[397]

As mentioned in Chapter 4, many in the judicial system began to embrace this evolving view of law and rejected the Christian understanding of absolute law rooted in a Higher Power. For example Supreme Court justice Benjamin Cardozo (appointed in 1932) said:

> If there is any law which is back of the sovereignty of the state, and superior thereto, it is not law in such a sense as to concern the judge or lawyer, however much it concerns the statesmen or the moralist.[398]

Relativism began to affect judicial philosophy and constitutional interpretation, as reflected in the words of Charles Evans Hughes, Supreme Court Chief Justice from 1930 to 1941: "We are under a Constitution, but the Constitution is what the judges say it is."[399]

A humanistic view of law, with its moral relativism, has spread to the point where today a majority of Americans embrace this idea. Its dissemination and influence is such that, according to one recent poll even a majority of those who claim to be Christian reject moral absolutes.[400]

As evolving law and the sovereignty of the state has replaced the absolutes of God's law, judges have also moved from making decisions based upon established law to becoming activists, legislating through their decisions. Activist judges are a great problem today. The three general eras of the Court[401] — (1) 1800-1895: Constitutional supremacy, (3) 1895-1950: Judicial supremacy, (4) 1950-present: Judicial activism — reflect the changing nature of law in America.[402]

Rise of Secularism in Government and the Economy

Statism is the general term we could use to describe a secular view of government and the economy. Statism began when Adam and Eve disobeyed God, desiring to determine for themselves what was good and evil (Gen. 3:5). The Tower of Babel was perhaps the first public expression of statism or socialism, with corporate man seeking to be his own god. So when Karl Marx's book, *The Communist Manifesto*, was published in 1848, it was not presenting new ideas. Marxist socialism had been around from the very beginning.

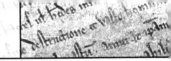

Socialism Is a Religion

Socialism has been one of the great enemies of liberty and of Christianity in the past. It will be one of the greatest threats to Christianity in the twenty-first century. Socialism can be defined as government control or ownership of property and/or the production of goods and services. Socialistic governments claim authority over all property. This is bad enough, but such states' claim of ownership goes much further — they also claim authority over the children in a nation. Thus, the state seeks to educate, provide for, direct and regulate their activities. The state seeks to be the parent.

God created individuals and three divine institutions: family, church, and state. He has given certain authority and responsibilities to each of these. No one institution has absolute authority over any other institution. Today, the state has come to be seen as the all-encompassing authority over men and other institutions. This is socialism. When government bureaucrats (elected or not) act under this belief they are like blind men, who will lead the blind into the ditch (Luke 6:39). To limit the all-powerful state, men must be self-governed under God and His law.

Only God is supreme and can exercise supreme power. No man or institution should ever exercise supreme power, especially regarding matters of the economy. Therefore, no central planning agency should rule over the entire economy (as in communist countries). The flow of authority should be from the bottom up, not the top down. In building the communist party in Russia, Lenin rejected the bottom upwards attempts of the less revolutionary socialists for a top down approach. He said, "My idea … is 'bureaucratic' in the sense that the Party is built from the top downwards."[403]

Socialism is a religion that assumes:[404]

1. All property belongs to society, that is, the state.

2. There should be no private property.

3. Men will work as hard for society in general as they would for themselves and their family.

These ideas have been shown not to work every time they have been attempted throughout history, even among Christians. But socialist adherents still press on to impose this philosophy on nations, even though it will bring stagnation and loss of liberty. Why? Because it is a religion to them.

Socialists have certain views about God, man, and law which are rooted in their faith, or fundamental presuppositions of life. They think the socialistic means of ownership and production will change the nature of man, will bring a utopia

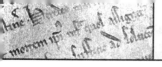
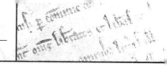

to earth, which is what people in communist U.S.S.R. were taught. They had not experienced a utopia yet, but they just needed more time to get rid of the left-over influence of free and private enterprise, and then it would come. These people were blinded by this false religion.

Productivity declines in a socialist state. Why? One reason is no individual incentive to produce, since individuals do not benefit directly from the fruit of their labor. Another reason is this: when men see that their property is easily confiscated by the state, which will then use it as it thinks best, then men are going to attempt to gain political power so they can control property. Gaining control of government then becomes more important than being productive. People will exert energy to gain control of government, using whatever means possible to do so, rather than using their energy to give to society needed goods and services. Economic productivity will decline.

Karl Marx

Socialism hates a flat tax or small head tax. Graduated taxation is the means of redistribution of wealth. Karl Marx's second plank of his program to destroy capitalism was a highly graduated income tax. Socialist governments seek to control by many means, most especially via taxation. As socialist governments assume more and more authority, they need more and more money to fulfill their ever expanding role in life.

Socialism and communism are forms of humanism, in that they all adhere to the idea of man as the supreme ruler. In socialism this supremacy is placed in political man — man exercising authority through the government.

4. Socialism says the world is naturally productive, but that human laws and institutions stifle man and nature from this natural productivity.

Socialists believe that if these laws and institutions could be removed or restructured, then this natural productivity could be released. Socialists think the central state planners must remove the obstacles. They must either own the means of production (which is communism or socialism) or direct the means of production (fascism or corporate state). In both cases a central elite body of planners claim to know what is best for everyone. They plan for everyone's life. These monopolistic central planners are acting like God, knowing what must be done in all areas of business, what unique skills of each person has, what the wants and desires of each consumer are. They are the agents to transform society; they are the agents of salvation. But they believe in salvation by force and by man-made laws.

Socialism claims authority over all property, including children. Thus, the so-

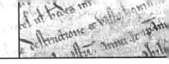

cialist state seeks to educate children, provide for them, and direct and regulate their business and activities. The state seeks to be the parent. In order to provide all that God says the family is to provide (including education, retirement, and so on), the state must seek higher and higher taxes. Thus, socialist leaders implement graduated income taxes, inheritance taxes, all kinds of licenses and fees, and more. The state becomes the substitute parent, but also the substitute child, by providing for people when they get old.

A society that rejects God's order for family responsibility will find the state becoming the educator and provider, and thus requiring a "double portion" of the inheritance (like the first born[405]), an ever-increasing tax burden, and an ever-increasing control, in order to fulfill its duties.

Socialism is ultimately demonic since it is Satan's attempt to control God's earth. At the Fall, Satan seized Adam's inheritance of the earth. Since Jesus has restored this to man, Satan continues to try to rob man of his inheritance in God. He uses the tool of the state to try to seize the capital of modern man, thus keeping man in bondage. Those who embrace the idea of the state as welfare agent are collaborating with the devil and delaying the advance of God's Kingdom in the earth. They are keeping man from the great blessing of his inheritance in God.

Growing Socialism in America

America is becoming more and more socialist. Seeds of socialism were planted in various colleges and schools in the early twentieth century and through various organizations like the Intercollegiate Socialist Society started in 1905 by Upton Sinclair, Jack London, Thomas Wentworth Higginson, J.G. Phelps Stokes and Clarence Darrow. These ideas began to influence public policy, including these past and recent actions:

- Graduated income taxes (beginning in 1913 with the 16th Amendment to the Constitution)
- Establishment of the Federal Reserve Bank (Fed), a central bank in hands of private bankers, in 1913[406]
- Rise of progressivism under President Woodrow Wilson
- Rise of the socialist state under President Franklin D. Roosevelt[407]
- Social security system
- Social programs under President Johnson. Since Johnson launched his war on poverty, America has spent trillions of dollars to help the poor, yet there are more people in poverty today than then. Most of the money (70-80%) for these social programs has not gone to the poor but to government workers to run the programs. Sadly, this well-intentioned but statist run war has destroyed many poor families in America, especially African-American families.

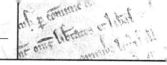

- Soaring government expenditures, especially in areas outside its jurisdiction. (Non-defense spending was 57% in 1965; it was 80% in 2005. Social security and Medicare/Medicaid spending was 40% of federal budget in 2005 and 53% in 2009.)

- Increased taxes and deficit spending. The tax burden has gradually increased on the American people during the twentieth century (with some reprieves here and there, as under President Reagan). But the American people can only be taxed so much, so our statist national government gets more money by borrowing it or creating money out of nothing (as blips on computer screens). This diminishes the wealth of people who have labored hard and saved over their lifetime, plus it lays a burden upon future generations. Our current national debt is over $16 trillion.[408]

Ronald Reagan said: "Government's view of the economy could be summed up in a few short phrases: If it moves, tax it. If it keeps moving, regulate it. And if it stops moving, subsidize it."

- Excessive regulation of land use and private property.

- Bailouts of AIG, Fannie Mae and Freddie Mac, and loans to American automobile corporations (with borrowed or newly created fiat money).

- $750 billion bailout agreed to in the fall of 2008, much of which was used to prop up faltering financial institutions.

- The election in 2008 of a socialist President and socialist leaders of both the House and Senate.

- In early 2009, the nearly one trillion dollar "stimulus plan" which was really primarily a socialist spending plan.

The effects of the massive recent spending by Congress will not produce the desired results of restoring the economy to a firm foundation. It will only increase our debt (increasing the burden on our children and grandchildren) and cause inflation (since any of this "money" not borrowed will be created from nothing). And worse, it will increase the power and size of government, which will result in loss of liberty and prosperity.

In 1986, Ronald Reagan summarized the modern socialist government: "Government's view of the economy could be summed up in a few short phrases: If it moves, tax it. If it keeps moving, regulate it. And if it stops moving, subsidize it."

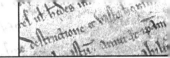
Rise of Global Government

The tendency of fallen man is to look to himself, in particular to corporate man via the state, as savior and provider. When problems arise in society, man usually seeks to centralize power to attempt a solution, which rarely, if ever, succeeds since all sinful actions begin in sinful hearts. Human governments cannot change the heart. In fact, man's "solutions" are usually worse than the problems. History reveals that more centralization of power leads to loss of liberty. The rise of secularism in America has led to greater centralization of power. A pagan view of government has also led the nations of the world to seek to centralize power globally, especially in the past century with the League of Nations, the United Nations, the European Union, and world courts. While working in union with those having a common worldview can be of benefit, the underlying secularism of the move to global government will only result in a continued loss of liberty.

Rise of Secularism in Science

Charles Darwin wrote his book *Origin of the Species* in 1859, but its evolutionary ideas did not become predominant in public education until after the Scopes trial of 1925. Evolutionary forces lost this trial but eventually won the battle of ideas. Evolutionists first argued for free expression of ideas, desiring evolution to be taught alongside of creationism. Today, evolutionists have a grip on public education and take great measures to suppress any mention of creationism or intelligent design, or of allowing any professors to consider such beliefs. Their behavior shows the great intolerance of the "tolerant" liberals.

Charles Darwin

While secularism was on the rise during the twentieth century, the fruit of Christianity was still evident in private and public life. Consider the government pamphlet on the right produced by the U.S. Department of Agriculture, Forest Service, in 1961. The Foreword states:

> There are many passages in the Bible that tell how our forests serve us and how we should protect them.... The Bible urges us to the protection and wise use of our forests, range, and woodlands.... As the Bible foretells, destruction of our natural resources will bring us punishment in the form of loss and misery.... In this booklet we selected Biblical passages of great wisdom and beauty.

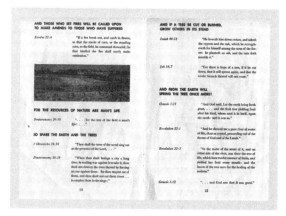

Even 50 years ago we still held to at least a form of godliness, yet as we have lost the power of the Christian faith, there has grown an increasing hostility to God in public (and private) life.

Pictures: Pamphlet front and back covers (top); two insides pages (below).

Rise of Secularism in Arts, Music, and Media

Music, arts, and the media are a means of communicating a worldview. While primarily Christian in our earlier years, today these are mostly humanistic. With the rise of secularism, the biblical Hudson River Painters, and others like them, who

 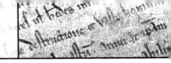

believed in truth and objective beauty, have been supplanted by relativistic artists who embrace a completely subjective view of beauty, and seek to shock viewers with more and more bizarre and perverted images.

Hollywood once produced many excellent biblical movies such as Sergeant York, Mr. Smith Goes to Washington, and Ben Hur, and never made immoral movies. They usually promoted a love of family, love of Christian character, love of God, and similar themes. Today, the opposite is true. While some good movies and television shows are produced today, the majority of them reflect non-Christian values and a secular worldview, and many are evil.

In early America, the church was the primary source of news. Ministers were the newsmen presenting events from a providential perspective. The first newspapers generally sought to communicate truth. Today, the secular bias of the major media helps to keep most Americans ignorant and in bondage.

America's Problem Today

Jesus taught that we are to render to Caesar the things that are Caesar's and to God the things that are God's (Matthew 22:15-21), but today Christians throughout the world have been rendering to Caesar the things that are God's. It is not surprising that secularists will do this because, since they have no god (but themselves), the state readily becomes their default god. However, it is surprising that Christians are worshiping this golden calf.

Does this mean they are worshiping the civil government? Do people have images of the Capitol in their house that they bow down to each day? Do they have Barak Obama bobble-heads on their coffee tables that they pray to each day? No, their idolatrous action is not so obvious.

The Second Commandment says, "you shall not make for yourself an idol" (Exodus 20:4-6). Habakkuk 2:18 says: "What profit is the idol when its maker has carved it, or an image, a teacher of falsehood? For its maker trusts in his own handiwork when he fashions speechless idols." Isaiah described well the absurdity and futility of those who worship the very thing they create. In chapter 44, verses 9-19, Isaiah tells how a man planted and raised trees, then cut one down and burned part of it to warm himself and prepare his food. "But the rest of it he makes into a god, his graven image. He falls down before it and worships; he also prays to it and says, 'Deliver me, for thou art my god'" (Isaiah 44:17).

We would consider it stupid to worship the thing we create with our own hands. Modern western man would not think of making a golden calf, setting it up in his living room, and bowing down before it. What he does is much more subtle.

Humanists are sophisticated idol makers. They are like the guy who carves an idol and worships it — they trust in their own handiwork. They create their own laws, think up their own value systems, form their own governmental and educational systems, and worship them, trusting in them to be "god" (that which is right and true). They can do this, but at their own peril, for if their work is not based upon God's truth, it will lead to ruin. Such idol worship produces bondage, not liberty.

Isaiah speaks of those who worship what they create, ending by asking, "Shall I fall down before a block of wood?" (Isaiah 44:19). Americans must ask themselves, "Shall we as a nation fall down before a block of wood?" "Shall we worship the creation of our own hand?" Shall we look to civil government to be our provider, our comforter, our savior, our god? Jeremiah warns that those who do "are altogether stupid and foolish" (Jeremiah 10:8).

While civil government is a divine institution with an important purpose, it is very limited in what it is suppose to do — it basically is to protect the life, liberty, and property of its citizens (Romans 13:4; 1 Peter 2:14). But we have made it like Babel, thinking the state (something of our own creation) will do much more than God says it is to do. We allow it to take on the role of God, the family, the church, and business. Many people look to the state to meet their needs from cradle to grave, to bring peace and utopia on earth, to help them in times of trouble, to solve all their problems, to care for them when they are sick, and to control and regulate all things. We as a nation have given over to the state many of the responsibilities that God says belong to individuals, the family, or the church.

Separation of Church and State

In His teaching on tribute to Caesar in Matthew 22:15-21, Jesus used a coin with Caesar's image upon it to illustrate that civil government has certain jurisdictional authority, such as in the area of taxation. However, Christ went on to pronounce that the state's jurisdiction is limited when He said that we are to render "to God the things that are God's." The inference is that there is a sphere of life where civil government (i.e. Caesar) has no jurisdiction at all. That sphere is implied here as involving the soul and mind of men, being made, not in Caesar's image, but in the image of God. Jesus was affirming that religious worship and

A denarius featuring Caeser

opinions, and any endeavor relating to thoughts or speech, must remain completely free from government control.

Jesus' teaching explains the biblical idea of the separation of church and state. It is not like the modern idea, which says we must remove God from public life. The principle of separation of church and state, the separation of school and state,

and the separation of the press and speech from the control of the state, which are articulated in the First Amendment of the United States Constitution, are rooted in this historic political teaching of Christ. Before Christianity, the pagan world always included religion and education under the jurisdiction of the state. It was a radical political concept for Christ to declare that Caesar's power should be limited, and, therefore, was used against Jesus when He was convicted of treason and crucified under Roman law. The Founders of America incorporated Christ's teaching on church-state relations into our government. Unfortunately, we have more recently been replacing this with the old pagan view.

Fruit of Statism

The fruit of statism or socialism — or the "Caesar mentality"— is loss of liberty, loss of prosperity, and loss of the ability for the church to disciple the nations. A statist government will suppress Christian involvement in government, education, and social life. It will seek to control not only what is taught in schools, but what is taught in homes and in churches. It will suppress Christian liberty.

Liberty is freedom to do God's will — freedom to do, not what I want to do, but to do what God wants me to do. The freedom of parents to educate their children is becoming more and more limited. We are not free to labor hard throughout life, and confidently save money that will have the same purchasing power it did when we earned it — this due to unbiblical action of the government (fiat money, fractional reserve banking, legal tender laws). We are becoming less free to provide for ourselves and our family because the state is taking more money from us and assuming control of more and more of our responsibilities.

Businesses are not free to operate based upon their moral convictions (like the photographers in New Mexico who were fined $6000 because they refused to photograph a homosexual union). In America, we are not free, in many ways, to govern the use of our property, especially upon death with inheritance taxes. We are experiencing a gradual loss of liberty to govern our children, live securely on our own property, freely worship, and freely speak.

If we turn over to the state control of the most important areas of education and property, we will have little positive long-term influence in reforming the nation. We must assume our responsibility to govern the education of our children and to place control of property in private hands if we hope to restore America.

War against Evil

While secularism was on the rise in America in the twentieth century, she

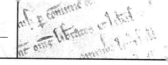

still adhered to much biblical truth and was involved in the battle against evil – in World War I and WWII; standing against Hitler and Nazism; resisting communism during the Cold War; and warring against Muslim terrorists. God raised up men for these battles, such as President Ronald Reagan who was instrumental in seeing communism collapse toward the end of the century.[409]

Even many secular thinking leaders, like President Franklin Roosevelt, understood the nature of evil and the source of liberty, declaring on November 1, 1940: "Those forces hate democracy and Christianity as two phases of the same civilization. They oppose democracy because it is

Franklin D. Roosevelt

Christian. They oppose Christianity because it preaches democracy."[410] In his State of the Union address, January 6, 1942, he said: "The world is too small...for both Hitler and God.... Nazis have now announced their plan for enforcing their...pagan religion all over the world—a plan by which the Holy Bible and the Cross of Mercy would be displaced by Mein Kampf and the swastika."[411]

This poster produced by the U.S. government to help sell war bonds during WWII reveals the Nazi's opposition to Biblical faith.

Our Forefathers and Founding Fathers both declared and lived the truth of the Christian faith. They understood that Christianity is the source of all liberty. More recent generations declared this truth, even if they did not live it. Unfortunately, as the fruit of secularism has increased, the majority of Americans today neither live nor understand this vital idea, that, in the words of Jedidiah Morse, "To the kindly influence of Christianity we owe that degree of civil freedom, and political and social happiness which mankind now enjoys."

The American Apostasy and Remedy for Decline

To summarize, America was founded upon biblical principles which produced much godly fruit — freedom, prosperity, advancement, spreading of liberty and charity. Christianity produced liberty of all kinds — personal, civil, religious, eco-

 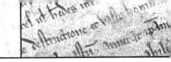

nomic. Personal, religious, and civil liberty made economic liberty possible. Freedom to work and invent, and benefit from the fruit of that labor, encouraged many advances leading to economic prosperity.

As the American republic grew, the influence of Christianity gradually diminished due to unbelief, corruption of doctrine, and neglect of institutions. What is the remedy for this?

Remedy for Decline

1. Unbelief – Revival

Christianity cannot prevail in society without mature believers and strong vibrant churches. These cannot exist without dedicated godly ministers. Biblical revival is the remedy for unbelief. Many people think that a revival is largely a move of God where individuals are converted and the church grows. While this does occur, true biblical revival is much more.

Noah Webster defines *revival*: "1. Return, recall or recovery to life from death or apparent death. 2. Return or recall to activity from a state of languor... 4. An awakening of men to their spiritual concerns."[412] Arthur Wallis said that, "Revival is necessary to counteract spiritual decline and to create spiritual momentum."[413] Revival is the inrush of the Spirit into a body that threatens to become a corpse. It is God bringing us to life that we might rejoice in Him (Psalm 85:6). According to Winkie Pratney, "revival makes the Church" – we His people – "whole and happy in God again."[414]

Methodist revival of 1839. Revival is needed to remedy the decline in America today.

Revival begins by the recovery of life from death, where people who are dead spiritually are supernaturally brought to life. These Christians whose hearts have been renewed also need renewed minds (Romans 12:2). How they act is dependent upon how they think (Proverbs 23:7). Many Christians today are brain-dead. Lack of a biblical worldview among many believers has contributed to the secularization of America and many nations. Revival causes spiritual life to flood into a nation, but it also causes a rising tide of biblical thinking which transforms the laws and institutions of the society.

Revival is a divine attack on society. Revival is God tearing open the heavens,

coming down to earth, and doing awesome things (Isaiah 64:1-3). We need the supernatural intervention of God in our lives and in our nation. We need to recover
the life that flows from the living God (personal transformation), and return to
activity from a state of languor. Our languor has enabled those who oppose God
to infiltrate all spheres of life (education, law, media, science, arts, and economics).
While we were sleeping the enemy came in (Matthew 13:25); while the watchmen
were asleep the horde invaded the city.[415] When we are revived by Him, we will
return to activity that will transform all society and all institutions – the family,
church, civil government, schools, and businesses.

2. Corruption of Doctrine – Restoration of New Testament Church and Biblical Truth

Biblical revival will impact every sphere of life, and involves the restoration of
truth. In fact, revelation and discovery of truth is central to revival. There can be
no revival without truth as revealed by God in the Bible. This truth includes theological doctrine and also biblical worldview, viewing and living life from a biblical
perspective.

3. Neglect of Institutions – Reformation of Society

Biblical revival and the recovery of truth will change the moral and social climate of a community. J. Edwin Orr writes, "The revived church by many or few is
moved to engage in evangelism, teaching, and social action."[416] According to A.W.
Tozer, "Revival must of necessity make an impact on the community and this is one
means by which we may distinguish it from the more usual operations of the Holy
Spirit."[417]

As mentioned above, revival results in the establishment of truth in man and
society. Charles Finney defined revival as "nothing else than a new beginning of
obedience to God."[418] Recovery of truth as revealed in the Bible is a central aspect of
any revival. Pratney writes that, "Revival is not magical. It is not mystical. It is, as far
as men are concerned, a heartfelt return to love and faith in the living and written
Word."[419]

Revival is not merely the conversion of many people, though this does occur
in revivals. Revival involves the conversion of men **and** institutions. Revival has not
occurred until truth is encoded within a nation via changed laws and societal institutions. History shows us that the entire culture is transformed when true biblical
revivals occur.[420]

We must continually fight spiritual entropy, a decline to a lower spiritual state.
We must constantly add fuel to the fire within us and keep the flames burning.

We must keep alive the passion and life within us. We must labor to be salt and light in our society, for as we do corruption shall subside, "the righteous will be in authority," and the people will rejoice" (Proverbs 29:2). God understands the need for renewed life and mercifully has sent His Spirit to revive mankind. He has come down many times to bring people and nations to life and He desires to do this today. As a remedy for decline, we need revival, restoration of truth, and the reformation of all society.

Review Questions

- What contribution did George Washington Carver make to America and the world? Do you think he could have accomplished this if he were not a Christian? Why?
- What are some of the biblical principles that John Wanamaker applied in his department stores?
- What are three reasons given by Rev. Morse for why the genuine effects of Christianity are diminished in any nation? Explain each one.
- What is secularism? Statism?
- Do you think our modern state financed, state directed, state controlled, and state mandated educational system is biblical? Why?
- Explain how the view of law has changed in America? What does Pound's statement, "the state takes the place of Jehovah" mean?
- What is socialism? Why is it a religion?
- What evidence is there that America is becoming more socialistic?
- The Bible teaches the principle of gradualism. Whether for good or evil, change comes gradually from the internal to the external. In light of this, how are we to go about reversing the rise of secularism in America?
- What is the biblical view of "the separation of church and state"?
- What is the remedy for unbelief, corruption of doctrine, and neglect of institutions?

CHAPTER 12

Being Watchmen on the Walls: Replanting the Seed of the American Republic

"I have posted watchmen on your walls, O Jerusalem; they will never be silent day or night." (Isaiah 62:6)

In Old Testament times watchmen were posted on the walls of cities to watch for the enemy and warn the people if they approached. Today, God appoints His people, especially leaders in the church as well as every sphere of life, to be watchmen on the walls – to guard the city and sound the alarm when the ungodly seek to take over. His watchmen performed this duty in the beginning of America.

Pastors and American Independence

In 1776 America was in the midst of war. Ministers, like Rev. James Caldwell, led the fight for freedom. Caldwell was pastor of the First Presbyterian Church of Elizabeth Town, New Jersey. Members of his congregation included William Livingston, the Governor of the State, Elias Boudinot, Commissary General of Prisons and President of the Congress, Abraham Clark, one of the signers of the Declaration of Independence, and more than 40 commissioned officers of the Continental Army. In 1776 Caldwell was chosen chaplain of the regiment that was largely composed of members of his church. Later he became Assistant Commissary General. The British placed a large bounty on his head. John T. Faris writes:

> The British called him the Fighting Chaplain, and he was cordially hated

because of his zeal for the cause of the patriots. His life was always in danger, and when he was able to spend a Sunday with his congregation he would preach with his cavalry pistols on the pulpit, while sentinels were stationed at the doors to give warning.[421]

Caldwell sought to defend himself from his enemies because he felt he was engaged in "the cause of God and that cause he did not consider would be advanced by yielding himself unresistingly into the hands of a skulking Tory to be dragged to the scaffold."[422]

The enmity of the British led to the burning of the chaplain's church, and the murder, a few months later, of Mrs. Caldwell. While she was sitting in a rear room at the house at Connecticutt Farms, where she had been sent for safety, surrounded by her children, a soldier thrust his musket through the window and fired at her.[423]

Rev. James Caldwell: "Now put Watts into them boys."

Mrs. Caldwell was killed. Soldiers then set the house on fire. Neighbors rescued the Caldwell's nine children and the body of Mrs. Caldwell. Upon hearing of this tragedy, Rev. Caldwell returned from camp to bury his wife. He then made arrangements for the care of his children and returned to the battlefield.

A few weeks later the following incident occurred:

The British under General Knyphausen, determined to drive Washington and his men from the New Jersey hills and to destroy his supplies, marched from Elizabeth Town on June 23, 1780. There were five thousand men, with fifteen or twenty pieces of artillery, in the expedition. A few miles away, near Springfield, was a small company of patriots, poorly equipped but ready to die in the defence of their country.

Warning of the approach of the enemy was given to the Continentals by the firing of the eighteen-pounder signal gun on Prospect Hill; twelve Continentals stationed at the Cross Roads, after firing on the enemy, had hurried to the hill. After firing the gun they lighted the tar barrel on the signal pole.

Instantly the members of the militia dropped their scythes, seized their muskets, and hurried to quarters. "There were no feathers in their caps, no gilt buttons on their home-spun coats, nor flashing bayonets on their old fowling pieces … but there was in their hearts the resolute purpose to defend their homes and their liberty at the price of their lives."

The sturdy farmers joined forces with the regular soldiers. For a time the battle was fierce. The enemy were soon compelled to retreat, but not before they had burned the village.... Chaplain James Caldwell was in the hottest of the fight. "Seeing the fire of one of the companies slacking for want of wadding, he galloped to the Presbyterian meeting house nearby, and rushing in, ran from pew to pew, filling his arms with hymn books," wrote Headley, in *Chaplains and Clergy of the Revolution*. "Hastening back with them into the battle, he scattered them about in every direction, saying as he pitched one here and another there, 'Now put Watts into them, boys.' With a laugh and a cheer they pulled out the leaves, and ramming home the charge did give the British Watts with a will."[424]

"Giving them Watts" was great symbolism. Pages from Watts Hymnal were being used as a physical weapon against the forces of oppression. It had been used as a spiritual weapon by the Americans for many years. Isaac Watts was an English Puritan dissenter, pastor, theologian, and hymn writer who helped to transform how congregations worshiped. The singing of his hymns was a great tool in transmitting the liberating truth of the Scriptures throughout America.

We are in a war today; not a war of guns and bullets, as fought by our Forefathers, but a war of worldviews. We have already mentioned this war between a biblical worldview and various man-centered worldviews (whether statism and its many forms, or false religions). Secularists have launched a great assault against God and truth in schools, in the public arena, in government, in courtrooms, in attempting to redefine the family, and in abandoning the concept of truth itself.

We should ask, "Why has the enemy been so effective in winning the various battles in the war of worldviews?" The enemy has been able to come in because the watchmen have been asleep. Contrary to God's command, they have been silent. To win the war and turn our nation around, Christians must awaken and fulfill their duties in all spheres of life.

The watchmen have fallen asleep.

The good news is that many times in history, "When the enemy comes in like a flood the Spirit of the Lord shall lift up a standard against him" (Isaiah 59:19). God did this in early America. Christians, and in particular ministers, were watchmen on the walls. They warned of the machinations of the enemies of God and gave birth to the nation. They provided leadership in all areas — they prayed, taught, led, and fought. They literally discipled this nation. We should follow their example.

Christians gave birth to America and were the watchmen on the walls.

Prayer was the foundation for all their action.

We have already given numerous instances of the central role of prayer in our history, including:

- At the founding of Virginia when Rev. Robert Hunt erected a cross at Cape Henry and led the first settlers in prayer on April 29, 1607
- Prayer by the Pilgrims upon leaving Europe for America, upon landing in New England, at the first Thanksgiving, and throughout the establishment of the Plymouth Colony
- Prayer was a vital part of early education, as revealed in an original rule of the first college, Harvard (1636): "And seeing the Lord only giveth wisedom, Let every one seriously set himselfe by prayer in secret to seeke it of him (Prov. 2:3)."
- The First Prayer in Congress by the Rev. Jacob Duche (1774)
- Prayer by the State of Connecticut on the day of the Battle of Lexington and Concord
- The first colony wide day of prayer held on July 20, 1775, in response to martial law imposed by Britain
- Prayer throughout the American Revolution by the Continental Congress (proclaiming 15 official days of prayer) and various states (issuing many prayer proclamations)

First Prayer in Congress

Pastors led the people in prayer, not only on the official days of fasting and prayer and thanksgiving, but also regularly in their churches and in their homes. They also prayed with the troops on the battlefield, many serving as permanent chaplains.

Presbyterian pastor and chaplain of the Pennsylvania militia George Duffield frequented camps, where "his visits were always welcome, for the soldiers loved the eloquent, earnest, fearless patriot." Duffield had become a chaplain after closing one Sunday sermon with the words: "There are too many men in this congregation.... Next Sunday there'll be one less!"[425]

Historian J.T. Headley gives the following incident of the courageous Duffield:

> When the enemy occupied Staten Island, and the American forces were across the river on the Jersey shore, he repaired to camp to spend the Sabbath. Assembling a portion of the troops in an orchard, he climbed into the forks of a tree and commenced religious exercises. He gave out a hymn…. The British on the island heard the sound of the singing, and immediately directed some cannon to play on the orchard, from whence it proceeded. Soon the heavy shot came crashing through the branches, and went singing overhead, arresting for a moment the voices that were lifted in worship. Mr. Duffield … proposed that they should adjourn behind an adjacent hillock. They did so, and continued their worship, while the iron storm hurled harmlessly overhead.[426]

General George Washington set an example for prayer, in private and public. He prayed at Valley Forge and throughout the war. He issued orders for troops to attend divine service numerous times. He ended his advice to the Governors in his Circular Letter (sent as the war was ending and he was preparing to disband the military and resign as Commander) with a prayer. In his first year as President, Washington issued a Proclamation for a Day of Prayer and Thanksgiving, November 26, 1789, stating: "Whereas it is the duty of all nations to acknowledge the providence of Almighty God, to obey His will, to be grateful for His benefits, and humbly to implore His protection and favor." Most Presidents since Washington have issued similar proclamations.[427]

Washington in prayer at Valley Forge.

Even non-Christians prayed. Jefferson penned a resolve as a member of the Virginia legislature setting aside a day of prayer in response to the Boston Port Act. Franklin called for the Constitutional Convention to pray in 1787 when they reached an impasse. There were well over 1400 days of prayer and fasting or prayer and thanksgiving proclaimed by governments at all levels from 1620 to 1813.[428]

President Ronald Reagan summarized the Founders' heart in his National Day of Prayer Proclamation, May 6, 1982: "The most sublime picture in American history is of George Washington on his knees in the snow at Valley Forge. That image personifies a people who know that it is not enough to depend on our own courage and goodness, we must also seek help from God, our Father and Preserver."

Pastors, civil leaders, and citizens prayed, but they also acted. Evangelization of the lost was an important part of their action, as evidenced in their founding charters, which stated they came to propagate the Gospel.[429] To assist in this work, over many

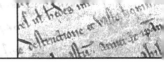

generations, they translated and published the Bible in about 100 different Native American languages. Scores of these Bibles are currently on display in the Native American museum in Washington, DC. Explanatory description on the display glass says: "Today the majority of Native people call themselves Christian." The European settlers in the Americas were so successful in fulfilling their vision to propagate the Gospel in the New World, that a majority of the descendants of the American Indians now call themselves Christians.

Bibles in various Native American languages on display in the National Museum of the American Indian, Washington, DC.

Their action affected individual lives, but it also impacted the public arena. As we have seen, Christians (and in particular ministers) colonized the states, wrote the laws and constitutions, started the schools and colleges, and served in leadership in every area of life.

Pastors Taught

Ministers were the primary educators in early America.

"To the pulpit, the Puritan pulpit, we owe the moral force which won our independence."[430] Thus wrote J. Wingate Thorton summarizing the role of the clergy in the birth of our nation. Such a significant role did not begin at the time of the American Revolution, but it was one that the church and her ministers had played from the beginning of the colonies.

As the primary educators of the colonial period, the clergy had a tremendous impact upon the character and thinking of the people. Professor Harry S. Stout of Yale University writes: "The average weekly churchgoer in New England (and there were far more churchgoers than church members) listened to something like seven thousand sermons in a lifetime, totaling somewhere

around fifteen thousand hours of concentrated listening." These statistics become even more significant when one considers there were essentially no "competing public speakers offering alternative messages. For all intents and purposes, the sermon was the only regular voice of authority."[431]

Ministers were the primary educators not only at churches but also at schools, academies, and colleges. Many of the Founding Fathers were tutored by ministers, including Thomas Jefferson, James Madison, George Mason, Patrick Henry, and Noah Webster. Those who attended college would have been trained by ministers as well. Through their biblical teaching, pastors guided the American people through their struggle for independence and freedom.

Rev. George Duffield was pastor of Pine Street Presbyterian Church from 1772 to 1790. He served as chaplain of the Continental Congress and of the Pennsylvania militia during the war. Duffield delivered many fiery, patriotic sermons to the many prominent men who attended his church. He inspired many to action, including John Adams, who was a member of his congregation while in Philadelphia.

In May 1776 John Adams listened to a sermon of Rev. Duffield that likened the way King George III treated the Americans to the way Pharaoh had treated the Israelites. Duffield concluded that God intended for the Americans to be liberated just as He intended the Israelites to be liberated. On May 17 Adams wrote to his wife:

> Is it not a Saying of Moses, who am I, that I should go in and out before this great People? When I consider the great Events which are passed, and those greater which are rapidly advancing, and that I may have been instrumental in touching some Springs, and turning some small Wheels, which have had and will have such Effects, I feel an Awe upon my Mind, which is not easily described. G[reat] B[retain] has at last driven America, to the last Step, a compleat Seperation from her, a total, absolute Independence.[432]

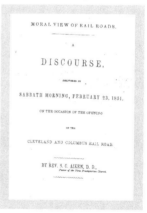

Sermons were often printed and distributed widely. They addressed every area of life, like this one on "Moral View of Railroads."

J.T. Headley writes of the influence of Rev. Duffield:

> The patriots of the first Congress flocked to his church, and John Adams and his compeers were often his hearers.... In a discourse delivered before several companies of the Pennsylvania militia and members of Congress, four months before the Declaration of Independence, he took bold and decided ground in favor of that step, and pleaded his cause with sublime

eloquence, which afterwards made him so obnoxious to the British that they placed a reward of fifty pounds for his capture.[433]

Later on in that sermon, Duffield delivered a prophetic word we must heed today: "Whilst sun and moon endure, America shall remain a city of refuge for the whole earth, until she herself shall play the tyrant, forget her destiny, disgrace her freedom, and provoke her God."[434]

We previously examined how Rev. John Witherspoon discipled the nation by training many of the Founding Fathers. If the pulpit had only given Witherspoon to the Revolution it would deserve everlasting remembrance. But the pulpit gave much more; ministers taught the nation. The clergy took the task of teaching all the truth of the Scriptures seriously.

In addition to sound theology and personal matters of faith, their sermons addressed all areas of life. A few sermon topics from the founding era include: education, marriage, ardent spirits, the poor, social justice, old age, sodomy, gambling, comets, earthquakes, soldiers and patriotism, artillery, fire, Stamp Act repeal, Thanksgiving Days, civil government, bridge building, eclipses, "Moral Uses of the Sea," discovery of a new planet, railroads, medicine, snow and vapor, property, election sermons, and execution sermons.

They also educated the nation through their books and writings. Moral and religious catechisms were common for use in the church and school. Rev. John Wise wrote "The Law of Nature in Government" in 1717 which was so influential that it was reprinted in 1772 and studied by the civil leaders. Sections of this work appear word for word in the Declaration of Independence. When Thomas Paine wrote his anti-Christian work, *Age of Reason*, ministers strongly responded, including Bishop R. Watson's excellent defense of the faith, *An Apology for the Bible*.

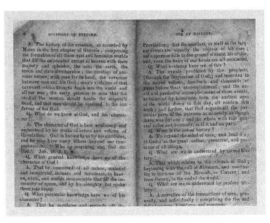

Pages from Frederick Butler's *A General History of the World*

Ministers wrote influential history books, such as *The Great Works of Christ in America* by Cotton Mather and *A General History of the World* by Frederick Butler,

educational books, such as Rev. William Holmes McGuffey's series of *Readers*, and many others. In addition, ministers started many schools and colleges, serving as professors and presidents, they were the primary newsmen, and they wrote laws, constitutions, and other civil documents. These and other factors led Alice Baldwin to write that "the Constitutional Convention and the written Constitution were the children of the pulpit."[435]

Pastors Led

Ministers led the fight for both religious and civil liberty from America's earliest years. Rev. Roger Williams and Rev. Thomas Hooker were champions of the idea of liberty of conscience. Williams, according to E.L. Magoon, was one of the first men to maintain

> that the civil magistrate has no compulsive jurisdiction in the concerns of religion; that the punishment of any person on account of his opinions was an encroachment on conscience and an act of persecution.... It is worthy of note, that the sentiments respecting toleration which he first proclaimed, and for which he was severely persecuted ... are now the unanimous opinions of this great nation.[436]

Another leader in the struggle for religious freedom was Francis Makemie. In 1680 Colonel William Stevens and a number of Presbyterians in Maryland asked the Presbytery of Laggan in Ireland to send a godly minister to help them form a church. In response Francis Makemie was sent, and under his leadership the first Presbyterian Church in Americ was organized and was called Rehoboth Church. It was named after Stevens' plantation which was begun in 1665. He had chosen the name

Narragansett Indians receiving Roger Williams.

from Genesis 26:22. For many years Makemie traveled and preached and organized churches. Though he had a certificate from the court to preach in Maryland, he still faced many trying times. His greatest trial, though, occurred in New York.

His arrest and subsequent trial in 1707 link him as a leader in the struggle for religious liberty. After preaching in the city of New York, a warrant was issued for his arrest. The charge, signed by Lord Cornbury, said that he had taken upon him-

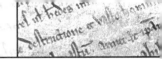

self "to Preach in a Private House, without having obtained My Licence for so doing, which is directly contrary to the known Laws of England."[437]

When brought before Lord Cornbury, Makemie said: "We have Liberty from an Act of Parliament, made the first year of the Reign of King William and Queen Mary, which gave us Liberty, with which Law we have complied." But Lord Cornbury replied: "No one shall Preach in my Government without my Licence.... That Law does not extend to the American Plantations, but only to England.... I know, for I was at Making thereof.... That Act of Parliament was made against Strowling Preachers, and you are such, and shall not Preach in my Government."[438] Makemie refused to pay bail and to agree to preach no more, so he was imprisoned. He defended himself at the trial and was found "not guilty," but was forced to pay all court costs. It cost Makemie more than 80 pounds (a tremendous sum) when all expenses were totaled for the trial.

The great burden of the arrest and trial hastened his death a few months later. But he had not suffered in vain, for his struggles for religious liberty were to bear much fruit in the years to come. It was another dissenting minister, John Leland of Virginia, who played an important role in the proposal and approval of the Virginia Statute for Religious Freedom (1786), which was a culminating event in the development of religious freedom.

Samuel Davies

Rev. Samuel Davies was a bold ambassador for Christ. In his desire to see the Kingdom of God come on earth as it is in heaven he served not only as a pastor but also as a lawyer, an ambassador to England, and president of Princeton College. Magoon writes that

Samuel Davies

> he had made himself a thorough master of English law, civil and ecclesiastical, and always chose to meet every persecuting indictment in the highest courts with his own plea. . . . [H]e went to England and obtained the explicit sanction of the highest authority with respect to the extension of the Toleration law to Virginia. It was during this mission that . . . George II and many of his court were in the congregation of this American Dissenter. His majesty, struck with admiration, or forgetting the proprieties of the occasion, spoke several times to those around him and smiled. Davies paused a moment, and then looking sternly at the king, exclaimed,

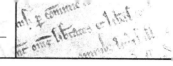

"When the lion roars, the beasts of the forest all tremble; and when King Jesus speaks, the princes of earth should keep silence."[439]

Davies, one of the greatest orators in colonial America, served as the mentor for the man Jefferson called "the greatest orator that ever lived" — Patrick Henry. When Patrick was around twelve years old his mother joined the church where Samuel Davies preached. Mrs. Henry would attend regularly and always take Patrick, who from the first showed a high appreciation for the preacher. Each Sunday as they rode home in their buggy, Mrs. Henry and Patrick would review the sermon. This greatly influenced Patrick and the development of his oratorical skills. Patrick even declared that Davies was "the greatest orator he ever heard."[440] But Patrick Henry also learned from Davies a sound biblical theology. William Wirt Henry writes: "His early example of eloquence … was Mr. Davies, and the effect of his teaching upon his after life may be plainly traced."[441] Pastors today should be mentors for our youth, inspiring and equipping them to lead in all areas of life.

Many other ministers provided leadership in significant ways. Rev. Jonas Clark of Lexington, Massachusetts, prepared his congregation to pay whatever price was necessary for liberty. Some of his church members were the first to give their lives for the cause of American independence on the morning of April 19, 1775. Rev. John Witherspoon not only signed the Declaration of Independence, but as president of the College of New Jersey (now Princeton) he trained one fifth of the men who gave us the Constitution, including its chief architect, James Madison.

Pastors Fought

Peter Muhlenberg

So many ministers participated in the War for Independence that the British called them "the Black Regiment," in reference to their pulpit gowns. One member of the "Black Regiment," Peter Muhlenberg, is honored by a statue in the United States Capitol Building. Benson J. Lossing writes of his beginning involvement:

In those days politics were preached in the pulpits and men were led to action on the side of freedom by faithful pastors. The eminent General Muhlenberg was one of this stamp. When the war for independence was kindling, he

Statue of Peter Muhlenberg in the Capitol.

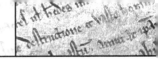

was a clergymen in Virginia, and at the close of 1775, he concluded a sermon with the words of Scripture: "There is a time for all things—a time to preach and a time to pray;" but those times, he said, had passed away; and then, in a voice that sounded like a trumpet-blast through the church, he exclaimed: "There is a time to fight, and that time has now come." Then laying aside his sacerdotal gown, he stood before his flock in the full uniform of a Virginia colonel. He ordered the drums to be beaten at the church door for recruits; and almost the entire male audience, capable of bearing arms, joined his standard. Nearly three hundred men enlisted his banner on that day.[442]

Rev. Peter Muhlenberg became one of Washington's primary Brigadier Generals in the Continental Army, serving with him in every major conflict from that time through the surrender of the British at Yorktown. When his brother Frederick, who was a pastor of a church in New York City, heard how Peter had left the ministry to get involved in civil and military affairs, he wrote him a letter opposing his action, stating: "You would have acted for the best if you had kept out of this business from the beginning. I now give you my thoughts in brief: I think you were wrong."[443] Peter responded:

> You say, as a clergyman nothing can excuse my conduct. I am a clergyman, it is true, but I am a member of society as well as the poorest layman, and my liberty is as dear to me as to any man. Shall I then sit still, and enjoy myself at home, when the best blood of the continent is spilling? Heaven forbid it! . . .
>
> But even if you was [sic] on the opposite side of the question, you must allow that in this last step I have acted for the best. You know that from the beginning of these troubles I have been compelled to have a hand in public affairs. I have been chairman to the committee of delegates from this county from the first. Do you think, if America should be conquered, I should be safe? Far from it. And would you not sooner fight like a man than die like a dog? I am called by my country to its defence. The cause is just and noble. Were I a bishop, even a Lutheran one, I should obey without hesitation, and so far am I from thinking that I am wrong, I am convinced it is my duty so to do, a duty I owe to my God and to my country.[444]

The next year, in 1777, British troops marched into New York City and destroyed or burnt 10 of the 19 churches in the city.[445] One of those they destroyed was that of Frederick Muhlenberg, after which he began to rethink his position on involvement in political affairs, realizing as did his brother Peter that if the church and her leaders do not take action in public affairs, there will be no liberty to worship or preach the Gospel. Frederick went on to serve in government, being elected a member from Pennsylvania of the first Congress under the U.S. Constitution. When the first Congress gathered in New York City in 1789, he was elected as the first Speaker

Rev. Frederick Augustus Muhlenberg, First Speaker of the House of Representatives, in the U.S. Capitol.

of the House of Representatives. As such, he also was one of only two people who signed the Bill of Rights. Thus, the first Speaker of the House of Representatives, Frederick Augustus Muhlenberg, was a minister who had been inspired by his minister brother to get involved in politics for the good of the nation and the good of Christ's Kingdom. His painting hangs in the Capitol Building today and reminds us of the important role ministers played in our history.

Pastors took the lead in the battle for American independence. They prayed, preached, taught, and fought. John Adams wrote to his wife from Philadelphia on July 7, 1775, telling her to make sure their minister was preaching patriotically: "Tell him [their pastor, Rev. Wibirt] the Clergy here, of every Denomination … thunder and lighten every sabbath. They pray for Boston and the Massachusetts—they thank God most explicitly and fervently for our remarkable Successes—they pray for the American army. They seem to feel as if they were among you."[446] America needs faithful pastors — those who will pray, who will preach liberty, and who will lead men to action on the side of freedom.

A Second American Revolution

Pastors and Christians were faithful watchmen on the walls. They led the American Revolution. We have great need today for a second American Revolution – an overturning of the unfruitful oppressive ideas of secularism and statism, replacing them with the liberating ideas from the Christian faith that have been proven to produce great blessing from our own history. For this to occur, God's people – the watchmen – must wake up, sound the alarm, and fulfill all their biblical duties and responsibilities.

George Washington takes the Presidential oath of office with his hand on the Bible, 1789.

The story of liberty continues in history. God continues to advance His purposes in the nations. The extent to which America experiences and propagates His liberty in the future depends upon His sovereign grace in conjunction with our obedience to His commands. The good news is that God, working through willing vessels, has transformed and brought great liberty to nations in the past. He can and will do it again, for His desire and plan is to liberate mankind. Hope remains for America to be "a city set upon a hill" and a place "to enlarge the glory of the Gospel." May God give us grace as we each do our part to advance His monumental story and restore America as the land of liberty.

Review Questions

- Who are the watchmen on the walls and what is their biblical duty?

- What do you think is the greatest threat to the Christian faith in America at this time? Why?

- What role did ministers play in the colonization of America?

- Give an example of prayer in public life in early America.

- How would you compare how ministers educated the people in early America to how they educate today?

- Give an example of how ministers provided leadership in early America. What do you think ministers can do today to help bring about a second American revolution?

- How can you be a watchman on the walls today?

- What do you believe God has called you to do regarding restoring America as the land of liberty? Be general and specific.

Endnotes

[1] America became an exceptional nation in history due to its foundation upon the Christian faith. As will be examined throughout this book, Christianity produced the character, self-government, and worldview upon which America grew in liberty and prosperity unlike any nation in history. See Stephen McDowell, *America, A Christian Nation*, Charlottesville: Providence Foundation, 2004, for more.

[2] For various figures and insight into what is being taught in state schools see, Bruce N. Shortt, *The Harsh Truth About Public Schools*, Vallecito, Cal.: Chalcedon Foundation, 2004, pp. 21, 51-52, and various other pages.

[3] http://www.guttmacher.org/pubs/fb_induced_abortion.html

[4] http://www.guttmacher.org/pubs/FB-ATSRH.html; and http://www.4parents.gov/sexrisky/teen_preg/teen_preg.html#72b

[5] http://www.cdc.gov/std/stats08/trends.htm ; http://www.usatoday.com/news/health/2008-03-11-std_n.htm

[6] http://www.washingtonpost.com/wp-dyn/content/story/2008/02/28/ST2008022803016.html

[7] "Land lock," *World Magazine*, April 19/26, 2008, pp. 60-61.

[8] See for example, "Believe or leave", *World Magazine*, Aug. 14, 2010, p. 8.

[9] Communism provides an example of the fruit of secularism/statism: in the 20th century communist nations killed over 100 million of their own citizens.

[10] This section is from Stephen McDowell, *The American Dream*, Charlottesville, Vir.: Providence Foundation, 2007, pp. 14-18.

[11] See Stephen McDowell, *The Economy from a Biblical Perspective*, Charlottesville: Providence Foundation, 2009.

[12] *Sources of Our Liberties, Documentary Origins of Individual Liberties in the United States Constitution and Bill of Rights*, edited by Richard L. Perry, American Bar Foundation, 1959, p. 60.

[13] *Colonial Origins of the American Constitution, A Documentary History*, edited by Donald S. Lutz, Indianapolis: Liberty Fund, 1998, p. 366.

[14] See *Colonial Origins of the American Constitution* and *Sources of Our Liberties*.

[15] *Sources of Our Liberties*, p. 158.

[16] *The Blue Laws of New Haven Colony, usually called Blue Laws of Connecticut . . . , By an antiquarian*, Hartford: printed by Case, Tiffany & Co., 1838, p. 145.

[17] Letter to the Clergy of Different Denominations Residing in and near the City of Philadelphia, March 3, 1797, *The Writings of George Washington*, John C. Fitzpatrick, editor, Washington: United States Government Printing Office, 1940, 35:416.

[18] *A Compilation of the Messages and Papers of the Presidents*, by James D. Richardson, Washington: Bureau of National Literature and Art, 1910, 1:205-216.

[19] Letter to Frederick Beasley, Nov. 20, 1825.

[20] *Notes of Debates in the Federal Convention of 1787*, reported by James Madison. New York: W.W. Norton & Co., 1987, pp. 209-210.

[21] Thomas Jefferson, *The Writings of Thomas Jefferson*, Albert Ellery Bergh, editor, Washington, D.C.: The Thomas Jefferson Memorial Association, 1904, Vol. XVI, p. 291, to Captain John Thomas on November 18, 1801.

[22] *Sources of Our Liberties*, p. 382.

[23] From a copy of the original "Last Will and Testament" in McDowell's possession, obtained via Wallbuilders.

[24] Ibid.

[25] Ibid.

[26] Ibid., for more wills of the Founders see, http://providencefoundation.com/wp-content/uploads/2011/08/Wills-of-Founders.pdf

[27] For more on Jefferson's religious beliefs see Stephen McDowell and Mark Beliles, *In God We Trust Tour Guide*, Charlottesville: Providence Foundation, 1998, pp. 205-221.

[28] Jefferson, *Writings*, 1904, Vol. XII, p. 315, to James Fishback, September 27, 1809.

[29] *The Works of Benjamin Franklin*, by Jared Sparks, Boston: Tappan, Whittemore, and Mason, 1840, p. 281-282.

[30] *Sources of Our Liberties*, pp. 264-265.

[31] Webster to James Madison, 16 October 1829, Madison Papers, Series 2, Library of Congress. Quoted in K. Alan Snyder, *Defining Noah Webster, Mind and Morals in the Early Republic*, New York: University Press of America, 1990, p. 253.

[32] *History of the United States*, New Haven: Durrie & Peck, 1833, p. v.

[33] Benjamin Rush, *Essays, Literary, Moral and Philosophical, Philadelphia*: printed by Thomas and William Bradford, 1806, p. 93.

[34] Election Sermon given at Charleston, MA on April 25, 1799.

[35] Cited in B.F. Morris, *Christian Life and Character of the Civil Institutions of the United States*, Philadelphia: George W. Childs, 1864, p. 328.

[36] W. DeLoss Love, Jr., *The Fast and Thanksgiving Days of New England*, New York: Houghton, Mifflin and Co., 1895, p. 41.

[37] Love, *The Fast and Thanksgiving Days of New England*. Love lists the days of fasting and thanksgiving. He also lists 622 fast and thanksgiving day sermons that were published, dating from 1636 to 1815.

[38] Catherine Drinker Bowen, *John Adams and the American Revolution*, New York: Grosset & Dunlap, 1950, p. 10-12.

[39] B.F. Morris, pp 530-531.

[40] Ibid.

[41] See Mark A. Beliles and Stephen K. McDowell, *America's Providential History*, Charlottesville, VA: Providence Foundation, 1989, p. 141, and Peter Force, *American Archives: A Documentary History of the English Colonies in North America*, Fourth Series, Washington: M. St. Clair and Peter Force, 1846, pp. 1278, 1471.

[42] *The Virginia Gazette*, Nov. 20, 1779, Number 4, Williamsburg: Printed by Dixon & Nicolson.

[43] Benjamin F. Morris, *Christian Life and Character of the Civil Institutions of the United States*, Powder Springs, GA: American Vision, 2007 (reprint of 1864 edition), pp. 675-678. See W. DeLoss Love, *The Fast and Thanksgiving Days of New England* for an extensive list of government proclamations for Days of Prayer.

[44] See *A Compilation of the Messages of the Presidents*, James D. Richardson, ed., New York: Bureau of National Literature, 1897.

[45] This section is from McDowell, *The American Dream*, pp. 18-20.

[46] To learn more see Stephen McDowell, *Building Godly Nations*, Charlottesville, Vir: Providence Foundation, 2003, Chapters 1 and 14, and Stephen McDowell, *Transforming Medicine and Business with Biblical Principles, Examples of Joseph Lister and John Wanamaker*, Charlottesville: Providence Foundation, 2010.

[47] See Stephen McDowell, *The Ten Commandments and Modern Society*, Charlottesville: Providence Foundation, 2000.

[48] John Adams, *The Works of John Adams*, Charles Francis Adams, editor (Boston: Little, Brown & Co., 1856), Vol. 6, *A Defense of the Constitutions of Government of the United States of America*, "Chapter First. Marchamont Nedham. The Right Constitution of a Commonwealth Examined."

[49] Gene Edward Veith, "The end of humanism," *World Magazine*, April 22, 2006, p. 30.

[50] Quoted in Rosalie J. Slater, *Teaching and Learning America's Christian History*, San Francisco: Foundation for American Christian Education, 1980, p. 251.

[51] This preceding section is from Stephen McDowell and Mark Beliles, *Liberating the Nations*, Charlottesville, Vir.: Providence Foundation, 1995, pp. 14-15 (chapter 1 was authored by McDowell).

[52] "A Letter to the Officers of the First Brigade of the Third Division of the Militia of Massachusetts, Oct. 11, 1798." In *The Works of John Adams, Second President of the United States*, Boston: Little, Brown and Co., 1854, 9:228-229.

[53] To learn more on the framework of Godly government see *Liberating the Nations*, pp. 141 ff.

[54] To learn more on the fundamental principles of Christian nations (or the power of free governments) see *Liberating the Nations*, pp. 3 ff. The five statues in the Forefathers Monument represent the power of free governments.

[55] B.F. Morris, *Christian Life and Character of the Civil Institutions of the United States*, Philadelphia: George W. Childs, 1864, pp. 239.

[56] William J. Johnson, *George Washington the Christian*, 1919, reprinted by Mott Media, Milford, Mich., 1976, p. 209.

[57] George Washington, "Circular to the Governors of the States," June 8, 1783, *The Writings of George Washington*, 26:496.

[58] Washington to Col. Lewis Nicola, May 22, 1782, *The Writings of George Washington*, 24:272-73.

[59] See *Building Godly Nations*, Chapter 13, pp. 231 ff., for "Qualifications for Godly Officials." Exodus 18:21 and Deuteronomy 1:13 present biblical qualifications for governing officials; Jesus said civil officials are to be public servants (Matt. 20: 25-26).

[60] James Thomas Flexner, *George Washington in the American Revolution, 1775-1783*, Boston: Little, Brown, 1967, p. 507, quoted in Stephen McDowell, *Apostle of Liberty, The World-Changing Leadership of George Washington*, Nashville: Cumberland House, 2007, pp. 204-206.

[61] Ibid.

[62] *The Christian History of the American Revolution, Consider and Ponder*, Verna Hall, compiler, San Francisco: Foundation for American Christian Education, 1976, p. 615. (Referenced as *Consider and Ponder* in later end notes)

[63] Bernard C. Steiner, *The Life and Correspondence of James McHenry*, Cleveland: The Burrows Brothers Company, 1907, p. 475, Charles Carroll to James McHenry on November 4, 1800.

[64] See McDowell, *Building Godly Nations*, chapter 11, "The Changing Nature of Law in America," pp. 183 ff.

[65] Andrew W. Young, *First Lessons in Civil Government*, Auburn, N.Y.: H. and J.C. Ivison, 1846, p. 16.

[66] Thomas Paine, "Declaration of Rights," *The Writings of Thomas Paine*, Collected and edited by Daniel Conway, New York: G.P. Putnam's Sons, Vol.3 , p. 129-130.

[67] See McDowell, *Building Godly Nations*, Chapter 7, "The Influence of the Bible on the Development of American Constitutionalism."

[68] For an examination of each of these points, see McDowell, *America, a Christian Nation? Examining the Evidence of the Christian Foundation of America* and "The Changing Nature of Law in America," Chapter 11, pp. 183 ff, in *Building Godly Nations*.

[69] Donald S. Lutz, "The Relative Influence of European Writers on Late Eighteenth-Century American Political Thought," *The American Political Science Review*, vol. 78, 1984, pp. 189-197.

[70] Sir William Blackstone, *Commentaries on the Laws of England*, Philadelphia: Robert Bell, Union Library, 1771, vol. 1, 38-42.

[71] James Wilson, *The Works of the Honourable James Wilson*, Bird Wilson, editor, Philadelphia: Lorenzo Press, 1804, Vol. I, p. 64, "Of the General Principles of Law and Obligation."

[72] James Wilson, *Works*, Vol. 1, pp. 103-105, "Of the General Principles of Law and Obligation."

[73] Rufus King, *The Life and Correspondence of Rufus King*, Charles R. King, editor, New York: G.P. Putnam's Sons, 1900, Vol. VI, p. 276, to C. Gore on February 17, 1820.

[74] *For the Colony in Virginea Britannia, Lawes Divine, Morall and Martiall, etc.*, compiled by William Strachey, edited by David H. Flaherty, Charlottesville: University Press of Virginia, 1969, pp. 10-11.

[75] See *Colonial Origins of the American Constitution* and *Sources of Our Liberties*.

[76] *Sources of Our Liberties*, pp. 349, 350.

[77] *The Constitutions of the Sixteen States*, Boston: Manning and Loring, 1797, p. 274, Tennessee, 1796, Article VIII, Section II.

[78] To learn some of the reasons for this change, see *America's Providential History*, Chapter 17.

[79] Benjamin Cardozo, *The Growth of Law*, New Haven: Yale University Press, 1924, p. 49.

[80] Charles Evans Hughes, *The Autobiographical Notes of Charles Evans Hughes*, David J. Danelski and Joseph S. Tulchin, editors, Cambridge: Harvard University Press, 1973, p. 144, speech at Elmira on May 3, 1907.

[81] Statism is the belief that man via the state or civil government is the ultimate authority. There are those who believe that man is the ultimate authority in the earth who do not espouse statism and think civil government should have very little power (for example, some libertarians). But in a society where each man is his own law-system, anarchy will increase, as every man is doing what he thinks is right. To maintain order, the state must assume more power and control – the more that each man acts as his own god, the more power the state must exercise to keep some degree of order. The end result is some form of statism, whether democracy, socialism, dictatorship, etc.

[82] "Preface," *Frame of Government of Pennsylvania*, April 25, 1682, in *Sources of Our Liberties*, p. 211.

[83] William Jay, *The Life of John Jay*, New York: J. & J. Harper, 1833, Vol. II, p. 376, Letter to John Murray, Jr. on October 12, 1816.

[84] Charles G. Finney, *Revivals of Religion*, Virginia Beach: CBN University Press, 1978, pp. 311-312.

[85] Noah Webster, *History of the United Sates*, New Haven: Durrie & Peck, 1833, pp. 307-308.

[86] See *Building Godly Nations* and *Liberating the Nations* for more on building and discipling nations.

[87] Deuteronomy 5:29; 28; Jeremiah 7:23-24; Deut. 28; Lev. 26.

[88] Elias Boudinot, "Oration at Elizabethtown, New Jersey, on the Fourth of July, 1793." *American Eloquence: A Collection of Speeches and Addresses, by the Most Eminent Orators of America*, New York: D. Appleton and Company, 1858, Vol. 1, p. 265.

[89] Robert C. Winthrop, "Address to Massachusetts Bible Society Meeting, May 28, 1849," *Addresses and Speeches on Various Occasions*, Boston: Little, Brown & Co., 1852, p. 172.

[90] *The Laws of the Pilgrims, A Facsimile Edition of The Book of the General Laws of the Inhabitants of the Jurisdiction of New – Plimouth, 1672 & 1685*, Wilmington, Del.: Michael Glazier, Inc., 1977, p. the Preface.

[91] Richard Morris, editor, *Significant Documents in United States History*, Vol. 1, New York: Van Nostrand Reinhold Co., 1969, p. 15-16.

[92] *Sources of Our Liberties*, p. 120.

[93] Ibid.

[94] Ibid., p. 123.

[95] *The Laws of the Pilgrims.*

[96] *Maxims of Washington*, compiled by John Frederick Schroeder, New York: D. Appleton & Co., 1854, p. 341.

[97] See Matthew 12:17-21; John 19:11; McDowell, *Building Godly Nations*, pp. 43 ff.; Beliles and McDowell, *America's Providential History*, pp. 29 ff.

[98] Rom. 13:1-5; 1 Pet. 2:13-14; for more on a biblical view of government see McDowell, *Building Godly Nations*, Chapter 3; and McDowell and Beliles, *Liberating the Nations*, Chapters 1, 11.

[99] Noah Webster, *History of the United States*, New Haven: Durrie & Peck, 1832, p. 309.

[100] William B. Reed, *Life and Correspondence of Joseph Reed*, Philadelphia: Lindsay and Blakiston, 1847, pp. 36-37.

[101] *The Writings of Thomas Jefferson*, XIV: 384. Letter to Colonel Charles Yancey, January 6, 1816.

[102] Richard Morris, editor, *Significant Documents in United States History, Vol. 1*, p. 19.

[103] "New England's First Fruits in Respect to the Progress of Learning in the College at Cambridge, in Massachusetts Bay," *America, Great Crises In Our History Told by Its Makers, A Library of Original Sources, Vol. 2*, Chicago: Americanization Department, 1925, pp. 155-156.

[104] Roscoe Pound, *The Spirit of the Common Law*, quoted in *Building Godly Nations*, p. 197.

[105] Shortt, p. 356.

[106] Noah Webster, "Education of Youth in America," *American Magazine* (March 1788): 212. Quoted in K. Alan Snyder, *Defining Noah Webster, Mind and Morals in the Early Republic*, New York: University Press of America, 1990, p. 114.

[107] *Life, Administration and Times of John Quincy Adams, Sixth President of the United States*, by John Robert Irelan, 1887, p. 16, quoted in Hall, *Consider and Ponder*, p. 605.

[108] Irelan, p. 16, in Hall, *Consider and Ponder*, pp. 605-606.

[109] Irelan, pp. 20-22, in Hall, *Consider and Ponder*, p. 607.

[110] "Connecticut Blue Laws," *Annals of America*, Vol. 1, Chicago: Encyclopedia Britannica, Inc., 1976, p. 203.

[111] Edward Kendall, *Kendall's Travels*, New York: I. Riley, 1809, Vol. 1, p. 299-305.

[112] "New England's First Fruits," (1643) in *The Pageant of America*, Ralph Henry Gabriel, ed., New Haven: Yale University Press, 1928, Vol. 10, p. 256.

[113] "New England's First Fruits in Respect to the Progress of Learning in the College at Cambridge, in Massachusetts Bay," *America, Great Crises In Our History Told by Its Makers, A Library of Original Sources, Vol. 2*, pp. 155-156.

[114] "Regulations at Yale College," *Annals of America*, Chicago: Encyclopedia Britannica, Inc., 1976, Vol. 1, p. 464.

[115] *The Pageant of America*, Ralph Henry Gabriel, editor, New Haven: Yale University Press, 1928, Vol. 10, p. 309.

[116] See McDowell, *Building Godly Nations*, Chapters 1 and 14 for more on biblical work.

[117] To learn more about these three elements see *Liberating the Nations, Building Godly Nations*, Providence Foundation Biblical Worldview University course on *The Principle Approach*, and Jim Rose, *A Guide to American Christian Education for the Home and School: The Principle Approach*, Camarillo, Cal.: American Christian History Institute, 1987.

[118] *The New England Primer*, Boston: Printed by Edward Draper, 1777. Reprinted by WallBuilders, 1991.

[119] Noah Webster, *The Elementary Spelling-Book*, New York: D. Appleton & Co., 1880, pp. 101, 121, 115.

[120] Definition of *immoral,* Noah Webster, *An American Dictionary of the English Language*, 1828, republished in facsimile edition by Foundation for American Christian Education, San Francisco, 1980.

[121] *Webster's New World Dictionary of the American Language*, David B. Guralnik, editor, Nashville: The Southwestern Company, 1969.

[122] Definition of *education* in Webster's 1828 Dictionary.

[123] Rosalie Slater, "The Christian History Literature Program," in *A Guide to American Christian Education*, by James B. Rose, p. 328.

[124] Jesus taught us to pray, "Thy kingdom come, Thy will be done, on earth as it is in heaven" (Matt. 6:10).

[125] Jesus commissioned us to disciple the nations: "All authority has been given to Me in heaven and on earth. Go therefore and make disciples of all the nations, … **teaching** them to observe all that I commanded you" (Matt. 28:18-20).

[126] Benjamin Rush, *Essays, Literary, Moral and Philosophical*, Philadelphia: printed by Thomas and William Bradford, 1806, p. 113.

[127] Robert Flood, *Rebirth of America*, Philadelphia: Arthur S. DeMoss Foundation, 1986, p. 127.

[128] A.A. Hodge, 1886, *Outlines of Theology*, Banner of Truth Trust.

[129] William J. Petersen, *Martin Luther Had a Wife*, Wheaton, Ill.: Tyndale House, 1983, 75.

[130] Mary-Elaine Swanson, *The Education of James Madison, A Model for Today*, Montgomery: The Hoffman Education Center for the Family, 1992, p. 53.

[131] Ibid.

[132] William V. Wells, *The Life and Public Services of Samuel Adams*, Vol. 3, Boston, 1865, p. 301.

[133] Galatians 5:1 NASB.

[134] Luke 17:20-21.

[135] Charles Clay, *An Artillery Sermon on The Governor Among the Nations*, c. 1777, contained in the Clay Family Papers (Mss 1c5795a), Virginia Historical Society, Richmond, Virginia.

[136] Milton E. Flower, *John Dickinson Conservative Revolutionary*, Charlottesville: The University Press of Virginia, 1983, p. 67.

[137] *Maxims of Washington*, compiled by John Frederick Schroeder, New York: D. Appleton & Co., 1854, p. 352.

[138] Noah Webster, *History of the United States*, New Haven: Durrie & Peck, 1833, pp. 273-274.

[139] This cry for freedom arises primarily in a Christian people or where Christian ideas affect society. Sin deadens the conscience of man and diminishes his quest for true freedom.

[140] Samuel Adams, *The Writings of Samuel Adams*, Harry Alonzo Cushing, editor, New York: G.P. Putnam's Sons, 1905, Vol. IV, p. 74, to John Trumbull on October 16, 1778.

[141] A letter to James Madison, 16 October 1829, *Madison Papers*, Series 2, Library of Congress. In Snyder, p. 253.

[142] John Adams, *The Works of John Adams, Second President of the United States*, Charles Francis Adams, editor, Boston: Charles C. Little and James Brown, 1850-1856, Vol. X, pp. 45-46, to Thomas Jefferson on June 28, 1813.

[143] For more on the principle of property, see *Liberating the Nations*, Chapter 1. Property rights are a foundational component of a free society. A person's property is whatever he has exclusive right to possess and control. We have God-given rights to both internal property (thoughts, opinions, conscience, ideas, mind, talents) and external property (land, money, possessions, freedom of speech, freedom of assembly). Signer of the Constitution, John Dickinson, reveals the Founders' view of how their right to property was being violated by the action of the English government, writing: "Man cannot be happy, without freedom; nor free without security of property; nor so secure, unless the sole power to dispose of it be lodged in themselves; therefore, no people can be free, but where taxes are imposed upon them with their own consent." (Flower, p. 58)

[144] William Wirt, *Sketches of the Life and Character of Patrick Henry*, Philadelphia: James Webster, publisher, 1818, p. 58.

[145] Francis Simkins et al, *Virginia: History, Government, Geography*, New York: Charles Scribner's Sons, 1964, p. 231.

[146] William Wirt Henry, *Patrick Henry, Life, Correspondence and Speeches*, Vol. 1, 1891, p. 83.

[147] Wirt, p. 58.

[148] Ibid.

[149] William Wirt Henry, p. 101.

[150] Ibid., p. 94. Patrick Henry reflected the faith of most of our Founders. In his last will and testament, bearing the date of November 20, 1798, and written throughout, as he says, "with my own hand," he chose to insert a touching affirmation of his own deep faith in Christianity. After distributing his estate among his descendants, he thus concludes: "This is all the inheritance I can give to my dear family. The religion of Christ can give them one which will make them rich indeed." (Patrick Henry's Will. From a photocopy in the author's possession.)

[151] The sermon is in John Wingate Thornton, *The Pulpit of the American Revolution: or, the Political Sermons of the Period of 1776*, Boston: Gould and Lincoln, 1860, pp. 105 ff. I would enjoy preaching a sermon to commemorate such good news today, that of a repeal of a tax; and especially to deliver it before our elected officials.

[152] See W. De Loss Love, Jr., *The Fast and Thanksgiving Days of New England*.

[153] Richard Frothingham, *Rise of the Republic*, 1890, quoted in Verna Hall, *The Christian History of the Constitution of the United States of America*, San Francisco: Foundation of American Christian Education, 1980, p. 328.

[154] Frothingham, quoted in Hall, *Christian History of the Constitution of the United States*, pp. 331-332.

[155] From a reprint of a Proclamation of the Virginia House of Burgesses for a Day of Fasting, Humiliation and Prayer on the 1st Day of June, Tuesday, the 24th of May, 14 GEO. III 1774. See Chapter 2 for a copy of this proclamation.

[156] Frothingham, quoted in Hall, *Christian History of the Constitution of the United States*, pp. 337.

[157] *The Patriots*, Virginius Dabney, editor, New York: Atheneum, 1975, p. 7.

[158] *Journal of the Proceedings of the Congress Held at Philadelphia September 5, 1774, A Facsimile of the Official Edition Printed in 1774*, Philadelphia: printed for the Library Company of Philadelphia, 1974, pp. 214-215.

[159] *The Book of Abigail and John, Selected Letters of the Adams Family*, 1762-1784, Cambridge, MA.: Harvard University Press, 1975, p. 76.

[160] Silas Deane, *The Deane Papers: Collections of the New York Historical Society for the Year 1886*, New York: Printed for the Society, 1887, Vol. I, p. 20, Wednesday, September 7, 1774.

[161] Ibid.

[162] Franklin Cole, ed., *They Preached Liberty*, Indianapolis: Liberty Press, p. 39.

[163] A copy of the Proclamation is in *Consider and Ponder*, p. 407.

[164] Ibid.

[165] A copy of the Proclamation is in *Consider and Ponder*, p. 510a.

[166] All colleges up until this time were started by churches or by Christians with a primary mission of training godly ministers. The instruction of these seminary/colleges covered theological training but also a biblical worldview of all spheres of life (law, science, history, etc.), so graduates pursued many vocations.

[167] Last Will and Testament of Robert Treat Paine, in David Barton, *The Practical Benefits of Christianity*, Aledo, Tex.: WallBuilder, 2001, 7-8. For more excerpts from the wills of America's Founders see, "The Last Will & Testaments of the Founders Reveal Their Christian Faith," compiled by Stephen McDowell, Providential Perspective, Vol. 19, No. 4, August 2005, published by the Providence Foundation.

[168] Last Will and Testament of Samuel Adams in David Barton, *The Practical Benefits of Christianity*, 7-8.

[169] From an autographed letter written by Charles Carroll to Charles W. Wharton, Esq., on September 27, 1825, from Doughoragen, Maryland; possessed by WallBuilders.

[170] Lewis Henry Boutell, *The Life of Roger Sherman*, Chicago: A.C. McClurg and Co., 1896, pp. 271-273.

[171] Benjamin Rush, *The Autobiography of Benjamin Rush*, George Corner, ed., Princeton: University Press for the American Philosophical Society, 1948, p. 166. For more on the Christian faith of the Signers, see Stephen McDowell, *America, a Christian Nation? Examining the Evidence of the Christian Foundation of America*, Charlottesville: Providence Foundation, 2005, and Barton, *Original Intent*.

[172] This is an anecdotal story reported by many sources using varying terminology. This quote is in Robert Flood, Men Who Shaped America, Chicago, 1968, p. 276. Another records Hancock said: "There, I guess King George will be able to read that" (The Annals of America, Vol. 2, Chicago: Encyclopedia Britannica, 1968, p. 449).

[173] *The Annals of America*, Vol. 2, p. 276. It cannot be confirmed if Hancock and Franklin actually made these statements, but these stories have endured because they were in character.

[174] Letter of Benjamin Rush to John Adams, July 20, 1811, quoted in *Our Sacred Honor*, edited by William J. Bennett, New York: Simon & Schuster, 1997, pp. 29-30.

[175] T.R. Fehrenbach, *Greatness to Spare*, Princeton, NJ: D. Van Nostrand Company, Inc., 1968, p. 23.

[176] Ibid., p. 247.

[177] Letter of John Adams to Abigail, July 3d. 1776, *The Book of Abigail and John*, p. 142.

[178] Franklin Cole, ed., *They Preached Liberty*, p. 39.

[179] From an *Address on American Independence* by Elias Boudinot, President of the Continental Congress.

[180] Ibid.

[181] Hall, *Consider and Ponder*, p. 47.

[182] See Beliles and McDowell, *America's Providential History*, for an expansion of some of these links on the Chain of Liberty.

[183] Richard Frothingham, *The Rise of the Republic of the United States*, quoted in *Christian History of the Constitution*, Verna Hall, ed., p. 1.

[184] Ibid., p. 2.

[185] David Barret, *Cosmos, Chaos, and Gospel, a Chronology of World Evangelization from Creation to New Creation*, Birmingham, Al., 1987.

[186] Seumas MacManus, *The Story of the Irish Race*, New York: The Devin-Adair Co., 1967, p. 126.

[187] Ibid.

[188] Ibid., p. 232.

[189] See Beliles and McDowell, *America's Providential History*, pp. 43-44 for more.

[190] G.V. Lechler, *John Wycliffe and His English Precursors*, quoted in Slater, p. 167.

[191] Charles Carleton Coffin, *The Story of Liberty*, New York: Harper & Brothers, 1878, p. 79.

[192] *Christopher Columbus's Book of Prophecies, Reproduction of the Original Manuscript with English Translation* by Kay Brigham, Fort Lauderdale, Fl.: TSELF, Inc ., 1992, pp. 178-183. For Columbus' faith revealed in his journal of his first voyage, see Stephen McDowell, *America's Providential History, a Documentary Sourcebook*, Charlottesville, Vir.: Providence Foundation, 2010, pp. 7 ff.

[193] B.F. Morris, p. 69.

[194] Henry C. Sheldon, *History of the Christian Church*, in Slater, *Teaching and Learning America's Christian History*, p. 169.

[195] Winkie Pratney, *Revival, Principles to Change the World*, Springdale, Penn.: Whitaker House, 1983, p. 48.

[196] Sheldon, *History of the Christian Church*, in Slater, p. 171.

[197] Ibid., pp. 170-171.

[198] See Douglas F. Kelly, *The Emergence of Liberty in the Modern World, The Influence of Calvin on Five Governments from the 16th Through 18th Centuries*, Phillipsburg, NJ: P&R Publishing, 1992. Those governments were Calvin's Geneva, Huguenot France, Knox's Scotland, Puritan England, and Colonial America.

[199] Sheldon, *History of the Christian Church*, in Slater, p. 171.

[200] J.H. Merle D'Aubigne, *History of the Reformation in Europe*, in Slater, pp. 334.

[201] Ibid., p. 336.

[202] Ibid.

[203] Ibid., p. 337.

[204] See Chapter 9, and McDowell, *Building Godly Nations*, Chapter 4, "The Bible: Rock of Our Republic," pp. 59 ff.

[205] For more on the development of these and other documents of liberty, see McDowell, *Building Godly Nations*, pp. 105 ff.

[206] *Bradford's History "Of Plimoth Plantation" From the Original Manuscript*, printed by order of the General Court of Massachusetts, Boston: Wright & Potter Printing Co., State Printers, 1898, p. 12. The spelling has been modernized.

[207] Ibid., p. 13.

[208] Ibid., p. 32.

[209] Ibid., p. 110.

[210] Ibid., the excerpts are from pages 11-121.

[211] Ibid., p. 116.

[212] Peter Marshall and David Manuel, *The Light and the Glory*, Old Tappon, NJ: Fleming H. Revell Co., 1977, pp. 130-132. See also, Bradford, pp. 116-117; and *Mourt's Relation: A Journal of the Pilgrims of Plymouth*, Plymouth, MA: Plymouth Rock Foundation, 1985, p. 48.

[213] *Mourt's Relation,* pp. 72-73; Marshall and Manuel, pp. 135-136; see also, *The Pilgrims and Plymouth Colony,* by the editors of American Heritage, New York: American Heritage Publishing Co., 1961, pp. 102-103.

[214] Bradford, p. 164.

[215] Ibid., p. 162.

[216] Ibid., p. 163.

[217] Ibid., p. 170.

[218] Ibid., pp. 170-171.

[219] Nathaniel Morton, *New England Memorial,* pp. 64-65.

[220] Bradford, p. 171.

[221] *A Compilation of the Messages and Papers of the Presidents,* Vol. 8, New York: Bureau of National Literature, Inc., 1897, pp. 3429-3430.

[222] William J. Federer, *America's God and Country,* Coppell, Tex.: FAME Publishing, Inc., 1994, p. 311.

[223] Noah Webster, *History of the United States,* New Haven: Durrie & Peck, 1832, p. 309.

[224] Lawrence A. Cremin, *American Education, the Colonial Experience 1607-1683,* Harper and Row, Publishers, 1970, p. 40.

[225] George Bancroft, *History of the United States, Vol. 2,* p. 402, in CD Sourcebook of American History, produced by Infobases, 1995.

[226] *Christopher Columbus's Book of Prophecies* by Kay Brigham.

[227] E.G.R. Taylor, editor, *The Original Writings and Correspondence of the Two Richard Hakluyts, Vol. 2,* London: Hakluyt Society, 1935, p. 211. For more on Hakluyt see McDowell, *The American Dream, Jamestown and the Planting of the American Christian Republic,* Chapter 3.

[228] The First Charter of Virginia, 1606, in *Sources of Our Liberties,* edited by Richard L. Perry, Chicago: American Bar Foundation, 1959, p. 40.

[229] George Bancroft, *History of the United States of America,* in Six Volumes, Boston: Little, Brown, and Co., 1879, Vol. 1, p. 241.

[230] Ibid., p. 269.

[231] Ibid., pp. 269-270.

[232] *Annals of America, Vol. 1,* Chicago: Encyclopedia Britannica, Inc., 1976, p. 103. See also *Sources of Our Liberties,* p. 94.

[233] Bancroft, 1:270.

[234] See Francis B. Simkins, Spotswood H. Jones, and Sidman P. Poole, *Virginia: History, Government, Geography,* Charles Scribners's Sons, New York, 1964, p. 133, and John Brinsley, *A Consolation for Our Grammar Schooles,* Scholars' Facsimiles & Reprints, New York, reprinted in 1943 from an original copy in the New York Public Library.

[235] *The Pageant of America,* Vol. 10, 1928, p. 312.

[236] *Sources of Our Liberties,* p. 120.

[237] Ibid., p. 169.

[238] William J. Jackman, *History of the American Nation, Vol. 2,* p. 390, in CD Sourcebook of American History, produced by Infobases, 1995.

[239] *Remember William Penn,* compiled by the William Penn Tercentenary Committee, Harrisburg, PA: Commonwealth of Pennsylvania, 1945, p. 74

[240] Ibid., pp. 85-86.

[241] "Frame of Government of Pennsylvania," in *Sources of Our Liberties,* p. 210.

[242] Samuel M. Janney, *The Life of William Penn: With Selections from His Correspondence and Autobiography,* Philadelphia: Lippincott, Grambo & Co., 1852, p. 407.

[243] *Sources of Our Liberties,* p. 256.

[244] Bancroft, vol. 2, in CD Sourcebook of American History, p. 284-285.

[245] Robert Dearden & Douglas Watson, *The Bible and the Revolution,* in Slater, *Teaching and Learning America's Christian History,* p. 142.

[246] *The Holy Bible*, As printed by Robert Aitken and Approved & Recommended by the Congress of the United States of America in 1782. Facsimile edition reprinted, New York: Arno Press, 1968.

[247] *Historical Almanac of the U.S. Senate*, p. 30, in CD Sourcebook of American History.

[248] *For the Colony in Virginea Britannia, Lawes Divine, Morall and Martiall, etc.*, compiled by William Strachey, Edited by David H. Flaherty, The University Press of Virginia, Charlottesville, 1969, pp. 10-11.

[249] *The Laws of the Pilgrims, A facsimile edition.*

[250] *Sources of Our Liberties*, p. 120.

[251] Ibid., p. 123.

[252] *Colonial Origins of the American Constitution*, Lutz, ed., p. 222.

[253] Bancroft, Vol. 1, p. 321.

[254] *Sources of Our Liberties*, p. 148.

[255] Ibid., p. 155.

[256] Ibid., pp. 158-159.

[257] *American Historical Documents*, The Harvard Classics, Danbury, Conn.: Grolier Enterprises, 1987, p. 90.

[258] *The Annals of America*, Vol. 1, p. 199.

[259] Ibid., p. 200.

[260] Ibid., p. 201.

[261] *Significant Documents in US History, Vol. 1*, Richard B. Morris, editor, New York: Van Nostrand Reinhold Co., 1969, p. 19.

[262] Ibid., p. 20.

[263] *The Pageant of America*, Vol. 10, 1928, p. 258.

[264] *Annals of America*, Vol. 1, p. 203.

[265] Edward Kendall, *Kendall's Travels*, New York: I. Riley, 1809, Vol. 1, p. 299-305.

[266] "New England's First Fruits in Respect to the Progress of Learning in the College at Cambridge, in Massachusetts Bay," *America*, Vol. 2, pp. 155-156 (spelling is modernized).

[267] *Annals of America*, Vol. 1, p. 464.

[268] Alexis DeTocqueville, *Democracy in America*, Vol. 2, p. 58, in CD Sourcebook of American History.

[269] *The Pageant of America*, 10:258.

[270] Noah Webster, *An American Dictionary of the English Language*, 1828, definitions of *right, governor, property*.

[271] *The Earliest Diary of John Adams*, ed. L.H. Butterfield, Cambridge, MA: The Belknap Press of Harvard Univ. Press, 1966, 1:9.

[272] Benjamin Rush, *Letters of Benjamin Rush*, L.H. Butterfield, ed., Princeton, New Jersey: American Philosophical Society, 1951, Vol. 1, p. 521.

[273] Benjamin Rush, *Essays, Literary, Moral and Philosophical*, Philadelphia: printed by Thomas and William Bradford, 1806, p. 113.

[274] *Works of Fisher Ames*, as published by Seth Ames (1854), edited and enlarged by W.B. Allen, Vol. 1, Indianapolis: Liberty Classics, 1983, p. 12.

[275] *Writings of Samuel Adams*, edited by Henry Alonzo Cushing, Vol. 4, New York, 1908. In Hall, *Consider and Ponder*, p. 82.

[276] William Wirt, *Sketches of the Life and Character of Patrick Henry*, p. 402.

[277] John Jay, *John Jay: The Winning of the Peace. Unpublished Papers 1780-1784*, Richard B. Morris, editor, New York: Harper & Row Publishers, 1980, Vol. 2, p. 709.

[278] *Letters of John Quincy Adams to His Son on the Bible and Its Teachings*, Auburn: James M. Alden, 1850, pp. 9-21.

[279] Cited in *A Christian History of the American Republic* by Walker Whitman, 1939.

[280] James Madison, *Notes of Debates in the Federal Convention of 1787*, New York: W.W. Norton & Co., 1987, p. 426.

[281] Jackman, Vol. 9, pp. 2690-2691.

[282] Edward Beardsley, *Life and Times of William Samuel Johnson*, Boston: Houghton, Mifflin and Company, 1886, pp. 141-142.

[283] *American Eloquence: A Collection of Speeches and Addresses, by the Most Eminent Orators of America*, Frank Moore, editor, New York: D. Appleton and Co., 1858, Vol. 2, p. 263.

[284] Noah Webster, *Value of the Bible and Excellence of the Christian Religion*, 1834. Republished by Foundation for American Christian Education, 1988, p. 78.

[285] Donald Lutz, "The Relative Influence of European Writers on Late 18th Century American Political Thought," *American Political Science Review*, LXXVIII (1984), p. 189-197.

[286] David Gegg, in Rosalie Slater, *Teaching and Learning America's Christian History*, p.40.

[287] Jonathan Edwards, *A Faithful Narrative of the Surprising Work of God in the Conversion of Many Hundred Souls in Northampton*, Edinburgh: Printed by Thomas Lumisden and John Robertson, 1738.

[288] Joseph Tracy, *The Great Awakening: A History of the Revival of Religion in the Time of Edwards and Whitefield*, Boston: Charles Tappan, 1845, p. 26.

[289] *The Autobiography of Benjamin Franklin*, edited by John Bigelow, New York: Walter J. Black, inc., 1932, p. 217.

[290] David Barton, "Worth Riding a Hundred Miles to Hear," in *The Founders' Bible*, Shiloh Road Publishers, 2012, p. 829.

[291] See John Wingate Thornton, *The Pulpit of the American Revolution*, Boston: Gould and Lincoln, 1860. W. DeLoss Love, *The Fast and Thanksgiving Days of New England*, New York: Houghton, Mifflin and Company, 1895. *Political Sermons of the American Founding Era, 1730-1805*, Edited by Ellis Sandoz, Indianapolis: Liberty Press, 1991.

[292] Bancroft, Vol. 4, p.95, in CD Sourcebook of American History.

[293] Bernard C. Steiner, *One Hundred and Ten Years of Bible Society Work in Maryland*, New York: G.P. Putnam's Sons, 1905, Vol. IV, p. 74, to John Trumbull on October 16, 1778.

[294] To learn more see McDowell, "The Bible, Slavery, and America's Founders" in *Building Godly Nations*, pp. 209 ff.

[295] Benjamin Rush, *Minutes of the Proceedings of a Convention of Delegates from the Abolition Societies Established in Different Parts of the United States Assembled at Philadelphia*, Philadelphia: Zachariah Poulson, 1794, p. 24.

[296] Bancroft, Vol. 4, pp. 233-234.

[297] "The Underground Railroad," Levi Coffin, *America*, Vol. 7, p. 157, in CD Sourcebook of American History.

[298] Jackman, Vol.4, p. 1097-1098.

[299] "Eliot's Brief Narrative (1670)," *American Historical Documents*, p. 141.

[300] DeTocqueville, Vol.2, p. 152.

[301] DeTocqueville, Vol.1, p. 322.

[302] DeTocqueville, Vol. 2, p. 374.

[303] Daniel L. Dreisbach, *Religion and Politics in the Early Republic*, Lexington, Ken.: The University Press of Kentucky, 1996, p. 113.

[304] Noah Webster, *Value of the Bible and Excellence of the Christian Religion*, p. 78.

[305] For a listing of biblical ideas contained in the Declaration see Stephen McDowell and Jim Arcieri, *Teacher's Guide to America's Providential History*, Charlottesville: Providence Foundation, 2005, pp. 80-81.

[306] See Beliles and McDowell, *America's Providential History*, Chapter 10-13.

[307] George Washington, *The Writings of George Washington from the Original Manuscript Sources*, 12:343.

[308] John Quincy Adams, *An Oration Delivered before the Inhabitants of the Town of Newburyport on the Sixty-First Anniversary of the Declaration of Independence, July 4th, 1837*, Charles Whipple, Newburyport, 1837, pp. 5-6.

[309] For more on the framework of the Constitution and Godly government, see *America's Providential History*, Chapter 13, *Liberating the Nations*, Chapter 11, and Mark Beliles and Doug Anderson, *Contending for the Constitution*, Charlottesville: Providence Foundation.

[310] Robert A. Rutland, ed., *The Papers of James Madison*, University of Chicago Press, 1962, Vol. 10, p. 208.

[311] W. Cleon Skousen, *The Making of America*, Washington, DC: The National Center for Constitutional Studies, p. 5.

[312] Washington to Jonathan Trumbull, July 20, 1788, *The Writings of George Washington*, Vol. 30, p. 22.

[313] Albert Henry Smyth, ed., *Writings of Benjamin Franklin*, Macmillan Co., 1905-7, Vol. 9, p. 702.

[314] *The Christian History of the Constitution of the United States, Self-Government with Union*, Verna Hall, compiler, San Francisco: Foundation for American Christian Education, 1979, p. 34.

[315] *Cyrus Hall McCormick, His Life and Work*, Herbert N. Casson, Chicago: A.C. McClurg &Co., 1909, p. 202. For more on McCormick see McDowell, *Building Godly Nations*, Chapter 14.

[316] Ibid., p. 40.

[317] Ibid., p. 47.

[318] Ibid., p. 53.

[319] Ibid., p. 54.

[320] Ibid., p. 58.

[321] Ibid., p. 79. To learn how McCormick applied biblical principles (that are used today by successful businesses) in founding his new business, see McDowell, *Building Godly Nations*, Chapter 14.

[322] Carleton Mabee, *The American Leonardo, A Life of Samuel F. B. Morse*, New York: Alfred A. Knopf, 1943, p. 279.

[323] Ibid., p. 275.

[324] Ibid., p. 276.

[325] Ibid., p. 280.

[326] Ibid.

[327] Ibid., p. 369.

[328] Charles Lee Lewis, *Matthew Fontaine Maury, The Pathfinder of the Seas*, New York: AMS Press, 1969 (reprinted from edition of 1927), p. 82.

[329] Other accounts say his wife read the Bible to him.

[330] Lewis, pp. 251-252.

[331] Ibid., pp. 240a-240b.

[332] Matthew Fontaine Maury, *The Physical Geography of the Sea and its Meteorology*, New York: Harper & Brothers, 1856, p. 80.

[333] John W. Wayland, *The Pathfinder of the Seas, The Life of Matthew Fontaine Maury*, Richmond: Garret & Massie, Inc., 1930, pp. 60-61.

[334] Lewis, p. xiv.

[335] Maury to Frank Minor, July 25, 1855, in Lewis, p. xiv.

[336] Wayland, p. 131.

[337] Lewis, p. 96.

[338] Lewis, pp. 98-99.

[339] Hildegarde Hawthorne, *Matthew Fontaine Maury, Trail Maker of the Seas*, New York: Longmans, Green and Co., 1943, pp. 154-155.

[340] Letter to David McClure, October 25, 1836, *Letters of Noah Webster*, Harry R. Warfel, ed., New York: Library Publishers, 1953, p. 453.

[341] Webster, *An American Dictionary of the English Language* (1828), Preface.

[342] William McGuffey, *The Eclectic Fourth Reader*, Cincinnati: Truman and Smith, 1838, p. x, facsimile edition republished by Mott Media.

[343] John H. Westerhoff III, *McGuffey and His Readers*, Milford, Michigan, 1982.

[344] *The Pageant of America*, Vol. 10, p. 315.

[345] Joe B. Frantz, *Gail Borden, Dairyman to a Nation*, Norman: University of Oklahoma Press, 1951, p. 166.

[346] See Stephen McDowell, *Kingdom Missionaries Marcus and Narcissa Whitman, The Founding of the Oregon Territory*, Charlottesville: Providence Foundation, 2011. A little more information is given about Whitman later in this chapter.

[347] *The Writings of Thomas Jefferson*, Andrew A. Lipscomb and Albert Ellery Bergh, Editors, Washington, DC: The Thomas Jefferson Memorial Association, 1903, 5:364.

[348] Ibid., 5:366.

[349] Joshua E. London, *Victory in Tripoli, How America's War with the Barbary Pirates Established the U.S. Navy and Built a Nation*, Hoboken, NJ: John Wiley & Sons, Inc., 2005, p. 23-24.

[350] Ibid., p. 25.

[351] Ibid., p. 11.

[352] See Stephen McDowell, *Abraham Lincoln's Faith*, Charlottesville: Providence Foundation, 2012.

[353] Joseph Banyard, *Daniel Webster, His Life and Public Services*, Chicago: Werner Company, 1875, pp. 131-133.

[354] Daniel Webster, *The Works of Daniel Webster*, Boston: Little, Brown, and Co., 1853, Vol.1, p. 49, from "A Discourse Delivered at Plymouth, on the 22nd of December, 1820."

[355] B.F. Morris, p. 270.

[356] David J. Hill, *Elements of Rhetoric and Composition*, Hills Rhetorical Series, 1884, p. 3.

[357] John M. Taylor, *Garfield of Ohio: The Available Man*, New York: W.W. Norton & Co., Inc., 1970, p. 180. Quoted from "A Century of Congress," by James A. Garfield, Atlantic, July 1877.

[358] James F. Cooper, *Knights of the Brush, The Hudson River School and the Moral Landscape*, New York: Hudson Hills Press, 1999, p. 17, Description on inside jacket cover.

[359] Ibid., Foreward.

[360] Ibid.

[361] Ibid., p. 23.

[362] Ibid.

[363] Ibid., pp. 23-24.

[364] For more on the Hudson River painters, including dozens of their paintings, see Cooper, *Knights of the Brush* (a copy can be ordered from the Providence Foundation, at providencefoundation.com). For a summary of Cooper's book, see the article on the Providence Foundation's website, http://providencefoundation.com/wp-content/uploads/2011/08/painters0001.pdf

[365] To learn about American literature from a Christian perspective see Rosalie June Slater, *The Noah Plan, Literature Curriculum Guide*, published by Foundation for American Christian Education, and Rosalie June Slater, "The Christian History Literature Program," in James B. Rose, *A Guide to American Christian Education, The Principle Approach*, Camarillo, Cal.: American Christian History Institute, 1987.

[366] William A. Mowry, *Marcus Whitman and the Early Days of Oregon*, New York: Silver, Burdett and Company, 1901, p. vi.

[367] To learn this fascinating story see Stephen McDowell, *Kingdom Missionaries Marcus and Narcissa Whitman, The Founding of the Oregon Territory*. (This can be ordered from providencefoundation.com)

[368] Mowry, p. 72.

[369] Mabee, p. 294.

[370] For more on Unitarianism see David Barton, *Original Intent*, Aledo, Tex.: WallBuilders, 2002, pp. 314-316.

[371] Kate Mason Rowland, *Life and Correspondence of Charles Carroll of Carrollton*, New York & London: G.P. Putnam's Sons, 1898, Vol. II, p. 321, to Robert Goodloe Harper, April 23, 1820. To learn more about the Founders and slavery see McDowell, "The Bible, Slavery, and America's Founders," in *Building Godly Nations*.

[372] Letter to Robert Morris, April 12, 1786, in George *Washington: A Collection*, ed. W.B. Allen, Indianapolis: Liberty Fund, 1988, p. 319.

[373] Quoted in Marshall Foster and Mary-Elaine Swanson, *The American Covenant, the Untold Story*, California: Mayflower Institute, 1983, p. 142.

[374] Frederick Douglass, *The Frederick Douglas Papers*, John Blassingame, editor, New Haven: Yale University Press, 1982, pp. 385-386, from "What to the Slave is the Fourth of July?", July 5, 1852.

[375] William J. Federer, *America's God and Country*, Coppell, Tex: FAME Publishing, Inc., 1994, p. 98.

[376] Rackham Holt, *George Washington Carver, An American Biography*, Garden City, NY: Doubleday, Doran, and Co., Inc., 1943, pp. 226-227.

[377] Ibid., p. 227.

[378] Ibid., p. 229.

[379] Charles E. Jones, *The Books You Read*, Harrisburg, PA: Executive Books, 1985, 132. Quoted in Federer, p. 96.

[380] Holt, p. 220.

[381] Federer, p. 97.

[382] James Manship, "George Washington Carver," notes of speech, 1998.

[383] Joseph H. Appel, *The Business Biography of John Wanamaker, Founder and Builder*, New York: The Macmillan Company, 1930, p. 205.

[384] Ibid., p. 206.

[385] Ibid., p. 208.

[386] Ibid., p. 55.

[387] Ibid., p. xv.

[388] Ibid.

[389] Ibid., p. viii.

[390] Ibid., p. xvi.

[391] Ibid., p. 197.

[392] Ibid., p. 291. For more on Wanamaker see, Stephen McDowell, *Transforming Medicine and Business with Biblical Principles, Examples of Joseph Lister and John Wanamaker*, Charlottesville: Providence Foundation, 2010.

[393] Verna Hall, *Christian History of the Constitution*, p. iv.

[394] To learn more about the practical implications of an incorrect view of these doctrines see Beliles and McDowell, *America's Providential History*, pp. 248-255.

[395] See McDowell, "Education and the Kingdom of God," in *Building Godly Nations*.

[396] See Herbert W. Titus, *God, Man, and Law: The Biblical Principles*, Oak Brook, Ill.: Institute of Basic Life Principles, 1994, pp. 3-6.

[397] Roscoe Pound, *The Spirit of the Common Law*, New York: The Legal Classics Library.

[398] Benjamin Cardozo, *The Growth of Law*, New Haven: Yale University Press, 1924, p. 49.

[399] Charles Evans Hughes, *The Autobiographical Notes of Charles Evans Hughes*, David J. Danelski and Joseph S. Tulchin, editors, Cambridge: Harvard University Press, 1973, p. 144, speech at Elmira on May 3, 1907.

[400] Barna Poll conducted in the Spring of 2002. See Chapter 4.

[401] Some people have suggested there have been four eras: (1) 1800-1835: National supremacy. (2) 1835-1895: Constitutional supremacy. (3) 1895-1950: Judicial supremacy. (4) 1950-present: Judicial activism.

[402] See Robert K. Dornan and Csaba Vedlik, Jr., *Judicial Supremacy: The Supreme Court on Trial*, Plymouth, Mass.: Plymouth Rock Foundation, 1986.

[403] Gary North, *Inherit the Earth*, Ft. Forth: Dominion Press, 1987, p. 34.

[404] Some of the ideas that follow in this section are from North, p. 41 ff.

[405] In ancient Israel, and in much of Christendom throughout history, the first born received a larger inheritance because it was his responsibility to care for his parents in their old age. In modern socialist states, the government is attempting to provide this (in the USA via social security), which adds to the destruction of the family, while greatly increasing the power of government.

[406] For more see Stephen McDowell, *Honest Money and Banking* and *The Economy from a Biblical Perspective*, both published by the Providence Foundation, 2009. Also see *Foundations of Biblical Economics, Business, and the Marketplace*, a Providence Foundation Biblical Worldview University course.

[407] See Burton Folsom, Jr., *New Deal or Raw Deal, How FDR's Economic Legacy Has Damaged America*, New York: Threshold Editions (Simon & Schuster), 2008.

[408] See McDowell, *Honest Money and Banking*, for more on fiat money.

[409] See Paul Kengor, *The Crusader, Ronald Reagan and the Fall of Communism*.

[410] *The Faith of FDR, From President Franklin Delano Roosevelt's Public Papers*, 1933-1945, compiled by William J. Federer, St. Louis: Amerisearch, 2006, p. 1.

[411] Ibid., p. 2.

[412] Noah Webster, *An American Dictionary of the English Language*, definition of *revival*.

[413] Wallis, *In the Day of Thy Power*, p. 45, quoted in Winkie Pratney, *Revival, Principles to Change the World*, Springdale, Penn.: Whitaker House, 1983, p. 15.

[414] Pratney, *Revival, Principles to Change the World*, p. 15.

[415] See Bruce Anderson, Mark Beliles, and Stephen McDowell, *Watchmen on the Walls*, Charlottesville, Vir.: Providence Foundation, 1995.

[416] Quoted in Pratney, p. 18.

[417] Quoted in Pratney, p. 18.

[418] Charles G. Finney, *Revivals of Religion*, 1978, p. 7.

[419] Pratney, p. 20.

[420] To learn more see Stephen McDowell, *Biblical Revival and the Transformation of Nations*, Charlottesville: Providence Foundation, 2013.

[421] John T. Faris, *Historic Shrines of America*, New York: George H. Doran Co., 1918, pp. 120-121.

[422] J.T. Headly, *The Chaplains and Clergy of the Revolution*, originally published by Charles Scribner, New York, 1864, republished by Christian Patriot Association, 1976, p. 63.

[423] Faris, p. 121. See Headley, pp. 65-67.

[424] Faris, pp. 138-140. Mr. Caldwell survived the war, in spite of the efforts of the British to capture him, only to be murdered on November 24, 1781, by a Continental soldier who was thought to have been bribed by those whose enmity the chaplain had earned during the conflict. (Faris, p. 121)

[425] J.T. Headly, p. 112.

[426] J.T. Headly, p. 101.

[427] For more on Washington's Christian faith see Stephen McDowell, *Apostle of Liberty, The World-Changing Leadership of George Washington*, pp. 135-153.

[428] See W. DeLoss Love, *The Fast and Thanksgiving Days of New England*.

[429] See for example the Charter of Virginia, the Mayflower Compact, the Charter of Maryland, the Charter of Rhode Island, and others, in *Sources of Our Liberties* and *Colonial Origins of the American Constitution*.

[430] John Wingate Thorton, *The Pulpit of the American Revolution: or, the Political Sermons of the Period of 1776*, Boston: Gould and Lincoln, 1860, p. XXXVIII.

[431] Quoted in Charles Hull Wolfe, *Three Churches, One Nation*, an unpublished manual.

[432] *The Book of Abigail and John, Selected Letters of the Adams Family, 1762-1784*, Edited by L.H. Butterfield, Marc Friedlaender, and Mary-Jo Kline, Cambridge, Mass.: Harvard University Press, 1975, p. 129.

[433] J.T. Headly, p. 101.

[434] Ibid.

[435] Alice Baldwin, *The New England Clergy and the American Revolution*, Fredick Ungar Pub. Co., 1928.

[436] E. L. Magoon, *Orators of the American Revolution*, New York: C. Scribner, 1857. Reprinted by Sightext Publications, El Segundo, CA, 1969, pp. 201-202.

[437] Faris, p. 213.

[438] Faris, p. 214.

[439] Magoon, pp. 207-208.

[440] William Wirt Henry, *Patrick Henry, Life, Correspondence and Speeches*, Vol. 1, p. 15.

[441] Ibid., p. 16.

[442] Quoted in Rosalie Slater, *Teaching and Learning America's Christian History*, p. 248.

[443] Paul Wallace, *The Muhlenbergs of Pennsylvania*, Philadelphia: University of Pennsylvania Press, 1950, p. 121.

[444] Quoted in J.T. Headley, *The Chaplains and Clergy of the Revolution, p. 37*. See also, Wallace, pp. 120-121.

[445] Daniel Dorchester, *Christianity in the United States from the First Settlement Down to the Present Time*, New York: Phillips & Hunt, 1888, p. 266.

[446] *The Book of Abigail and John, Selected Letters of the Adams Family*, p. 95.

About the Author

Stephen McDowell is co-founder and President of the Providence Foundation, a Christian educational organization whose mission is to train and network leaders of education, business, and politics to transform their culture for Christ. In 30 years of full time work with the Foundation, Stephen has trained people from 100 countries to apply Biblical truth in all spheres of life. He has traveled to 35 nations in six continents where he has consulted with government officials, assisted in writing political documents, advised political parties, and started Christian schools and Biblical worldview training centers. He has authored over 30 books, videos, and training courses including Liberating the Nations and America's Providential History. His books and writings have been translated into 18 languages and distributed to more than one million people. McDowell holds a master's degree in geophysics, served for several years as a pastor, and has been an adjunct professor at Regent University. Stephen and his wife Beth live in Charlottesville, Virginia, and have four children and three grandchildren.

CONTACT INFORMATION:

Email: info@providencefoundation.com
Website: providencefoundation.com
Work phone: 434-978-4535